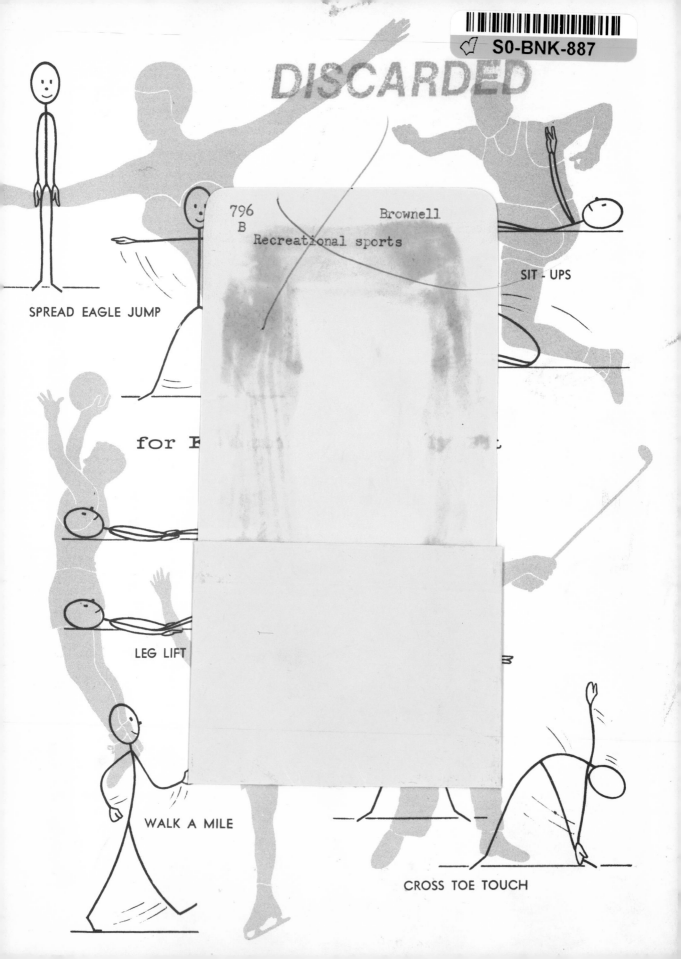

SO-BNK-887

DISCARDED

796
B

Brownell

Recreational sports

SPREAD EAGLE JUMP

SIT - UPS

for

LEG LIFT

WALK A MILE

CROSS TOE TOUCH

DISCARDED

Recreational

Sports

CES

Creative
Sports Series

BASEBALL

FOOTBALL

BASKETBALL

TRACK AND FIELD

GOLF

SWIMMING

TENNIS

ARCHERY

BADMINTON

BOWLING

CANOEING

HANDBALL

FIGURE SKATING

SKIING

TABLE TENNIS

VOLLEY BALL

WATER SKIING

Physical Fitness Program

RECREATIONAL SPORTS

by

Clifford L. Brownell, Ph.D.

CHAIRMAN, DEPARTMENT OF PHYSICAL EDUCATION, COLUMBIA UNIVERSITY, NEW YORK

Roy B. Moore, Ph.D.

CHAIRMAN, DIVISION OF HEALTH AND PHYSICAL EDUCATION, MANKATO STATE COLLEGE, AND STAFF

ARCHERY . . . . Don W. Buchanan
BADMINTON . . . . Dee Whitlock
BOWLING . . . . Einar A. Olsen,
Don W. Buchanan
CANOEING . . . . Ruth Shellberg
FIGURE SKATING . . . . . Jack S. Wilson
HANDBALL . . . . Roy B. Moore
SKIING . . . . Ruth Shellberg
TABLE TENNIS . . . . . Robert D. Johnson
VOLLEYBALL . . . . Clem Thompson
WATER SKIING . . . . . Herbert L. Loken

CREATIVE EDUCATIONAL SOCIETY, Inc., Mankato, Minnesota

1966 Edition

© Copyright 1961, 1962 by the
Creative Educational Society, Inc.
Mankato, Minnesota

1965 PRINTING
ALL RIGHTS RESERVED
PRINTED IN THE UNITED STATES OF AMERICA

Library of Congress Catalog Card Number: 62-19618

PICTURE ACKNOWLEDGMENTS

AAPHER 225

A. A. U. 105

American Bowling Congress . 61, 62

A. M. F. Pinsetters, Inc. .... 63, 64, 65, 66, 68, 69, 70, 71, 72, 73, 74, (lower left) 75, 76, 77, 79, (upper left) 80, 81, 82, 84, 87

Athletic Institute .... 12, 13, (lower left) 14, 17, 19, 20, (lower sequence) 23, 78

Bear Archery Co. .... (upper) 23

Brunswick-Balke-Collender Co. .. 67, (upper right) 72, (upper right) 75, (lower) 80, 83

Cypress Gardens .... 228, 229, (lower left) 231, 232, 233, 234, 235, 238, 239, 248, (upper left, lower left, middle right, lower right) 249

Fresno F. A. 28

Ice Center, Mpls., Minn. 127, 128, 129, 130, 131, 153

Mankato State College 30

Mercury Motors .. (lower right) 231, 236, 240, 241, 242, (upper right) 243, (upper right) 245, 246, 247, (upper right) 249, 250, 251

Northland Ski Co. 230, 237

Pop Musical Ice Revue Co., St. Paul, Minn. 124, 151

Sports Illustrated Magazine 115, 116

Stallcup, Dr. Leonard B., Official Photographer, U. S. Volleyball Ass'n 203, (upper) 205, (lower left) 211, 218, 220, 224

U.S. Volleyball Ass'n .... (lower) 205, 208, (sequence) 211, 217

Foreword

RECREATIONAL SPORTS ARE assuming a greater importance in our modern living where it is becoming more difficult to maintain for all age groups an adequate level of physical fitness. Our nation in late years has frequently been characterized as physically soft, a criticism which caused Dwight D. Eisenhower to issue his presidential proclamation in 1959 for a National Youth Fitness week.

Many physicians have indicated that physical activity of at least a mild nature is essential for healthful living and that such activity prevents children and adults from becoming overweight in addition to providing relaxing and joyful play experiences so essential in our fast-moving world.

The recreational sports found in this volume were selected by experts as representative for all ages; children, boys and girls and men and women. Special attention is given to adaptations of these activities for the beginner and experienced person.

Skills learned in recreational sports can be carried over into later school and adult life. Carry-over activities of the type found in this book are being recognized as of increasing value by authorities in the field. A person will continue to participate in an activity he enjoys and in which he has developed a certain degree of skill.

This volume can be used by individual students who want to learn and study more about these recreational sports, their history, skills and rules. Parents will want this volume for the family library as it can be used in planning for individual and family recreational projects. Teachers can use it to supplement teaching of the sports in school situations.

In short, this book has been written to help children, youth, adults, parents and teachers to learn more about recreational activities in order that they may participate in enjoyable, relaxing and invigorating physical practices now and in future years.

CLEM W. THOMPSON
Professor — Health and
Physical Education
Mankato State College

EDITORIAL BOARD

John Lowell Pratt, EDITOR-IN-CHIEF
Donald Schiffer, MANAGING EDITOR

EDITORIAL CONSULTANTS

Clifford L. Brownell, Chairman, Department of Health, Physical Education and Recreation, Teachers College, Columbia University

Carl L. Nordly, Chairman, Department of Physical Education, University of California, Berkeley, California

Kenneth L. Wilson, Former Commissioner, Big Ten (Western Intercollegiate Conference), President, U. S. Olympic Committee

Clifford B. Fagan, Executive Secretary, National Federation of State High School Athletic Associations

Theodore P. Bank, President, The Athletic Institute

Walter Byers, Executive Director, National Collegiate Athletic Association

Robert Kingery, Chief of the Preparation Division, New York Public Library, Library Consultant

William E. Jones, Reading Consultant—Lancaster Public Schools, New York

Clyde Overmyer, ART EDITOR

Roy Swanson, COVER ARTIST

Paul Siegel and John Biehl, PHOTOGRAPHERS

AUTHORS AND EDITORS

FOOTBALL. J. R. "Bob" Otto

BASEBALL. Frank F. DiClemente

BASKETBALL. Joe Hutton, and Vern B. Hoffman

TRACK AND FIELD. Earl "Bud" Myers and Rich Hacker

GOLF, SWIMMING, and TENNIS. Otis Dypwick, Einar Olsen, Helen H. Jacobs

RECREATIONAL SPORTS. Clifford L. Brownell, Roy B. Moore and Staff.

Introduction

A NATION IS AS STRONG as the people in it who possess courage, conviction, and calm determination. This strength comes not only from satellites revolving in space and the multitude of labor-saving devices, but also from proper diet, moderation in daily living, and a measure of healthful activities pursued during leisure hours. Fortunately, most persons in these United States appreciate the benefits to be derived from recreational sports available to citizens of all ages.

Recreation implies many things. Webster's Collegiate Dictionary defines recreation as ". . . a refreshment of strength and spirits after toil; a diversion or a mode of diversion, play."

The visual story in the pages that follow is designed to help individuals maintain strength and vigor while enjoying themselves at the same time. Many of the activities described can bring equal satisfaction to youths and adults, none of the events require superior physical skill, and hence entire families may join in healthful participation.

A person who engages in vigorous and wholesome activity during his leisure hours usually is better prepared to face day-to-day responsibilities than the one who "recreates" from the sidelines. Most persons gain emotional perspective by active participation in recreational sports, like those described herein.

For a more pleasurable and healthful life — people of all ages, in all walks of life — do something that refreshes body and spirit.

Clifford L. Brownell

CLIFFORD L. BROWNELL
Teachers College
Columbia University, N. Y.

7

Contents

ARCHERY

Don W. Buchanan

Through the Ages of Archery

Thousands of years ago the ability to shoot a bow and arrow was necessary for survival. The use of the bow was wide spread. Its main use was for hunting and warfare. The Asiatics, Europeans, and American Indians used the bow and arrow in warfare for centuries.

The bow remained significant until the gun displaced it. Only with the development of gun powder and the use of iron (later forms of steel were to replace iron) did the bow and arrow disappear as a weapon of protection and warfare.

Drawings and sketches made on rocks in caves indicate the extent to which the bow and arrow was used. Animals of various descriptions were drawn on the walls of caves and cliffs in the Mediterranean lands, the Near East, and in North Africa.

The Hebrews used the bow and added strings to it and made a crude harp.

The Greeks used the bow and arrow as a symbol of love—associated then with Diana and Cupid.

William Tell's use of the cross bow and Robin Hood's use of the English Longbow have become legendary in our time. They have been the basis for opera and motion picture film.

Today the more primitive peoples of Africa, South America, and the East Indies Islands are the remaining peoples using the bow and arrow as a means of getting food and for self defense. The European and American sports enthusiast may hunt exclusively with a bow but he does so because of a specialized interest.

The older bows of our ancesters were not very accurate weapons. The user's inaccuracy was compensated for by having the archers shoot volleys of arrows at what appeared to be the best time to do the most damage to the enemy. The American Indian was not a very accurate shot with bow. His success with the weapon was possible because he could stalk game and the enemy exceptionally well. Close shots taken at a few feet were the rule with the American Indian.

Archery was first fostered as a sport by King Charles II of England in 1676 and for years afterward it flourished among the European countries. Its popularity took hold in America early in the nineteenth century and led to the organization in Philadelphia in 1828 of the first archery club. Equipment originally was imported from England. But after the Civil War, with increased interest in the skill of the sport, Americans constructed their own equipment.

In 1879 the National Archery Association was founded in Crawfordsville, Indiana, and held its pioneer national tournament in Chicago. This Association has established the rules for target archery and annually fosters a national championship tournament.

Today the NAA has a membership of over two hundred clubs with thousands of archer-members. Colleges and universities sponsor intercollegiate and interschool indoor and outdoor target meets as well as mail tournaments. The Camp Archery Association sponsors an all year round program indoor and outdoor, in which schools, Y's, recreation clubs and camps participate. Tournaments are not only conducted on regional and national levels but also on international levels. The Olympic Bowman League conducts indoor winter mail match competition on an international basis to determine world champions. Archery ranges have been made available to thousands of enthusiastic bowman, positive proof of the fascinating challenge of the bow and arrow.

14

Archery Tackle

Archery equipment has kept pace with the number of archers. Tackle nowadays is of the highest caliber ever. Any bow or arrow is not only the result of centuries of experience but also the product of high level engineering.

Bow. — For target archery a good bow to start with is the American flat bow, either a self bow (made from a single piece of stock—solid wood, plastic, metal, a backed bow,) or a laminated bow. The latter is like the self bow except that it has a backing of fiber for greater strength and longer wear.

Most bows made today are of recurve design. A few companies make straight end laminated bows because there is still some preference for them among some of the experienced archers.

The parts of a bow are designated as follows:

HANDLE: the middle and thickest portion, about 4 inches in length. This is where you grip.

LIMBS (upper and lower): the working parts, between the handle and the tips.

ARROW PLATE: ornamental trim inlaid in the side of the handle where the arrow rubs it. The arrow plate facilitates recognition of the upper limb of the bow.

ARROW REST: a shelf at the top of the handle. Without this the arrow must rest on the top of the hand which holds the bow handle.

NOCKS (upper and lower): the notches in the bow at either end.

BOWSTRING: The string of the bow, usually made of dacron threads. The end loops of the bowstring go around the bow tips and into the bow nocks. Frequently the string has only one loop which can be fitted into the upper nock; the other end is plain so that it can be tied into a timber hitch to fit it to the length of the bow. The bowstring holds the bow to a braced position and casts or throws the arrow.

SERVING: a wrapping of thread to protect the bowstring from finger tab, armguard and arrow wear.

NOCKING POINT: a mark on the serving at right angles from the bowstring to the arrow rest where the arrow fits onto the serving. This is a constant place so that you shoot each arrow from the same position on the bowstring.

BACK: the side of the bow farthest from the string or facing away from you.

BELLY: the side closest to the string or facing toward you.

The bow you select must endure being bent often and to an extreme degree and must spring to its original shape when you release the strain on it. The best woods, those which can take this strain, are Osage Orange, yew, and lemonwood.

Your bow also must fit you in weight and length. Bow weight means the necessary pounds or pull required to draw the bow to the exact length of the arrow. Bow length is determined by your draw. Authorities have calculated a person's draw length, the proper arrow length, to be about 38 per cent of the total arm span — the "spread eagle" — measuring from fingertip to fingertip; and the bow length (this for a self bow) to be about 2½ times as long as the arrow. If your draw length measures for a 26-inch arrow, for example, your bow length should be 5 feet 5 inches, measured between the string nocks; the longer your draw, the longer your bow. Draw weight often is marked below the bow handle and is shown for a 28″ draw because a 28-inch draw is the average. A bow becomes set to a draw of a certain length arrow. Be sure you choose a bow you can draw without strain or you never will learn to shoot properly. It does not follow that the heavier the bow the faster and longer the arrow will fly. Work toward a heavier bow, however, because your accuracy will improve as you increase the weight of your bow.

Left-handed archers must be certain to use a bow which has an arrow rest to the right side of the bow. An archer wishing to purchase a bow must specify a left-handed model or the order will be filled with a right-handed bow.

The strength of the bowstring must be related to the weight of your bow, with a large margin of strength to take care of the tremendous momentary strain to which the string is subjected as the bow snaps back at the instant the arrow leaves it.

As a general rule, the string should be approximately 3½ inches shorter than the length of the bow. When measuring the bow, measure from nock to nock along the back of the bow.

The strength of a bow string is decided by the number of threads used to make up the thickness of the string. A 25-30 lb. bow requires a string made up of 9 threads; whereas, a bow of 55-60 lbs. requires a 24 thread string.

As a general rule proper string length will brace a bow to fistmele height (six inches). Test this by placing your clenched fist on the handle and fully extending the thumb. Your fist and thumb should span the distance from handle to string. Depending on the type of bow, the fistmele may vary between 6 to 8 inches. You had better check with the manufacturer of your bow to see what fistmele is recommended; then use a ruler rather than your fist and thumb to check the correct distance.

Arrow. — Arrows range in length from 24 inches to about 30 inches. Target archery arrows must be less than an ounce in weight and 5/16 of an inch in diameter. They must be rigid enough to withstand the sudden push of the string and at the same time, springy. For target archery all arrows must be as nearly identical as possible. An arrow's parts consist of the following:

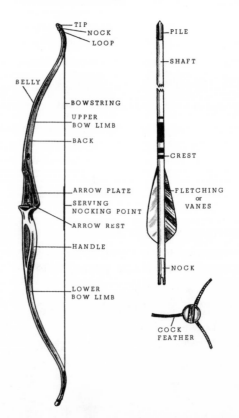

STELE OR SHAFT: the main part of the arrow. Upon this part the whole behavior of the arrow in flight depends. The footing and pile are part of the shaft.

SHAFTMENT: the end portion of the arrow that bears the crest and feathers and the groove (nock).

FEATHERS OR VANES: Stiff, durable and flexible, these help guide the shaft. In number the vanes range from 3 to 8. One feather is usually of a different color from the others, set at right angles to the arrow's nock. This is the cock feather. The others are called hen feathers.

CREST: the decoration which serves to identify the arrows.

NOCK: a groove at the end of the shaftment. The bowstring fits into this groove.

FOOTING: a hard, dense piece of wood, spliced on the end of the shaft, to make the arrow stronger.

PILE: the tip or head of the arrow, made of metal to aid penetration of the target.

The first choice for wooden arrow shafts is Port Orford cedar; second choice, Sitka spruce. Both of these woods are scarce. Other wood shaft material is white birch which is tough but has a tendency to warp; fiber glass (tubular type) which is strong, straight, and impervious to moisture; and aluminum which is light and durable.

Targets and Backstops. — One of the most hazardous phases of archery is the possibility of an arrow not stopping in the intended distance.

Commercially-made targets and backstops can be purchased at a nominal cost. The types sold are of several varieties; such as, a wound grass target, tied straw, or a paper box target filled with straw.

Other arrow-stopping materials are common bales of hay or excelsior bales.

Archers who wish to shoot in their basement would normally shoot into a commerical target or a bale and also use some type of material to make a back-drop. This back-drop can easily be an old rug or other material large enough to cover an adequate space behind the target itself. This back-drop is generally thought of as a protective device — protecting the arrows from undue damage.

The "back-yard" archer must be certain of adequate back-stops to eliminate any danger of an arrow ricocheting away from the target itself. Extra bales will serve the purpose; however, a mound of dirt will be more successful.

There is a definite procedure to follow when removing arrows from a target. The proper method is to press one hand against the target face and pull the arrow with the other hand. Pulling arrows in this manner eliminates the possibility of tearing the target face.

Sundry Gear. — Though not absolutely essential, these items of equipment will make your shooting more comfortable.

BRACER OR ARMGUARD: a piece of stout leather which you can lash to your bow forearm just above the wrist. The lashing should be on the outside so the bowstring has a smooth surface on which to strike. This arm guard protects you against bruises or welts. When you loose the string, depending on the shape of your arm and how you hold the bow, it may give you a hard whack on the inside of your left forearm. If you wear a jacket an armguard is not necessary, but you should tie up the wrist of the jacket with a piece of string or tape.

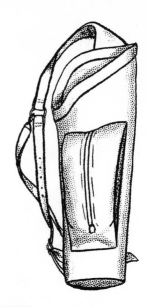

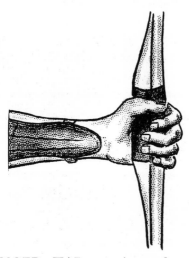

FINGER TAB: a piece of supple leather cut to fit your shooting fingers. Use leather about 1/16 inch thick. Cut two holes to slip over the fore and third fingers and to project so as to cover all three of your working fingertips. Cut a slot between the fore and second finger so the shaft may come through. You will need this tab to protect your fingers as you draw the bowstring, because the tip of the forefinger, on its inside surface, may get pinched in the angle between the string and the shaft.

QUIVER: a device for holding or carrying arrows. A ground quiver, used by target archers, has a pointed end which can be forced into the turf a few inches. Fashioned from a steel rod, the upper end has a circular loop and a pair of extended bent rods, which serve as arrow and bow supports respectively. Some archers use a side quiver which hangs from the belt around their waist. A back quiver, used by roving and field archers, comes in various styles and sizes, and holds from one to three dozen arrows. Popular, too, with these archers is a bow quiver, a device attached above and below the bow handle which holds about four arrows.

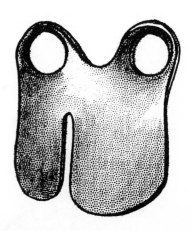

Fundamental Skills and Techniques

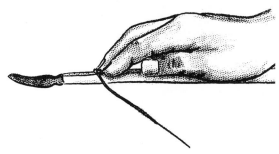

The first skill to learn in archery is how to string your bow. Then master the stance, the grip, nocking, drawing, anchoring, aiming and releasing. Consistency in these skills will cause your bow to cast each arrow correctly. Timing and rhythm will become automatic with practice.

Stringing the Bow. — Before you prepare your bow for action, first make sure it is not upside down. The longer of the two limbs must be uppermost. Then to limber it, bend it gradually and progressively several times. To string it:

1. Standing with your feet apart, grasp the handle with your left hand. Place the tip of the lower limb against the instep of your left foot — don't let the tip touch the ground. Brace your left arm against your hipbone.

2. Put the heel of your right hand on the flat side of the upper limb near the nock. Let your middle finger rest behind the loop of the string on the back of the bow (above).

3. Bend the bow, with your instep as a brace, by pulling back with your left (bow) hand and pressing down on the back of the bow with the heel of your right (string) hand.

4. Work your hand toward the tip of the bow and guide the loop into the nock with your fingers.

When you have your bow strung, the string should be at least 6 inches (one fistmele) away from the grip of the bow.

To unbend the bow, because you must never put it away fully strung, brace the bow against your left instep, push with your right hand and pull with your left to take the tension off the string. Then use your fingers to ease the loop out of the nock (below).

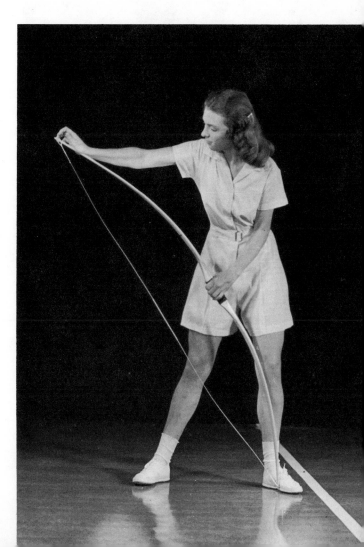

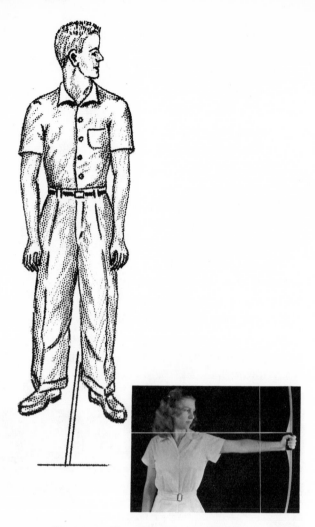

Stance. — To address the target properly for target shooting, your body and shoulders must line up in the direction of flight at all times (above).

1. Stand astride the shooting line at right angles to the target, with the shoulder of your bow arm in the direction of the arrow's flight.

2. Keep your knees straight but not stiff and your hips and shoulders directly over your feet which should be about 10 to 12 inches apart.

3. Hold your chest high, with head erect and turned so that you look directly at the target. Let your arms hang loosely at your sides.

Placing the Bow in the Bow Hand. — Your grip is the way the handle of the drawn bow seats itself comfortably into the V of your hand, formed by the base of the forefinger and the base of the thumb. This requires holding the bow with the fingers closed very lightly about the handle so that the bow is not twisted from alignment and also means that your elbow joint of the bow arm must be in a somewhat vertical position, otherwise the bowstring will strike your arm after it is released. Therefore:

1. With your bow horizontal to the ground, bowstring toward you, and your bow arm extended, back of the bow hand up, grasp the handle over the bowstring as you would grasp a suitcase handle, with a V made by your thumb and forefinger. With your string hand pull on the bowstring a bit to make certain you feel the pressure against the heel of your hand and not down the middle of your palm (below).

2. Rotate the bow hand only, from the wrist, until your bow is in a vertical position. Keep your wrist straight but not stiff.

3. Gripping lightly on the handle, raise the bow toward the target until your arm is parallel to the ground. Turn your elbow out and back. It should "lock" in a bent, almost vertical, position. Keep your shoulders perfectly level.

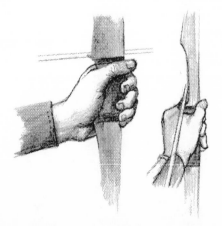

If your wrist is right you should be able to see a fairly straight line down your forearm from the elbow extending on through your thumb.

Nocking the Arrow. — You are ready to put your arrow in the bow — to place the arrow's nock on the bowstring at the nocking point.

1. With the correct grip on the handle hold the bow down in front of your left hip and parallel to the ground, string toward the side of your body. The back of your bow hand is up.

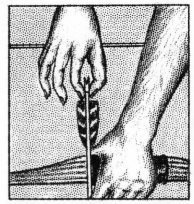

2. Use your thumb and index finger of your string hand to grasp an arrow behind the vanes, cock feather up, and lay it over the top side of the bow's upper limb on the arrow rest. Lacking an arrow rest, lay the arrow on the first knuckle of the bow hand against the bow.

3. Place the index finger of your bow hand lightly over the arrow shaft to hold it in position against the bow.

4. To slide the arrow toward the nocking point until the nock is lying on top of the bowstring nocking point, slip the index finger (which is under the arrow nock) under the bowstring. The thumb will keep the nock in position.

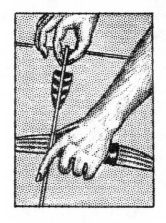
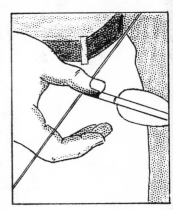

5. Again, hold the arrow nock with the thumb and index finger and place it onto the nocking point of the string. If you have nocked your arrow correctly and your bow hand is in the right position, the arrow and string make a perfect right angle.

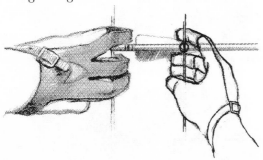

Your arrow is now ready to draw. Remember before you start the draw to return the index finger of the bow hand where it belongs. Your arrow will be immediately de-nocked if you start to draw while holding the arrow against the side of the bow with the index finger of your bow hand.

Drawing the Bowstring. — With a proper stance, a relaxed grip, and an arrow nocked you are ready to spread the bow. You do this by drawing (pulling) the bowstring with your string hand to your anchor point.

1. Place the index finger of the string hand above and just touching the arrow and the two next fingers below the arrow. (Keep your thumb and little finger out of the way.) Hold the bowstring at the first joint of the fingers, or slightly nearer the tips. Keep the wrist straight so that the back of your string hand aligns with your forearm (below left and center).

2. Push slightly with your bow arm and pull straight back from your shoulders with the string arm until your index finger reaches your anchor point. Equalize the push and pull—both hands should come to the position of full draw at the same time.

The anchor point is a place upon or against your face where you hold the hand which has drawn the bowstring. Once you establish an anchor point you draw exactly to it every time you draw. Your anchor point may be either of two places: (1) The center of your chin. This brings your forefinger under the chin, firmly pressed against your jawbone. The bowstring should cut the middle of your chin and if your head position is correct, the string should also rest on the point of your nose. (2) The side of your chin. This brings the thumb up and along the side of the cheek or directly behind the jawbone and the string to the side of your nose (below right).

Take a breath as you draw and hold your breath until you release. At full draw your string arm is a continuation of the arrow.

Releasing the Bowstring. — At the instant you adjust your aim, you release the bowstring by allowing the string fingers to relax and quit holding. The string slowly rolls off your fingertips. This sets the arrow on its flight. While aiming or at the moment of release you must not allow the arrow point to move forward of the back side of the bow. This is a "creeping on the draw" action which consumes some of the original cast and leads to inconsistent shooting. If you jerk at the release or if you permit the string to roll off your fingers too suddenly the arrow will wobble on its flight to the target.

As you release and the pressures are relieved, your hands will move apart slightly in their respective directions of force. This is the follow through, a natural involuntary action. Keep your shooting position — don't lower either arm — until the arrow, hits the target (below).

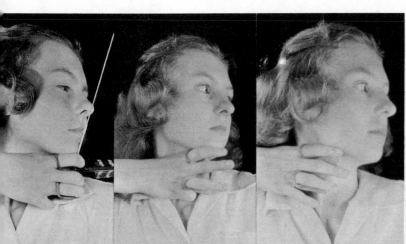

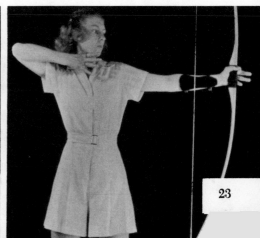

Aiming. — The way in which an arrow is released results in the arrow's taking off in an upward direction. Thus the flight of an arrow describes an arc. This arc is called the arrow's trajectory. With any given bow and arrow there is only one distance at which you can shoot and hit the target by aiming directly at the gold. This is the point blank range. At any other distance you have to change the angle of take-off so the flight of the arrow will be interrupted by the target. Once you have figured out this angle for your bow you must release each arrow at that same angle. Since each bow has a different trajectory, you have to determine the correct angle of release for your arrows at each different range — at, for example, 50 yards, 40 yards, and 30 yards.

Point of Aim Method — For target shooting the most satisfactory system of aiming is the point of aim method. With this method you use a specific object, for example, a block of wood on the ground (C), or an object in a tree (A), at which to aim. When this object is in proper position and when the arrow point is sighted on it at full draw, the correct trajectory is given the arrow. If you do not use a point of aim and if you stand farther from the target than the point blank range (which certainly at first you won't know) and aim at the gold, your arrow will fall short of the target. Or if you stand nearer to the target than the point blank range and aim at the gold, your arrow will probably fly above the target.

If your distance from the target is short, you must adjust your sight line (your aim), to bring the arrow's flight line to the center of the target.

Therefore you sight (aim) low in front of the target. This compensates for the fact that you cannot get your eye in a direct line with the arrow's flight. To determine where on the ground to aim you will have to experiment, using a marker or point of aim. Your marker must be in a straight line from you through the center of the gold. To get it in this line, take your stance at the shooting line. Now hold your bow out at arm's length, with the bowstring vertical and passing through the center of the gold. Your point of aim should be along the bowstring. So have someone place your marker on the ground about a third of the distance from the target and in direct line with your bowstring.

Use the marker, your point of aim, as an aiming point and shoot a few arrows. You may have to adjust the point of aim a few feet closer to or farther from the target so your arrows will hit the target. If your shots are too low (below the gold), you must raise your point of aim. Therefore move the marker closer to the target. Once your arrows begin to group on the gold, you have a proper point of aim for your present distance from the target.

As you put more distance between you and the target, your point of aim moves closer to the target. When your point of aim coincides with the center of the gold, you have found point blank range. Mov-

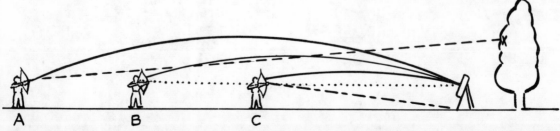

A   B   C

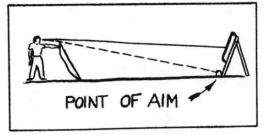

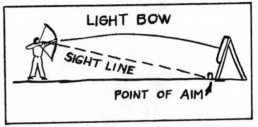

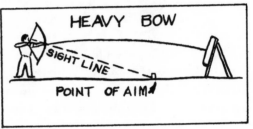

ing still farther away, probably 50 yards or more, means that your point of aim now will have to be on the target or be an object above the target: the longer the range the h i g h e r t h e point of aim. Whether high or low, the point of aim must be along the straight line (the bowstring, here) from your eye through the center of the gold.

Once you have worked out the location of your aiming points for the distances you plan to shoot (for example for 50, 40, or 30 yards from the target) with your bow, you will not have to experiment again if you record these on a rangefinder.

A slat of wood about 6 inches long and about the size of a tongue depressor — on which you can write — makes an adequate rangefinder. The top of your slat should have one square corner. Mark a red dot in this corner (below).

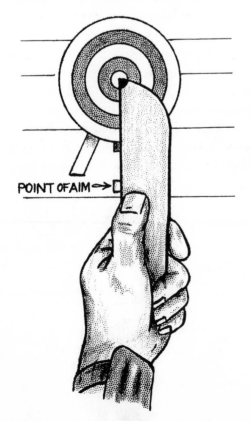

POINT OF AIM →

Now using your bow to steady your aim, stand at your shooting line and hold the slat out at the full extent of your bow arm toward the target (top above). Raise or lower the stick until in your line of vision (usually the right eye) the red dot in the top square corner lines up with the center of the gold and with your point of aim. Put your thumb on this spot on the stick. Then with a pencil draw a line across the stick and note the distance. Now you have a permanent measuring rod to tell you the exact spot for your point of aim the next time you shoot from this distance. By this method you can add the other range marks after you have established their aiming points.

Remember, your range finder will work only for the bow for which you made it. Points of aim vary with the weight of the bow (above), length of the arrow, height of the archer, distance between the eye and the chin of the archer, and the distance of the archer from the target.

Whenever you get a grouping of arrows away from the gold after you have established a point of aim, you probably are aiming properly but are missing one of the fundamentals of shooting. Bad habits show up on the target. For example:

If your arrows are high on the gold, you may be overdrawing, bringing the string back beyond the anchor point, or "peeking" (looking up to watch arrow flight).

If your arrows are low, you may not be drawing all the way back to your anchor point, or dropping the bow at the instant the arrow is released.

If your arrows are going to the right, you may be holding the string too far in on your string fingers, or "Relaxing," (letting your drawing hand move forward).

If your arrows are going to the left, you may be moving your string hand away from the anchor point, or "Hunching" (lifting the left shoulder), or "Throwing the bow arm" (moving the bow arm toward the target).

Bowsight Method.— More experienced archers use a bowsight to simplify the procedure of aiming. A bowsight is a horizontal pin or bar which can be fastened on the back of the bow just above the arrow rest and which can be moved up or down. Some bowsights have peep holes, some have pin-type aim indicators, others have ground glass lenses for distances. The most common, a horizontal aiming bar, can be used for distances from 10 to about 80 yards. To use this bar you first must determine the distance the arrow will be drawn below the eye or the exact location of the arrow point. Then you move the aiming bar this same distance above the arrow rest. Try shooting your arrows now from 10 yards, lining up the sight with the center of the target. Follow the arrow loca-

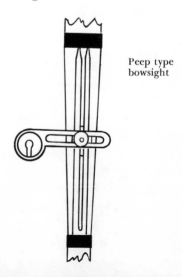

Peep type bowsight

tion with the sight bar. Now shoot a few more arrows. If they go to the left, move the sight out to the left; if they group high, raise the sight a bit. Once all is correct for 10 yards, you must move the sight bar down the bow limb towards the upper end of the bow handle about $\frac{1}{2}$ inch to $\frac{5}{8}$ inch for each 10 yards you move away from the target. After you have located the sight bar for each distance, record your calibrations on a piece of adhesive tape and attach the tape to the back of your bow.

Instinctive Method. — Field archers follow the instinctive method of shooting — a natural method of shooting the bow — without benefit of point of aim, bowsight, or distance measurement. T h e y must learn to adjust shooting to range rather than to yardage. Instinctively, shooters aim the way a person would point a finger to indicate an object. The shooter will draw his arrow, elevate his bow arm to what he considers the proper height, and then release his arrow. His main concern is to keep his line of sight directly on the target. Most instinctive archers use the side of chin anchor point.

The instinctive archers are called "instinctors" and the National Field Archery Association places them in the "bare bow" classification for tournaments.

To learn to shoot by the instinctive method, follow this procedure:

1. Spread your feet well apart for a brace against wind and body motion. Keep your body at right angles to the target.

2. Incline your bow slightly to keep the string away from your face.

3. Tilt your head slightly, so that your right eye is over the arrow. Tilting your head improves your sight line.

4. Hold the bow lightly and firmly. A tight grip means you are tense.

5. Rest your bow against the thumb-side of your palm. In this way the weight of your draw will be against your thumb.

6. Keep your b o w a r m firm and straight.

7. Anchor the bowstring high on your cheek, the top finger touching the corner of your mouth.

8. Use both eyes.

9. Use a full draw for hitting power. Beware of creeping.

10. Hold your shot for the single moment that you need to get set and aim.

Your accuracy depends upon the keenness of your judgment — your ability to adjust your aim quickly in relation to your judgment of distance and your target. If you experience difficulties in releasing, you probably are too tense. If your arrows are not going to the target, check these points:

1. Arrows going to the left may mean your grip is too tight, or you are anchoring too far to the right of your eye.

2. Arrows going to the right may mean that your feet are not placed correctly in relation to the target or your bow grip may be moving to the left after your release.

3. If you are overshooting or undershooting you may be releasing the arrow too far above or below your anchor or you may be dropping your bow hand.

And if you still are wide of the target your arrows may be either too stiff or too limber. The best procedure now is to check w i t h a n experienced field archer.

Target Archery

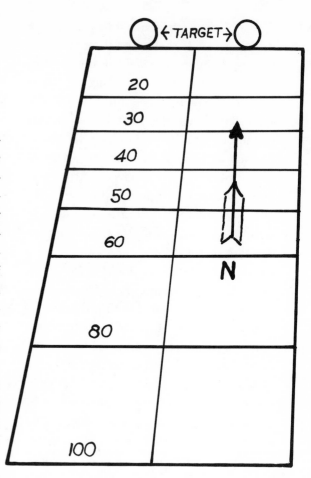

Target archery involves shooting arrows from fixed distances at a bull's-eye in a regulation circular target. The scoring system is set; the outcome of competition is based on either individual or team scores or both. Archers shoot a specified number of ends (an end is six arrows) in a round (a given number of ends from more than one distance). In target shooting a definite system of aiming is essential either by point-of-aim or bowsight, since consistent accuracy is the objective.

Range. — A target archery range is a carefully measured area, the shooting lines parallel to the regulation targets on the range and at set distances from these targets. The archers shoot on lanes, not more than four to a target. The ideal range runs north and south, with targets at the north end (right).

Rounds. — In target archery, archers are required to shoot a given number of consecutive ends (termed a range). When these are shot from more than one given distance, the archer shoots a round. Rounds are classified for specified age groups. "Junior" in the name of a round means that only boys and girls under 15 years of age can participate in the round. Boys and girls between the ages of 15 and 18 are "intermediates." Some rounds are for men only, others for ladies only. The most common rounds for target archery competition are outlined here. The chart shows the total number of arrows to be shot at specified distances. For example, in an American Round, 90 arrows must be shot as follows: 30 at 60 yards, 30 at 50 yards, and 30 at 40 yards.

COMMON TARGET ROUNDS: MEDIUM TO LONG RANGE

Rounds		Target Size	Total No. Arrows	Distance (Yards)	Scoring
American men, ladies and intermediates ..		48″	90	60-50-40	9-7-5-3-1
Junior American		48″	90	50-40-30	9-7-5-3-1
Columbia (ladies)		48″	24	50-40-30	9-7-5-3-1
Junior Columbia		48″	24	50-40-20	9-7-5-3-1
Scholastic		48″	24	40-30	9-7-5-3-1
Junior Scholastic		48″	24	30-20	9-7-5-3-1
Team					
ladies, juniors		48″	96	50	9-7-5-3-1
men's		48″	96	60	9-7-5-3-1
intermediates		48″	96	40	9-7-5-3-1

COMMON TARGET ROUNDS: SHORT RANGE

Rounds	Position	Target Size	Total No. Arrows	Distance (Yards)	Scoring
Chicago		16″	96	20	9-7-5-3-1
Olympic		48″	90	30	9-7-5-3-1
Flint	1	8″	4	17	
	2	6″	4	20 (feet)	
	3	8″	4	20	
	4	6″	4	14	
	5	8″	4	15	
	6	6″	4	10	
	7	8″	1	20	
			1	18	
			1	16	
			1	14	

Scoring: Dot and Inner Ring: 5 pts. Outer Ring: 3 pts.

Note: Normal Rounds is 56 arrows (twice through the seven shooting positions).

NFAA NATIONAL INDOOR ROUND

Uses variable distances.
Ten targets are shot, with
four arrows per target.
The round is shot as two units of
five targets each.
For the 20-yard indoor range
it would be as follows:

UNIT ONE

Distance	Target
20 feet	8 inch
30	8
40	12
50	12
60	12

UNIT TWO

25 feet	8 inch
35	8
40	12
45	12
55	12

For the 30-yard indoor range it is:

UNIT ONE

40 feet	12 inch
50	12
60	16
70	16
80	16

UNIT TWO

30 feet	12 inch
45	12
60	16
75	16
90	16

Scoring: Same as the Flint round.

Target Scoring. — Archers are assigned to targets, with usually four to a target and no more than two shooting at the same time on one target. Shooting follows the order the archers' names appear on a score card. In shooting, the archer must stand with one foot on each side of the shooting line and, when shooting in turn shoots three arrows, yields his place to his mate, and then in his turn shoots the other three arrows. Each archer shoots a set number of ends in a round. Shooting for each end begins at a signal from a Field Captain (men) or a Lady Paramount (ladies). Any type of bow except a cross bow may be used. Arrows of each archer should have a distinctive mark (crest) for identification. Points of aim used for aiming may not be more than 6 inches above the ground and may never be placed on the target.

The colors on the target face represent scoring values: gold, 9 points; red, 7 points; blue, 5 points; black, 3 points; white, one point. The center of the gold shall be 4 feet from the ground. An ar-

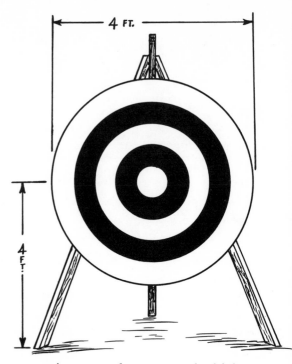

row cutting two colors counts the higher value. Those arrows shot at distances of 60 yards or less which rebound from the scoring face of the target count 7 points.

Upon the completion of an end, all archers go to the target to score their hits (below left). Those hits of the highest value are withdrawn and recorded first, and each hit is separately itemized on the score sheet. Each target has a designated captain who draws the arrows and calls the value of each. Each target has two scorers who record the values. As all ends for each distance are completed, the scorers total the number of hits for that distance and also the score for all ends from that distance. This is the range score. When the round is over, the scorers total the complete number of hits and total the complete score. This is the archer's final score. In team competition, the team score is the compilation of scores of all team members shooting the same round.

Field Archery

Interest in field archery has grown by leaps and bounds ever since some expert target archers in California in 1930 took to the field after small game. To foster the development of field archery and bow hunting, the National Field Archery Association was founded in 1939 at Redlands, California. Its activities include hunting with the bow, roving (shooting at various inanimate objects while strolling through meadows or woods), and shooting field round roving or field archery courses. The first national tournament for field archers, sponsored by the Association, was held at Allegan, Michigan, in 1946. Since then the Association has held annual tournaments, the national champion being selected from the instinctive shooting class under the field round roving rules.

In field archery, the arrows are shot from distances known to the archers and at various types of regulation targets or animated targets by the instinctive method of aiming or free style method. In competition, the archers shoot around a specially laid out field archery course. These field round roving courses are in units of 14 target layouts, with a specific scoring system. In match or team play, the outcome is decided by totaling the points each archer has made on all the targets. A round constitutes the shooting of the complete target course.

Robin Hood clubs for junior field archers are popping up everywhere to offer the young enthusiast an opportunity to enjoy all aspects of field shooting.

Membership in the NFAA today exceeds 2000 clubs, with nearly 20,000 archers participating in field shooting competition sponsored by individual clubs, state associations, and the National Field Archery Association.

The field archery range is a simulated hunting area, and might be compared to a golf course with its hazards and long and short distances. The targets, generally 14 in number for a field round roving course, are set at varying distances and are of varying sizes. The archers following the numbered posts shoot around the range in groups of not less than three.

Archers shoot in groups from three to five in number over a 14-target course. The course plus all the official shots is a unit. A round is two units or twice around one. Each archer shoots four arrows (an end) at each of the 14-target layouts in a unit. In ten cases this means the four arrows from a single post (shooting position) at a single target face. In the other four cases it means either: (1) shooting one arrow from each of four posts at a single face; or (2) shooting all four arrows from a single post but at four separate faces. Four face sizes are used. The outside ring of the targets is black. *Field Scoring.* — The bull's-eye is white and the aiming spot black. Animal targets with these official round faces may be used. An archer scores 5 points for hitting the bull's-eye, including the spot, and 3 points for the outer circle. A standard unit consists of the following 14 shots, 4 arrows at each distance:

Layout of a 14 Unit Roving Range

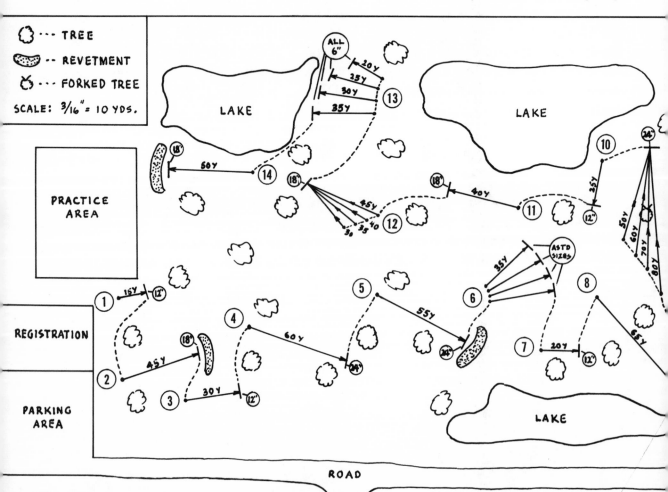

 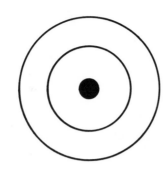 

15, 20, 25, and 30 yards at a 12-inch target;

40, 45, and 50 yards at an 18-inch target;

55, 60, and 65 yards at a 24-inch target.

Four position shots — each arrow shot from a different position or at a different target:

35 yards — 18-inch target, all from the same distance but from different positions or at different targets;

30, 35, 40, and 45 yards at an 18-inch target;

50, 60, 70, and 80 yards at a 24-inch target;

20, 25, 30, and 35 feet at a 6-inch target.

Any kind of bow except a crossbow and any kind of arrow except broadheads (those with large metal tips) may be used. A Field Captain appoints a target captain and two scorers for each shooting group and designates the order in which groups are to shoot or assigns posts from which each group is to start. Shooting is in the order of the scores made on the last previous target, the highest scorer first and so on. Archers shall stand with both feet back of the shooting line, and no one may approach the target until all have finished shooting. The target captain orders the shooting at his target and draws all arrows for recording. An arrow cutting two rings is scored as being in the ring of greater value. Witnessed bounces and arrows passing through the target are scored three points. All targets are numbered and yardages are posted on most ranges.

In tournament shooting, instinctive and free-style archers are divided into separate classifications. Instinctive archers compete only against other instinctive archers. The different rounds are called Field Round, Hunters Round, and Big Game Round, and each has specifications which must be followed in the shoot.

In some meets, free style shooters (those using a bow sight) may compete in the same tournament with instinctive shooters, as long as the bowsight is not calibrated for the course. Scores for free style archers must be kept in a separate division or class, however, and not with the instinctive class.

Archery Safety Rules

1. Inspect bow for cracks.
2. Inspect loops and serving of bow for fraying.
3. After stringing the bow, make sure the distance between the serving and the bow handle is no greater than one fistmele (6 inches).
4. Examine arrows for
   a. proper length
   b. cracks or checks in shaft
   c. proper fletching
   d. proper tip.
5. Never draw bow string without an arrow.
6. Inspect target area to determine that other persons will not be endangered by your shooting.
7. Nock arrow only when you are ready to shoot.
8. Never stand in front of another archer — always be in "line" with him.
9. Retrieve all arrows at the same time when two persons or more are shooting.
10. Shoot only at the target.
11. Never shoot an arrow straight up into the air.
12. Never shoot arrows for distance unless you can see over twice as far as you expect the arrow to travel.
13. Call "timber" if you wish to warn persons that you are ready to shoot.
14. Avoid "trick" shots; such as allowing another person to hold a target for you.
15. Handle the bow and arrow as a deadly weapon — it has been!

Bibliography

Burke, Edmund: *Archery Handbook*. New York: Arco Publishing Co., 1954.

Burke, Edmund: *The History of Archery*. New York: William Morrow and Co., 1957.

Elmer, Robert P.: *Target Archery*. New York: Alfred A. Knopf, 1946.

Forbes, Thomas A.: *A Guide to Better Archery*. Harrisburg, Pa.: Stackpole Company, 1955.

Grogan, Hiram J.: *Modern Bow Hunting*. Harrisburg, Pa.: Stackpole Company, 1955.

Hochman, Louis: *Complete Archery Book*. New York: Arco Publishing Co., 1957.

Hodgkin, A. E.: *The Archer's Craft*. New York: The Ronald Press Company (N.D.).

Hougham, Paul: *The Encyclopedia of Archery*. New York: A. S. Barnes and Co., 1958.

Jaeger, Eloise: *How to Improve Your Archery*. Chicago: The Athletic Institute (N.D.).

Reichart, Natalie and Gilman Keasey: *Archery*. New York: The Ronald Press Co., 1940.

Whiffen, Larry C.: *Shooting the Bow*. Chicago, Ill.: Bruce Publishing Co., 1946.

Guides and Rules Books:

Official Archery — Riding Guide, Division of Girls and Women's Sports, American Association for Health, Physical Education and Recreation, Washington, D.C.

Official Target Archery Rules, The National Archery Association, Santa Ana, Calif.

Official Field Archery Rules, National Field Archery Association, Redlands, Calif.

BADMINTON

Dee Whitlock

Origin and Growth

BADMINTON IS AN IDEAL sport for every-one. Just about anyone, in a matter of minutes, can learn to hit the shuttle back and forth across the net well enough to immediately enjoy playing the game.

However, those who wish to become skilled badminton players must realize that this is one of the fastest and most active sports.

Research has shown that a man who is a topflight player, engaged in a game of singles, uses more arm action than a base-ball pitcher who plays a full nine-inning game, where the average number of pitches is 100. In one game of singles, a top player runs further than a running back or end who plays a full sixty min-utes of football!

There is a feature in this game which makes it different from any other sport. The range of speed is greater than in any other sport. When gently tapped, the shuttle floats more slowly than any object hit in any other game, but when hit hard and timed just right, the shuttle travels at a speed of over 110 miles per hour! It can easily be seen that there can be a change of pace in badminton not equalled in any other sport.

With all these features, badminton has fun and excitement to offer to all levels of players including the family that enjoys using the back yard set and the young competitive man or woman who takes part in tournaments.

Although played differently long ago than it is now, the game of badminton is actually hundreds of years old. It had its beginning in India where it was called Poona. The natives played it with tiny rackets and a feathered shuttlecock. In the 1860's English Army officers stationed in India saw the game and tried it. Several years later some of the officers went back to England on leave. They attended a party at the Duke of Beaufort's country estate called Badminton, where they played Poona. After that time, Poona became known as the game of Badminton.

At that time the rules were not clear and different people had different ideas about the way the game should be played. Therefore, in 1887 the Bath Badminton Club in England fitted the game to English ideas and standardized the rules. In 1895 several English clubs met and formed the Badminton Association of England. This group set up rules which still govern the game throughout the world.

At this time the game was only played by the wealthy class of people. It was simply a gentlemanly batting back and forth a shuttle over a net. While "playing", the men wore Prince Albert coats, high button shoes and silk hats. Women also dressed in the height of fashion, usually wearing large hats and long gowns. Once a club even expelled a player who went so far as to remove his coat during the heat of the game!

The game was introduced to the United States in 1876. It was being played throughout the country some fifty years later and by 1937 the first National Championships were held.

Competition reached world-wide proportions in 1949. Sixteen countries, including our own country, competed for the Thomas Cup, the equivalent of the Davis Cup Matches in tennis and run along almost identical lines.

Badminton in the United States does not have the excellent playing facilities as in other countries such as Denmark and Canada. Also, it does not receive the emphasis that a major spectator sport does. In Malaya it is front-page headline news whenever a Malayan player wins an important tournament.

In spite of the above factors, our country has produced some outstanding players. Dr. David Freeman of Pasadena, California, held an amazing record of not having been beaten in singles play (including Thomas Cup Matches) over a ten year span! In 1949 he won the All-England Singles Championship in London, England, against the best players from Malaya, India, Denmark and other countries.

American women were well represented in this tournament by Mrs. Clinton Stephens. She and her husband, Mr. Stephens, won the world's top honors in the Mixed Doubles Championship.

Equipment and Playing Area

A good deal of badminton's appeal results from the fact that the equipment is light and easy to handle. Because the racket is light and the shuttle can be so quickly directed at various speeds, the game has more possibility for deception than any other sport.

Racket. — No official specifications or limitations are prescribed for the size and weight of a badminton racket; the average length is about 26 inches, and the weight, when strung, is about 5 ounces. A heavier racket will give a little more slugging power, but this advantage is more than lost by lack of speed and handling. The most important factor in a racket is balance.

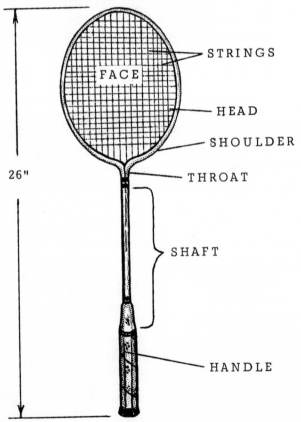

26"

STRINGS

FACE

HEAD

SHOULDER

THROAT

SHAFT

HANDLE

Wood rackets of ash, beech and hickory are greatly used, although steel rackets and rackets with a steel shaft are available generally at a somewhat higher price.

When selecting your racket, choose a handle that fits snugly and comfortably into your hand and fingers — one that feels just right when you try a few swings.

Test your choice by holding the racket by the top of the head and the handle. There should be an even bend along the full length of the racket.

The best material for stringing, to give liveliness and resilience, is gut. There are different gauges or thicknesses of gut; twenty gauge is a good playing average, while twenty-one gauge is a light, delicate tournament weight.

Nylon stringing qualifies well for wear and its quality has improved greatly in the last several years.

When not in use, be sure to keep the racket in a press to prevent the wood from warping. A waterproof cover is necessary to keep moisture away from the gut strings.

Shuttlecock. — The shuttlecock, commonly called shuttle or bird, is designed with precision, weighing from 73 to 85 grains for indoor and outdoor play. Each grain adds about 4 inches to the length of the flight. The base is made of cork, 1 inch to 1⅛ inches in diameter,

CORK

covered with fine, light, kid leather. Inserted into this base are 14 to 16 goose feathers from 2½ to 2¾ inches in length.

It takes one goose to supply enough suitable feathers to make one shuttle, so treat the shuttles that you use with due respect!

The ends of the feathers are either pointed or rounded — the pointed-end feather will give more distance than the rounded-end of the same weight.

Shuttles are marked either by weight or as slow, medium, or fast. The warmer the room the faster the shuttle; the average weight shuttle for heated courts is 76 grains pointed-end or 79 grains, rounded-end. Keep shuttles in a cool, moist place, such as a humidifier. If they dry out they break up quickly.

Plastic or synthetic shuttles are available in standard weights for indoor or outdoor practice.

Costume. — Wear a costume which will allow you full freedom of movement. White clothes are preferred — all contestants in National Championships must wear white. Your feet get a good pounding during a game, so use a light shoe with good tacky soles, well cushioned inside. Two pairs of heavy wool socks (never cotton, or you are likely to blister) help provide a cushion, too.

Court. — A badminton court has two sets of lines, one for singles play (when two players compete) and one for doubles play (when two players on each team compete). Court size is 20 x 44 feet.

Good facilities should have at least two feet of clear space on the sides of the court and not less than four feet clear-

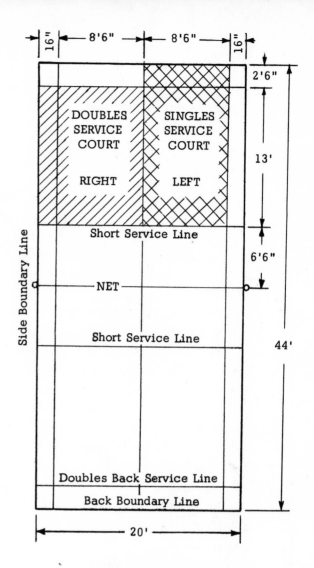

ance at each end. Overhead space of twenty-four to thirty feet is good. National and international competition requires a safe height of well over thirty feet.

A net, 5 feet high from the floor in the center and 5 feet one inch high at the post ends, is suspended across the middle of the court, from post to post. The official net, fine tanned cord of ¾ inch mesh, is 2 feet 6 inches in depth. The parts, lines and dimensions of the court are shown in the illustration above. The lines should be 1½ inches wide.

Rules. — The game is played by one player (singles) or two players (doubles) on a side. Service is determined by a toss, the winner having the option of serving first, not serving first, or choosing ends. A player on the "in" or serving side starts the game from the right-hand service court, hitting the shuttle underhand diagonally to the right-hand court of the receiving side, the "out" side (below). If the receiver of the service returns the shuttle successfully, the shuttle is hit by alternate sides until a fault (violation) is made. If the fault is made by the serving side a handout (loss of service) is declared; therefore the serve goes to the opposite side. If the fault is made by the receiving side, the serving side scores one point. As long as a side remains "in," the service is delivered alternately from each half of the court into the opponent's court which is diagonally opposite. Only the server scores; he continues to serve as long as he wins points.

In the singles game the long narrow service court is used. The service is always from the right-hand service court when the server's score is zero or an even number, and from the left-hand service court when his score is odd or an uneven number.

In the doubles game the short, wide service court is used. The player in the right-hand court always makes the first serve of every inning (the side's turn to serve). Both partners serve in turns alternating courts (right to left and left to right) until a hand-out occurs for each. On the first service of the game, however, only one partner serves — only one hand-out is permitted.

Scoring. — The doubles and men's singles game consists of 15 or 21 points as may be arranged. In a game of 15 points, if the score is tied at 13 the side which first reached 13 has the option of "setting" the game to 5 more points; or if tied at 14 the side which first reached 14 has the option of setting the game to 3 more points. After a game has been set, the score is called "love all," and the side which first scores 5 or 3 points wins.

The ladies' singles game consists of 11 points. If the score is tied at 9-all, the player first reaching 9 has the option of setting the game to 3; if tied at 10-all the player first reaching 10 has the option of setting to 2.

In both singles and doubles the side winning a game always serves first in the next game. In doubles, either of the winners may serve and either of the losers may receive.

Players should change sides of the court at the beginning of each new game.

In a third game the players change ends when the leading score reaches:

(a) 6 in a game of 11 points;

(b) 8 in a game of 15 points;

Unless other arrangements are made the winning side should win two out of three games.

Faults. — A fault constitutes an out if it is made by the serving side and a point for the opponents if made by the receiving side. These are faults:

1. If in serving, the shuttle, when struck, is higher than the server's waist, or if any part of the head of the racket is above the server's hand. (Illus. 1)

2. If the shuttle on service falls outside the boundaries of the diagonally-opposite court.

3. If the server or receiver steps out of his court or on the line before the serve, or fails to keep some part of both feet in contact with the ground until the serve is delivered.

4. If in play the shuttle falls outside the court boundaries, passes through or under the net, fails to pass over the net, touches sidewalls or touches the person or clothing of any player. (Illus. 2)

5. If in play the shuttle is hit by a player before it crosses to his side of the net. It is acceptable, however, to "follow-thru" across the net, providing the racket does not touch the net.

6. If in play a player touches the net or post with his racket or person. (Illus. 3)

7. If the shuttle is hit twice in succession by either the same person or players on the same side.

8. If a player obstructs an opponent by invading his court with racket or person.

9. If a player holds the shuttle on the racket during a stroke, or "throws" the shuttle in contact with the racket while stroking the shuttle.

10. If a player hits the base of the shuttle with the frame around the head of the racket.

When a let (replay) is in order, that play does not count and the player who served repeats his serve. It is a let, if in service, the shuttle touches the net (providing the service is otherwise good); or if in service, or in a rally, a shuttle, after passing over the net, is caught in or on the net. If, during a service, the shuttle touches the top of the net and is then struck by the player served to, it is also a "let" or a replay.

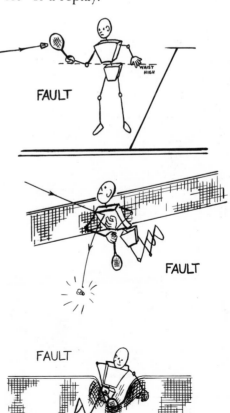

Fundamentals and Techniques

For many of the following explanations it would be a good idea for you to take a badminton racket in hand and actually try to "get the feel" of the grip and various strokes as you read about them.

A most important word of advice at this stage is to read carefully these basic facts and use them always during practice. Your chances of becoming a top notch player are good only if you build a good foundation now.

Holding the Racket. — The following explanation will be made for right-handed players. Left-handers may simply reverse the directions.

For all badminton strokes one uses either a forehand or a backhand grip. The forehand strokes include overhand or underhand strokes on the right side of your body (the forehand side). Backhand strokes are those on the left side of the body or across the body.

Forehand Grip. — For the forehand grip the fingers are comfortably spread with the heel of your hand touching the end of your racket handle. Take your grip this way:

1. Hold your racket by the shaft in your left hand. Extend your arm directly in front of you, with the racket face perpendicular to the ground.

2. Place the heel of your right hand on the handle so that the heel rests against the end of the handle.

3. Close your hand around the handle, fingers slightly spread. Your index finger should be slightly apart from the others, running down and around the handle; and your thumb should angle down and around the handle, too. Feel the pressure of the grip against your thumb, index finger, and little finger. The V between your thumb and index finger should be slightly to the left of the top of the handle.

With a correct grip you can see four knuckles; however, if your hand is small only three may show. If you hold your racket out, it should look like an extension of your arm.

Backhand Grip. — For shots on the left side or across your body, you must contact the shuttle with the opposite side of the playing surface of the racket from that used for forehand strokes. Therefore you must change your forehand grip slightly for backhand shots.

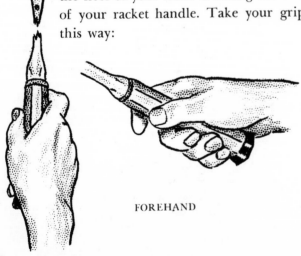

FOREHAND

BACKHAND

1. From a forehand grip turn the racket handle slightly to the right in your fingers. (The racket head turns away from your body.) Move your thumb up so that it rests flat against the side of the handle, in line with the nonhitting side of the racket head. Your thumb acts as a lever and helps to guide the racket forward to meet the shuttle.

2. Keep your index finger slightly apart from the others, running down and around the handle at an angle of about 45 degrees.

In the backhand grip your racket handle lies diagonally across your fingers; in the forehand it is in the palm of your hand. On all backhand strokes your little-finger side of the hand leads the way, palm of your hand facing the ground as your racket goes forward. This simple change from forehand to backhand grip soon becomes an automatic movement whenever you see the shuttle flying toward your left side of the court.

Grip Summary. — There is a mistake made by almost 100% of beginning players that you should know about so that you can avoid making it. This is simply gripping the racket handle too tightly. Never bunch your fingers together and hold your racket as though it were a club. For all strokes your fingers and thumb hold the racket firmly but not tightly. If your grip is too tight your wrist and arm muscles become tense and taut. You will be forced into a push or punch movement rather than into a relaxed hitting and throwing action, which, of course, is the correct and desirable action.

Wrist and Forearm Action. — Learning to rotate the wrist is a basic part of a good stroke. Your forearm must rotate to bring the face of the racket into a flat hitting position, otherwise you will either produce a slicing effect or worse, hit the shuttle with the edge of your racket. Illustration 1 shows the principle of wrist rotation brought into a forehand overhead stroke.

Finger control is very important. You get more sense of feeling in your fingers as you develop more delicate or exacting control. Net shots are almost entirely controlled by the wrists and the sensitive feeling in the fingers. In contrast, the smash shot uses the fingers and forearm muscles to their fullest extent.

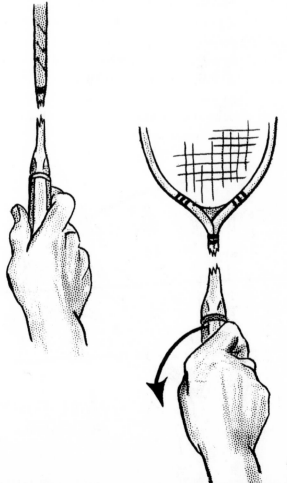

A rigid or stiff wrist provides no driving force to the racket head. The wrist must be cocked back for all shots. A simple check for you to use to discover whether or not you are getting your wrist "into" the stroke is this: take a full swing at an imaginary shuttle — if your wrist is locked there won't be much sound, but but if the wrist is cocked and then "uncorked" halfway through the swing, you will hear a definite swishing sound. The amount of cocking varies according to the speed and power of your stroke. Some cocking must be present on even the most delicate shots.

Your hitting range — the last three feet of the racket's motion to strike the shuttle — holds the key to hitting power, speed, control, and deception. At the end of any backswing the wrist is fully cocked backward and the face of the racket is open. When your arm comes forward, your forearm rotates forward to meet the shuttle squarely. The release of the wrist must be timed so that your arm and racket always form a straight line at contact.

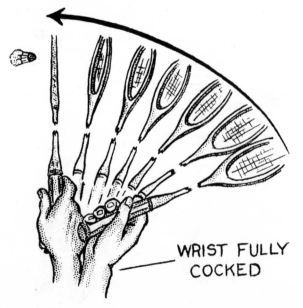

WRIST FULLY COCKED

Footwork. — The development of good strokes definitely depends upon the development of good footwork. You must move around the court forward, backward, or sideways, so that you can hit the shuttle with the greatest amount of power and control and the least amount of effort. Foot action is extremely fast in badminton. Quickness in starting and turning is even more important than sheer speed. A good thought to keep in mind is that the quicker you move into position, the more time you have to carry through your shot.

When waiting for returns, face the net and keep relaxed with your weight on the balls of your feet; in other words, with your weight forward. Keep the weight evenly balanced and knees somewhat flexed or bent. Try to get the feel of an easy, bouncing action in the knees, ready to move in any direction.

It adds a great deal to your game to have your weight move forward from the back to the front foot when hitting so that you can hit the shuttle well ahead of yourself. Meeting the shuttle as early as possible gives a cleaner, crisper, and more controlled stroke. This gives your opponent *less time* to reach your return.

Equally as important as reaching forward to contact the shuttle is always meeting the shuttle at the *highest* possible level. If the shuttle is allowed to drop two or three feet lower than necessary, then it has the same distance to travel upward to go back over the net — and the opponents are allowed additional time to reach these returns.

Improved accuracy has to accompany meeting the shuttle higher and nearer the net. It is a simpler task to become accurate when the shuttle has less distance to travel.

Understanding and practicing these important concepts will help you a great deal toward becoming a fine stroke player.

To get to the back of the court for forehand overhead returns, use a sideways skipping action. Turn your body sideways by pivoting on your left foot and drawing your right foot back so that your left shoulder is toward the net. Then with a low, sideways skipping run move toward the back line. Your body arrives in the correct hitting position since your right foot has led the way. You must go back far enough to position your body behind the falling shuttle so that you can transfer your weight forward to your left foot to add power to your strokes, and so that you can hit the shuttle well ahead of your body.

Reaching Range. — Many badminton players are not aware of the reaching possibility that they possess on the court. Each player should make this easy check to discover his own reaching range. Stand on the center line facing the net. Now take an average step toward either side line with your front foot being nearer the net; next, balance your weight on your front foot, stretch your arm and racket so that they are fully extended and notice how far away from your original position on the center line it is possible for you to reach without strain. Players of average height can reach almost to the singles side line.

Forehand Action. — The action for the forehand is similar to that of throwing a ball. The left side is turned toward the net, and the arm, bending fully, brings up the wrist, cocked back, to pause for just a moment near the right shoulder. For a full backswing, bring your arm up and cock your wrist back so that the head of the racket touches or nearly touches you between the shoulder blades. It is as though you are a spring coiled up waiting to be released at the right moment.

Now, instead of throwing a ball, you "throw" the racket head at the shuttle. Be relaxed and deliberate, and for additional deadly accuracy, *watch the base of the shuttle as closely as possible all the way into the un-corking of the shot.*

Your follow through is a normal continuation of the stroke. To assure a clean hit you must let the racket head continue in the direction of your actual shot.

For overhead forehand strokes your backswing describes a long circular arc, using the shoulder as the center of the circle. This brings the racket head up behind your shoulder blades, ready for a forward upswing. Straighten your arm out overhead and "uncoil' your legs and body to add strength to the overall forward thrust toward the shuttle. Though your arm is straightened out do not uncock the wrist until the last moment before contact. For the overhead smash, stretch your body, arm, and racket to the utmost to meet the shuttle at its highest point. Your follow through ends well down on the left side of your body. Your follow through for an overhead clear will not be as long as that for the smash, since much of your power for the clear is directed upward rather than downward.

Backhand Stroke Action. — As in the forehand, you have in your backhand action a backswing, forward swing, and follow through, whether you meet the shuttle about chest high, below the knee, or above the shoulder.

In a full backswing for a backhand stroke your right hand must always be alongside your left shoulder at the time your feet are positioned for the final stroking step. In the backswing the elbow acts as a hinge. It must be bent so that it can help the wrist in adding power and speed when it straightens out in a forward swing. As you bring your hand and racket toward your left shoulder, point your elbow directly at the shuttle: down for low shots, about net high for drives, and up for overhead clears, drop shots, and smashes. On the backhand you do not get quite the power from your wrist since it can be bent only half as much sideways as it can backward. Much of this disadvantage is offset by the extra snap given from the pressure of the thumb which is behind the racket handle.

To start the forward motion of your backhand stroke do two things: transfer your weight from the back foot to the front foot and, with your elbow pointing directly toward the shuttle, straighten it and allow your wrist to whip the racket forward to hit into and through the shuttle. The forward punching action of the elbow carries the weight of your body forward from the back to the front foot, and makes it much more possible to hit a solid blow.

Never stop your racket at contact. Permit it to continue forward in a long, flat arc; this gives the racket head a better chance to meet the shuttle squarely. In this follow through your wrist rotates and rolls over slightly, turning the palm of your hand sideways. In net play, especially for the girl or woman in mixed doubles, a long follow-through is not called for since shots so close to the net require little strength. Quickness in bringing down the shuttle with a short, flicking shot is the best bet in this situation.

Chest High   Low   High

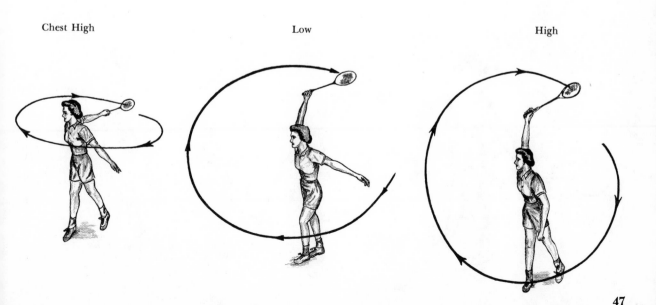

Serving and Receiving. — The most important single stroke in badminton is the serve. Since this is a game in which you can score only when serving you must serve well to win. Keep in mind that in the service the shuttle must be below the waist at contact with the racket, and the head of your racket must not be higher than any part of your hand holding the racket. The two most used serves are the low, short, serve in doubles and the high, deep serve in singles.

The badminton player who is using his head keeps in mind that in a serving situation he has more time available than in any other phase of the game. There is no other time when the shuttle and racket are under such control. So be comfortable and deliberate in carrying out the service.

Stance and Delivery. — 1. Stand near the center service line approximately 3 feet behind the short service line, left foot ahead of the right.

2. Place your racket back, wrist slightly cocked back, ready for the forward swing.

3. Hold the base of the shuttle between the first finger and thumb of your left hand. Extend your arm out shoulder height so that you can drop the shuttle well ahead of your body in line with your right foot. Your weight should be leaning slightly over your back foot.

4. Open your index finger and thumb and let the shuttle drop straight down; at the same time allow your right arm to swing the racket forward easily. It should meet the falling shuttle at arm's length ahead of your body and continue into the follow through.

5. As you deliver the serve, ease the weight of your body forward from the back foot to the front foot.

Low or Short Serve. — In the low or short serve you practically guide the shuttle over the net; little wrist movement is necessary. Try to cause the flight of the shuttle to reach its highest point on your (server's) side of the net. It will fall as it crosses over the net very close to the net tape to drop inside the short service line.

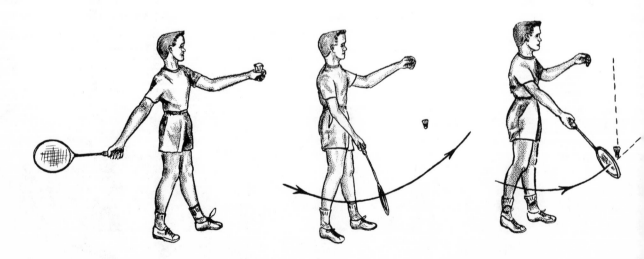

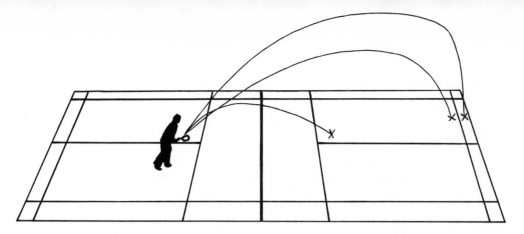

High or Long Serve. — Although you use the same basic swing for the high serve as you do for the low serve, you need more power to make the shuttle go high and deep to the base line. To get this power, keep your feet wider apart, bring your racket back farther in the backswing, and cock your wrist back more. Start your vigorous forward swing by transferring your weight from its prepared balanced position over the back foot, forward onto the front foot. The impetus of the swing will carry the racket forward and upward above head level in a long, smooth follow through, and your shuttle will fly high and deep. At the end of your follow through, your weight should be balanced on the ball of your front foot, toe of the rear foot still in contact with the ground.

Receiving the Serve. — The server must serve from *below* his waist level into a limited area. This fact helps to give the receiver the offensive advantage. So the receiver should see to it that he retains this natural advantage with his return. It must be stressed that all serves should be met *above* waist level; the higher above this level the better.

Your purpose in the receiving position is to be ready and able to meet any low serve as high and as early as possible and yet be able to move back to hit down any high serve.

In singles, your receiving position should be about 4 or 5 feet behind the short service line; in doubles, you should plan to move a little closer toward the net since the doubles service court is shorter (and wider). Since your forehand will usually be your strongest offensive weapon, take your receiving stance in the right court near the center line; in the left court, about 3 feet away from this line.

The main line of movement in receiving the service will be either forward or backward. So in order to be able to "push off" quickly either toward the net to meet a low serve or away from it to take a high serve, you should take a stance with the feet somewhat spread apart and the left foot ahead of the right. In this way you will be partly sideways, facing the right side line. This is the ideal position for the quick use of the sideways, low sliding action to get back to meet a deep, high serve. You ought to be able to get to the back of the service court in time to hit all high serves in a downward direction with an overhand shot.

Remember to reach forward and meet the shuttle as high and early as possible. In doubles, you should be able to meet all low serves *in front of the short service line*. This will call for the most that you have in alertness and cat-like movement.

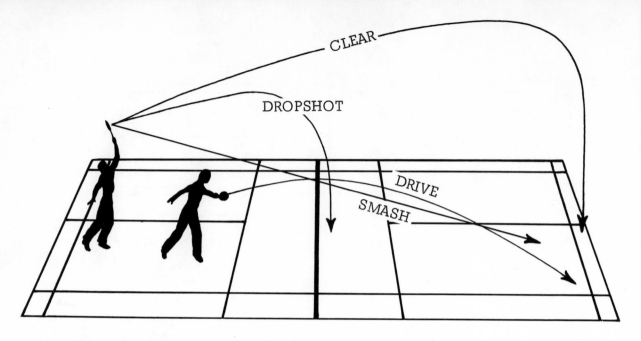

CLEAR

DROPSHOT

DRIVE

SMASH

Basic Strokes

The shuttle goes exactly where it is directed. It will fly one way or another, fast or slowly — limited only by your skill. The course it follows is known as the flight or trajectory. In badminton, there are four major flights. These flights and the action called for from you to create these flights make up the four major strokes in the game (above).

Before going into this area, be very sure that you understand the fundamentals of good footwork and the make up of the forehand and backhand action. The *smash,* the *clear* or lob, the *dropshot* and the *drive* are the four basic strokes. Each of them can be played with either the forehand or backhand.

Smash. — The smash or kill shot is the main point-winning stroke in badminton. Since you must hit the shuttle downward when smashing, you should have the feeling of the racket head coming over on top of the shuttle. Generally, learn to hit a smash from a normal forehand position at a point *above* and *ahead* of the right shoulder. Reach up and forward to meet the shuttle at the highest possible point. The all-important action of your wrist "throwing" the racket head at the shuttle adds to the snap of the well-hit smash. The more wrist snap you throw in, the more sharply the shuttle will fly down.

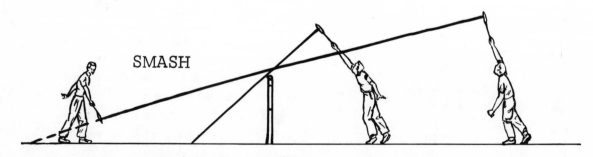

SMASH

Speed is important, but as the defense of your opponents improves, speed without placement will boomerang. Remember that the faster a shuttle travels over the net, the faster it can be returned, thus giving you, the smasher, less time to reach any return. So speed is first when there is an opening and placement is first when an opponent is in a good defensive position. In doubles you can try more all-out smashing because your partner can take advantage of an opponent's return which, in singles, might cause you difficulty. Remember that a well-aimed smash directly at an opponent's body can be just as devastating as one aimed out of reach.

It is not good to jump off the floor in the process of smashing. When learning, you ought to have a good toe-hold with at least the toes of your front foot on the floor at the moment of contact.

The return of the smash is purely defensive. About all that can be done is to block the shuttle so that it will rebound from the racket because of its own momentum. If possible, an underhand drop shot is sometimes a successful return. If the smash is aimed at your body, a backhand stroke is best for a return.

A good smash raises the value of your other strokes. Once an opponent finds out that you have high speed under control, he is likely to make mistakes in his eagerness to not give you a chance to use this menacing weapon.

The Clear. — The clear or lob, is a stroke which sends the shuttle high into the air above the opponent's court. It is mostly a defensive shot and is often used for gaining time to get into a good defensive position.

Good length is the very heart of good clearing. A short clear gives your opponents the easiest of returns—the set-up smash. Use the *full* length of your opponent's court. The difference of a few inches in the length of clears has decided a great number of international matches.

If you are continually "being smashed" or caught on drop shots, then you should realize that your clearing is not of good length.

Height of the clear must be considered also. As you need more time to recover your position, the higher you should smack the shuttle into the air. Remember that the higher the shuttle goes up, the straighter down it will fall. This is worth knowing and using because the shuttle that falls straight down is much more difficult to time and hit cleanly than one traveling on a flatter arc.

The overhead forehand clear should be hit (use the same motion as a smash) directly above the head. Never let the shuttle get behind your body! Naturally the higher and sooner you meet the shuttle the less distance it has to travel. Taking it high also presents the threat that you may hit down.

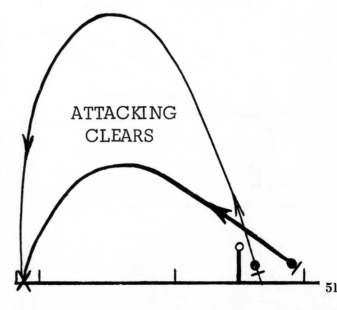

ATTACKING CLEARS

Experienced opponents check early to see if you can clear well from the deep backhand side. In making this return be sure that your body is turned away from the net. Then your arm and wrist have plenty of freedom to get the racket well back before snapping it powerfully upward and forward. Meet the shuttle as high as the arm and racket can reach.

BACKHAND CLEAR

The underhand high clear resembles the long, high serve. This is a generally effective shot to use following an opponent's drop shot to your forecourt.

Deep, accurate clearing — when possible, to your opponent's backhand side — is the backbone of defense.

The Drop Shot. — The drop shot is a stroke which causes the shuttle to drop steeply close to the net in the opponent's fore court.

This shot is used on offense to make an unexpected return of any stroke. It is well used when your opponent is in the back court or running hard toward the back court. The main purpose is to make your opponent hit a high return from below net level so that you, or your partner in doubles, can gain the attack by hitting down.

Do not make the common mistake of over-using the drop shot. It usually is not smart to play a drop shot when there is an opportunity to hit down more quickly.

The drop shot has the slowest flight of any stroke; so it must be accurate, and equally important, it must be *deceptive*. This becomes even more true the farther back in court that you attempt the drop shot, since the shuttle has a greater distance to travel.

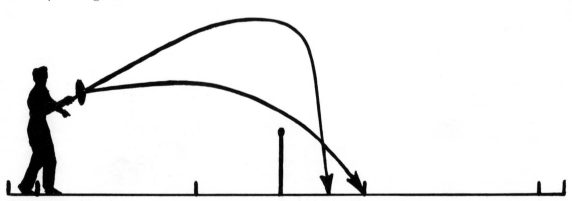

There isn't much deception if you use one type of swing for a hard shot and another for a softer shot. So your preliminary action for a drop shot should indicate that it is to be a power stroke. But as the arm comes forward, you should release the wrist in a kind of slow-motion action. The racket should gently and *firmly* guide the shuttle over the net. For an overhead drop shot, deceive your opponent into thinking that you are going to smash; for drop shots from around knee level, suggest by your action that a clear shot to the back court is your intention.

Drop shots played from the area near the net are called "net shots." You should guide all these net shots over with extreme accuracy so that the shuttle will turn over and fall straight down just as it crosses the top of the net. The sooner it drops, the less possibility for a good return.

As soon as you have played a net shot which hugs the far side of the net, stay alert with your racket up ready to flick down any poor return made by your opponent.

Learn to play the straight-ahead (hair pin) and cross-court net shots. For a cross-court shot, reach for the shuttle near the *top* of the net and aim the shot near the tape of the net toward the opposite side line.

When the shuttle has dropped below net level the hair pin stroke is required. It is simply a reaching stroke, with a slight flick upward so that the shuttle will loop over the net with practically no clearance.

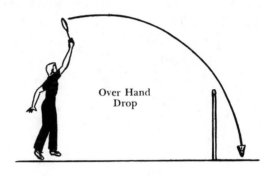

Over Hand Drop

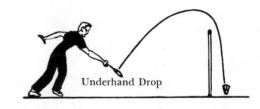

Underhand Drop

Net Shot

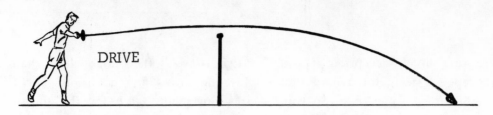

DRIVE

Drive. — The drive is a flat sidearm stroke, either forehand or backhand, which sends the shuttle skimming low over the net in a line somewhat parallel with the floor. It is most effective when delivered from between head and chest level. It should land behind the opponent's short service line.

Keep in mind the always important action of reaching forward and as high as possible to drive back the shuttle. If the fundamentals of good footwork are put in play, this shot should not cause you a great deal of difficulty.

When driving, your objective is not to give your opponents a chance to meet the shuttle at a higher level than the level at which you contacted the shuttle at the start. If this happens, he can return with a smash.

Use the drive on offense to pass an advancing opponent or to intercept a shuttle coming at you net high. Your best placement is down the side line; sometimes driving the shuttle directly at your opponent.

Learn to use the drive intelligently and avoid any costly interception. It can be second only to the smash as an attacking weapon.

FOREHAND DRIVE

BACKHAND DRIVE

Simplified Court Tactics

Fundamental Tactics.—You should realize that the tactics change constantly during the game.

This is the distinction:

> You are on defense when hitting up.
> You are on the attack when hitting down.

This applies to play in the fore and back court; in singles and in doubles play.

Singles Play.— The singles game situation should find the player taking a position in the center of the court — about 4 feet behind the short service line. As soon as you move to return a shot, move again, *immediately*, back to your home position in mid-court. When you are forced to make a return that takes you way off base you are at a disadvantage and need to gain time. This is the place for your time-taking high, deep clear so that you can again get to the middle of the court.

Good length is the first essential of a good singles player. If, as a beginner, you learn to hit high, deep serves and clears to within just a few inches of the backline, you will have an invaluable shot to help you through any caliber of play. These strokes are the mainstays of singles defense. Remember that placing the shuttle to the opponent's backhand side is very often a good shot to make.

Clean hitting calls for quick, decisive thinking. As the shuttle comes to you during a rally, notice the position on court of your opponent and your own position. With this in mind, decide on the best shot to play — and always carry through with it to the very best of your ability.

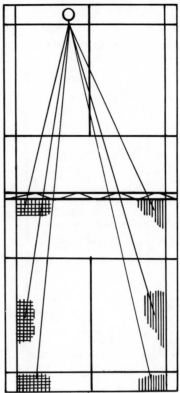

Choice of return shots after receiving a high serve

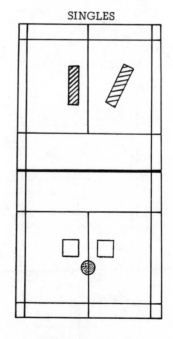

SINGLES

○   Your base

☐   Serving Positions

▨   Receiving Positions

55

BASE or HOME POSITIONS
in DOUBLES PLAY

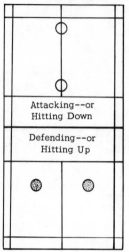

Attacking--or
Hitting Down

Defending--or
Hitting Up

◉ The base of your play
when you are on the
defense. Each player
must take any return
on his side.

○ The base of your play
when you are on the
attack. Each player
must take his own
area. All the front or
all the back.

MEN'S and LADIES'
DOUBLES

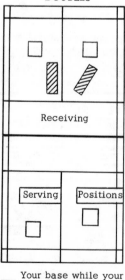

Receiving

Serving   Positions

☐ Your base while your
partner is serving or
receiving

▨ Serve from anywhere
within this area

Men's and Women's Doubles. — The position of the partners changes constantly as they move from a defensive situation into an attacking one and vice versa.

When on defense you and your partner should be midway back in the court. In doubles, when one partner hits downward, the other partner should move up near the short service line to hit down any loose returns that come to the forecourt.

Use the low serve as your basic serve with the idea of making the receiver hit the shuttle up so that you or your partner can hit down.

Doubles is an attacking game — you and your partner should smash at every opportunity. Don't hit up unless there is no choice. When forced to hit up, however, help your defense by clearing the shuttle high and deep into your opponent's court so that you and your partner will have more time and a better chance to return the shuttle.

Court Positions for Mixed Doubles

Mixed Doubles. — In mixed doubles the woman usually plays in the front part of the court and the man in the back court, both ready to hit down at every opportunity. Because she has less time to hit returns from the opponent's court the woman should cover only from the front service line to the net (6½ feet). Since there is so little time at the net the woman must always hold her racket up ready to "kill" off all returns above net level.

MIXED DOUBLES

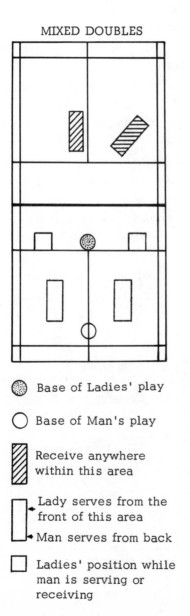

⊛ Base of Ladies' play

◯ Base of Man's play

▨ Receive anywhere within this area

⬚ Lady serves from the front of this area
Man serves from back

☐ Ladies' position while man is serving or receiving

GENERAL STRATEGY

In the normal situation the player who wins is the one who uses the standard strokes most efficiently. Those who follow the game into advanced playing find out that there comes a time when the difference is a matter of lightning-fast brainwork *and* the ability to play consistently well under pressure.

Always take immediate and careful note of every part of your opponent's game. Test his speed on the court. If he moves slowly, use placement to run him all over the court. Discover if he has a stroke that is not dependable, then pound that weakness.

Be very aware of the high cost of carelessness. Three rallies have to be won to overcome one error made when the opponent serves; one rally to gain back the serve, two to get even again, and three to go ahead.

One of the great attractions of badminton is that there is no one formula for strokes and tactics. The qualities that have produced some of the greatest players have included great variations.

But among these qualities have always been:

1. Untiring practice in perfection of skills.
2. Great endurance and stamina.
3. A great determination to win.

Badminton Terms

Ace — One point. Unit of scoring. Synonyms: "score," "point."

Alley (side) — Narrow strips of court (1½ feet wide) between outer-most boundary lines.

Backhand — All strokes played with playing arm and racket across body; for right-handed players, strokes on left side of the body.

Bird — Common term for shuttle.

Clear (or lob) — A stroke which sends the shuttle high and deep to the back of the opponent's court.

Cross-court — A stroke that sends the shuttle across the court diagonally from one side to the other.

Doubles — The game played with four players, two on each side of the net.

Down — Loss of service caused by the server's failure to score. In doubles, each side has two downs (except in the first inning of the game). In the first inning, the side first serving has only one down.

Drive — A stroke in which the shuttle is hit hard and takes a fast horizontal flight.

Drop shot — A stroke in which the shuttle falls just over the net and drops to the floor.

Fault — A term used to indicate a violation of the rules. Often used in connection with a serve that did not land in the proper court, or was not properly served.

Fore court — The area near the net; generally between the short serving line and the net.

Forehand — Stroke played with the playing arm and racket on the natural side of the body; for right-handed players, strokes on the right side of the body.

Hand-in — Term used to show that the player serving still keeps the service.

Hand-out — Normally used in doubles to show that one partner is "down", that is, he already has had his turn at serving.

Inning — A side's turn at serving.

Love-all — A term used in scoring to indicate o-o.

Match — A series of games, best two out of three to determine a winner.

Mixed doubles — A game in which a man and a woman play as partners on each side of the net.

Placement — A shot directed with control into an area where it will be difficult for an opponent to make a return.

Singles — Game in which there is one player opposing another player on the other side of the net.

Smash — A stroke in which the shuttle is hit downward with great overhead power.

Throw or Sling — A carrying contact between shuttle and racket, usually caused from the feathers being caught in the strings. This is a "fault", according to the rules.

Bibliography

Davidson, Kenneth R., and Gustavson, Lealand R. *Winning Badminton.* New York: The Ronald Press Company, 1953.

Last, F. W. *Introduction to Badminton.* New York: Associated Booksellers, 1955.

American Badminton Association. *Official Laws of Badminton.* Wellesley Hills, Mass.: The Association, latest edition.

Division of Girls' and Women's Sports. *Official Tennis-Badminton Guide.* Washington, D.C.: American Association for Health, Physical Education, and Recreation, published biannually.

BOWLING

Einar A. Olsen

Don W. Buchanan

History of Bowling

Primitive men rolling stones at "Sheep Joyntes."

Bowling, PROBABLY THE most ancient of sports, is now considered one of the most popular participation sports in the United States, and millions of boys and girls, men and women, regularly enjoy it today, in its modern version.

How ancient is the sport of bowling? It has been authentically placed at 5200 B.C. in Egypt, although many authorities believe that the sport is even more ancient. Some historians have indicated that primitive men made a sport of rolling stones at upright bones or sticks.

Northern Italy is believed to be the site where bowling in Europe was first practiced. The Helvetii living in the Alpine regions during Caesar's time (50 B.C.) were said to have played a game similar to the present day Italian bowling game called "Boccie," a form of lawn bowling.

The Puritans utilized ninepin bowling rather extensively, taking advantage of slate as the material out of which they constructed their beds.

The Egyptian game of bowling dates back to 5200 B.C.

Ninepin alley in Switzerland that is over 200 years old

Bowling at pins began in Europe in the 3rd or 4th century A.D. as a religious ceremony. William Pehle, in his book "Bowling" writes, "The ancient chronicles of Paderborn reveal that the first bowling was done in the cloisters of cathedrals. It was the custom of the church dignitaries to have parishioners, in turn, place their pins at one end of the cloister. This represented the "Heide," meaning heathen. The parishioner then was given a ball, and asked to throw it at the "Heide." If a hit was scored, it indicated that the thrower was leading a clean and pure life and was capable of slaying the heathen; if he missed, it meant that a more faithful attendance at services would help his aim."

After a time, "kegeling" ceased to be a religious gesture and became a sport. Various forms of the game were introduced in all sections of Europe. "Ninepins" was the favorite game in Holland; "Skittles" was an English version; "Quilles" in the French Pyrenees; and the Scots began a bowling game on ice called curling, a sport still very popular today in Canada and parts of the U. S.

The Dutch are credited with bringing ninepin bowling to early America. The game first became popular in and around New York but soon spread throughout the Colonies.

Bowling began to lose popularity about the middle of the 1800's because of gambling and fixed matches. Connecticut and other states passed laws forbidding the game of ninepins to be played. To get around the laws a new game "Tenpins" was originated, thus setting the stage for today's version of bowling. The game has continued to develop, with modifications in rules and equipment under the American Bowling Congress, and today it is one of the leading participation sports in the U. S.

— • Bowling Under Sheds • —

Our Modern Era of Bowling

THE BOOM IN modern bowling which started shortly after World War II is still continuing as the sport steadily gains in popularity.

The rapid increase in suburban populations has resulted in the building of new, attractive bowling establishments in these areas.

Bowling lanes that had been in business in the downtown areas for years, remodeled and expanded to keep pace with the new competition. It was as if the sport had had a rebirth with a new character emerging that pleased everyone.

The new bowling lanes have become symbols of modern thinking in sports and recreation.

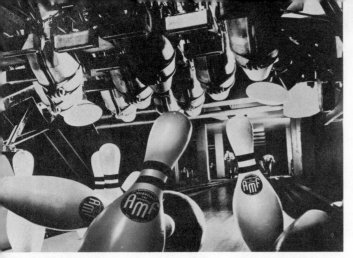

There's nobody to see this view of a bowling strike now that AMF's Automatic Pinspotter has replaced the pin boy of yesteryear's bowling lanes.

A panoramic view of one of the new, modern, large bowling centers equipped with AMF Automatic Pinspotters, is a product of American Machine & Foundry Company. The Pinspotter employs electronic and mechanical principles.

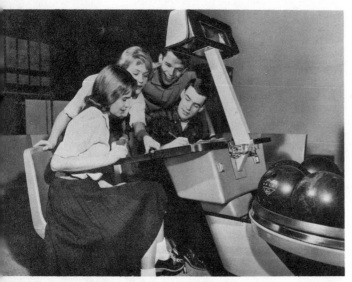

Teen agers go for bowling in a big way.

With automation has come automatic pin setting machinery. New innovations of interior design and use of baffles and other sound absorbing materials have helped to eliminate noise.

Today's bowling establishment contains equipment displays, lockers, snack bars and comfortable seats for bowlers and spectators alike. Nursery rooms are available to accommodate families with small children.

Modern lunch counters, like this one, serve hungry or thirsty bowlers.

Well equipped nurseries keep the kids happy while Mom and Dad bowl a few lines.

The "Telescoping Pin Distributor of the AMF Automatic Pinspotter moves pins on an endless belt to cups on the "Spotting Table" from which the pins are actually placed on the lane surface.

This is a view of the "electronic brain" that controls the hairline precision and rhythmic performance of the AMF Automatic Pinspotters.

Many proprietors are trained to help bowlers select proper equipment and offer instruction to all age groups.

Boys, girls, men, and women love and enjoy bowling on each age level, mixed or stag, in pairs, groups or leagues, and especially as a family.

League bowling offers competition at one's own skill level.

Bowling is a wonderful family sport.

A bowler can buy almost any equipment he needs right his favorite bowling center.

Start them young — kids enjoy bowling and it's good exercise.

Equipment. — A person, going bowling today, will find that the alley can provide the things he needs such as the ball and shoes. Shoes are usually rented by beginners or occasional bowlers but most regular bowlers want shoes and other equipment of their own.

Each alley has a large selection of balls of different weights and grips. In duckpin or candlepin bowling, the balls do not have finger holes although they may be of different weights. A bowler should learn, first of all, to find, or ask the attendant to help him find, a suitable ball. Much of the success of bowling depends upon using the proper equipment.

Bowling shoes are necessary, not only because ordinary shoes might damage the lanes and approaches, but, because bowling shoes are constructed in such a way that the bowler has good traction as he walks forward in his approach and, yet, allows him to slide on the last step of his delivery. This slide is needed for proper timing, smoothness of delivery, and balance.

In purchasing shoes, one has to indicate whether he is a left- or right-handed bowler as a right-handed bowler wants his sliding shoe to be on his left foot. Rental shoes are designed for use by either left- or right-handed bowlers.

Proper attire for women and girls depends upon local custom but a skirt and blouse or a dress loose enough to permit free movement of arms and legs is usual. Men usually wear a loose fitting long or short-sleeved sport shirt and comfortable slacks.

Selecting a Ball

Weight. — Balls provided for use in modern bowling centers usually range from 9 to 16 pounds. You should select a ball which is light enough to be held and controlled, as you swing it, and still heavy enough to knock down the pins. One should try different balls until the desirable weight is found. Beginners should avoid using a ball that is too light for good pin action. Most women find that a suitable ball will range from 12 to 15 pounds. Boys and girls can start with a lighter weight ball, even a 9-pounder, and work up to a heavier one, as they increase their bowling skill.

Grip. — Balls provided by the alleys have holes drilled for the thumb and the middle and third fingers.

First, try the thumb-hole. It should be snug but not too tight, or the ball will "hang" as you release it. Most stars recommend that you place your thumb down as far as it will go. (See picture C above, right.)

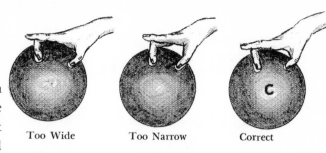

Too Wide	Too Narrow	Correct

Without lifting your thumb from the hole, rest your finger across the finger holes. The second joints of the middle and third fingers should extend about a quarter-inch past the front edges of the holes, for the correct fit.

Most regular bowlers prefer to purchase their own ball and modern alleys are prepared to help in selecting the weight and grip best suited to the individual. There are other grips, besides the conventional grip, that are also used with good results. The semi-finger tip has the finger-holes approximately mid-way between the first and second joints of the middle fingers, while the full fingertip has the holes out to the first joint. These are two popular variations. Most beginners do best by learning the basic bowling skills with a conventional grip ball.

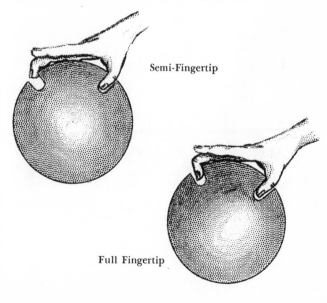

Semi-Fingertip

Full Fingertip

Fundamental Skills and Techniques

Wrong method of picking up the ball. You can get your fingers injured severely if a ball rolls onto the rack and drives another ball against your hands.

As in most all sports the basic fundamentals are the tools you need in constructing a solid foundation on which to build your more skillful techniques and become better than average. Bowling is no exception. In fact it is a sport that requires the coordination of several basic actions into a combined skill that takes just a few seconds to complete.

It takes education and understanding of all the basic maneuvers and plenty of practice to become an accomplished bowler.

This is the wrong way to pick up the ball, too. You can sprain your fingers or hurt your arm.

Position and Stance

Position. — After picking up your ball, take your position for beginning the delivery. In the diagrams on the opposite page common beginning locations are shown for the various kinds of balls thrown. Beginners should try the straight-ball position first.

The straight-ball bowler takes a position slightly to the right of the center of the lane. Proper distance from the foul line (the line which determines the

The proper method of picking up the ball from the rack, weight evenly balanced in both hands and fingers on the sides where they will not be pinched.

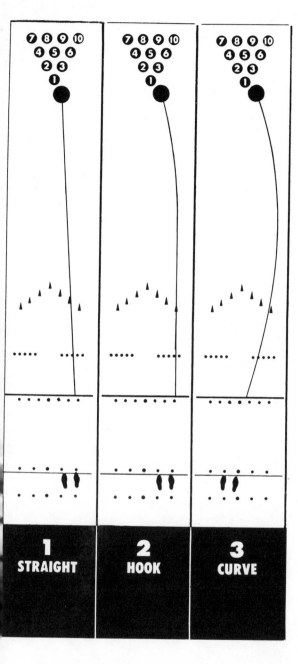

| 1 STRAIGHT | 2 HOOK | 3 CURVE |

Stance. — Bowlers vary on the stance they take to begin the delivery, but the style shown here by Buzz Fazio, Brunswick Advisory Staff, is one that is popular with many bowlers. The body is erect but relaxed, and the feet are spread enough for good balance. Some bowlers prefer to have the left foot slightly advanced, as demonstrated by Fazio. The ball is held near waist-level, or slightly above, and the weight of the ball is supported almost wholly by the left hand. Note the bowler's concentration on his target.

beginning of the lane) is determined by the size of the individual and his natural length of step. You can find this starting point by walking back from the foul line four and one-half steps. Adjustment from this can be made later as skill progresses.

The Four-Step Delivery

There are several acceptable methods of approaching the foul line. Every bowler should try to select the one which gives him a smooth, easy stride and swing. The four-step delivery is most commonly used.

In this sequence, Fazio demonstrates the beginning of the four-step delivery. Much of the success of this delivery lies in starting the ball and right foot in correct timing.

The First Step. — The bowler should begin his motion with the push-away, as the right foot is advanced. In the push-away, the ball moves forward and downward in a continuous arc. When the body weight is over the right foot, the ball has started its pendulum swing.

The Second Step. — As the left foot takes the second step, the ball continues back-

ward in the pendulum swing. The arm is quite straight, hanging down from the shoulder, and the ball is allowed to swing back on its own momentum. This step is slightly longer than the first.

The Third Step. — As the third step is taken, the ball reaches the height of the backswing and, as the step is completed, the ball is coming down in a full-arm sweep (pendulum swing now coming forward).

The Fourth Step. — The last step is a step and slide. The body is lowered slightly as the left knee bends and the body leans forward. The slide insures proper body balance and permits a gradual checking of the forward movement.

The ball should be nearing the bottom of the swing when the slide begins. The hand should be in correct position for delivery. As the ball passes the left foot, it is released towards the target.

Release

Whether you roll a straight ball, a hook, or a curve, the release comes as the slide nears completion. On release, the thumb leaves the thumb hole and the ball is set in motion by a lifting action of the fingers. The ball should be lifted over the foul line from 6 to 18 inches, and no higher.

Marion Ladewig shows perfect release. The thumb, at moment of delivery, leaves the ball first and the "V" formed by the thumb and finger points toward the target.

Lee Jouglard demonstrates correct way to throw a straight ball, easiest for bowlers who do not have time to practice.

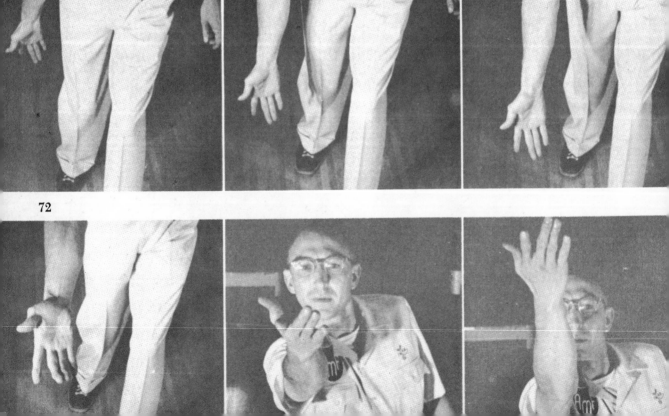

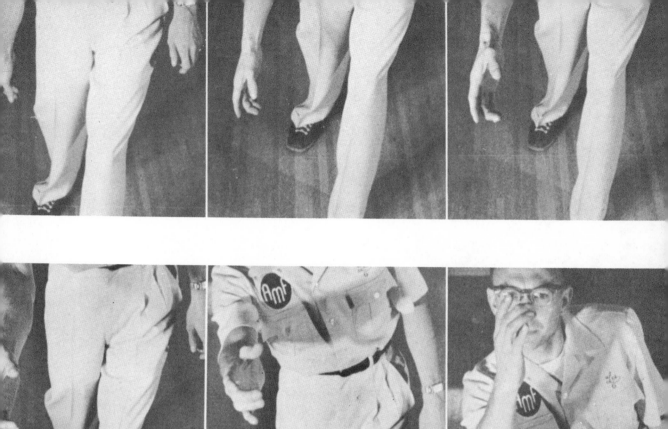

Pictured, above, is the hand action on the popular hook ball. Notice that there is no twist of the hand or wrist.

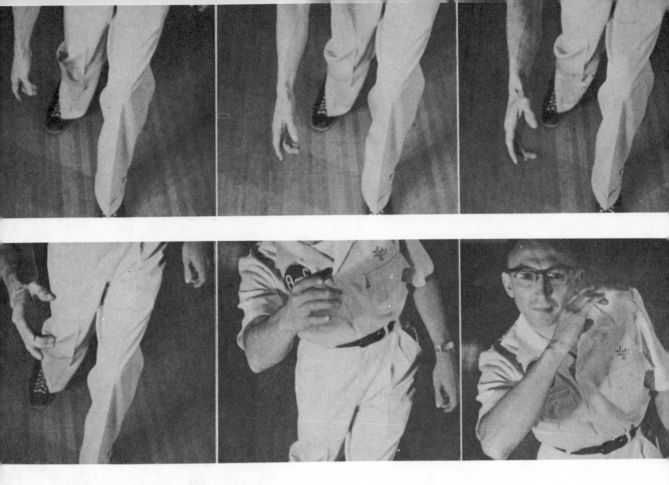

The above sequence shows the hand action used in throwing the curve ball. Note the "lift" given by the hand and wrist.

Follow-Through

Whether you pitch a baseball, hit a golf ball, or roll a bowling ball, follow-through is an important part of the skill. Failing to follow-through properly is one of the more common errors in bowling, yet it is fairly easy to correct.

Follow-through is the arm motion which comes after the release of the ball. The Beginner, and even many bowlers who have bowled for some time, stop that smooth pendulum swing the instant the ball is released. Actually the

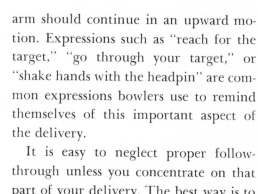

Brunswick star, Marion Ladewig, also shows beautiful follow-through form.

arm should continue in an upward motion. Expressions such as "reach for the target," "go through your target," or "shake hands with the headpin" are common expressions bowlers use to remind themselves of this important aspect of the delivery.

It is easy to neglect proper follow-through unless you concentrate on that part of your delivery. The best way is to exaggerate the follow-through and hold the final pose until the ball is half-way down the alley.

Ed Lubanski, member of the AMF Bowling Promotion Staff, demonstrates good follow-through form (left). Note the arm continuing upward and also the good body balance with the left foot pointed toward the pins.

Lubanski shows how the body should face directly toward the pins.

The Three-Step Delivery

The three-step delivery, popular with duckpin and candlepin bowlers, is used only by a few leading tenpin bowlers.

Good timing and balance are more difficult to attain because the bowler must compress all the movement, described previously in the four-step approach, into three steps. To get the proper timing, the push-away of the ball must be started before the first step is taken. Note how Welu, in the pictures below, has the ball well into the backswing before he completes his first step. The backswing is kept low and reaches its peak as the second step is completed.

As the bowler begins his third step-and-slide, the ball is still behind him, and he now needs a strong arm-pull to complete the delivery in time. This forcing of the arm movement tends to make it difficult to maintain timing and balance.

Billy Welu, nationally famous bowler, demonstrates proper form for Three-Step delivery.

The Five-Step Delivery

Many high-scoring bowlers use the five-step delivery. It is slightly more difficult to master than the four-step. In fact, it would be better for the novice to work at this delivery after he has mastered the four-step.

Note in the pictures below, demonstrating the five-step delivery, how Welu takes a very short first step.

The push-away of the ball is started as the first step is completed and the heel of the right foot picks up for the start of the second step. The ball moves out and down and reaches the low point of the pendulum swing as the second step is completed.

On the third step, the ball is nearing the height of the backswing. This swing should not be higher than the shoulders.

Each successive step finds the body lower and lower as the knees bend more. See how low Welu is on this fourth step and also note how the ball is just ready to start down from the top of the backswing.

As the last step-and-slide are taken, the shoulders are facing squarely at the pins. A straight arm and a slightly dropped right shoulder keep the ball at the correct distance from the floor.

The release of the ball and the follow-through are the same as in the four-step delivery.

Aiming for Accuracy

The beginning bowler is often confused when he hears such terms as "grooving the ball" or "put it in the pocket." These are bowling terms used to describe strike action.

A right-hand bowler gets the most consistent pin action if the ball comes in from an angle to the right of the "head" pin and rolls into the "1-3 pocket," shown below. There are two widely used methods of aiming — pin bowling and spot bowling — the latter is the most popular with today's bowlers.

Pin Bowling

In pin bowling, the point of aim is the 1-3 pocket itself. That is, from the time the stance is taken and throughout the delivery, the bowler keeps his eye on the strike pocket. You aim at what you want to hit. This method seems natural for beginners, especially those rolling a straight ball.

As shown in the diagram below the pin bowler starts his delivery from the right of center. He walks straight toward the target and releases the ball fairly close to the right-hand edge of the lane.

Spot Bowling

Spot bowling makes use of directional markers built right into the lane bed. Two rows of markers are on the approach, another at the foul line, and a fourth row is 7 feet beyond the line. Just beyond this last row of markers is a series of darts, sometimes called "diamonds," arranged like an arrowhead pointed down the lane.

Every bowler has to find the best starting position and "spot" at which to aim. However, the bowler who starts just slightly to the right of the center of the approach will find the second dart, in from the right side, very close to being his "spot."

If the right-handed bowler is not hitting the 1-3 pocket, he can compensate by changing his starting position. If the ball is hitting to the right of the pocket, the bowler should move his starting position slightly to the right. If the ball is to the left, move the starting position to the left. It is best not to change the point of aim while making this starting adjustment.

Curve-ball and hook-ball bowlers generally find the "spot" bowling method most satisfactory.

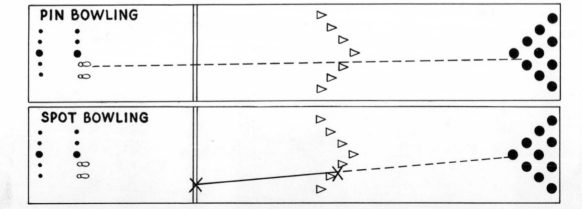

Pinfall

The goal of every bowler is the perfect game — a 300 score. A 300 requires that the bowler throw 12 strikes in a row. High scores cannot be made unless the bowler can consistently roll strikes.

You cannot expect a strike with each roll, so it becomes necessary to convert the "spares." A bowler who occasionally gets strikes, but consistently picks up the spares, will add 20 to 40 points to his average.

Learning how to make spares takes study and practice. One must recognize the spare leave and know where the ball

should roll to hit the pins in the right spot.

Some spare leaves, such as the 5 pin, can be converted with a normal strike ball. Most bowlers find strike position spares the easiest to convert.

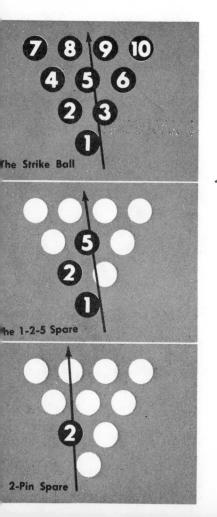

The Strike Ball

The 1-2-5 Spare

2-Pin Spare

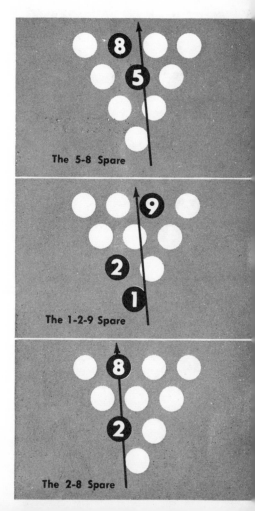

The 5-8 Spare

The 1-2-9 Spare

The 2-8 Spare

Left-Side Spares

Right-handed bowlers usually find left-side spares easier to convert than right-sided spares. The starting position for left-side spares is usually from the right of center. The ball is thrown cross-alley and its path is generally slightly left of the head pin if pin bowling, or between the second and third darts from the right if spot bowling.

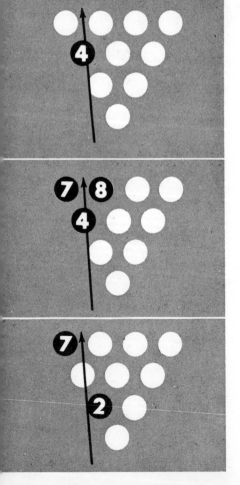

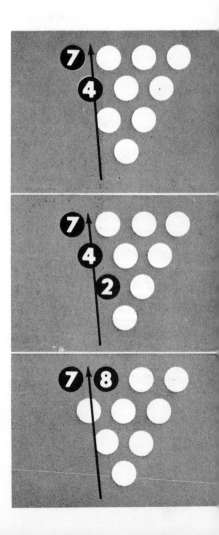

Right-Side Spares

Right-handed bowlers find right-side spares harder to convert than left-side spares. The beginner should use the same cross-alley technique that was indicated for left-side spares. Hook-ball or curve-ball bowlers will find it ex-tremely difficult to hit the 10 pin unless they move to the left. Even the straight ball bowler will find that the cross-alley ball gives the best results. As the experts say, "Use all the lane" which means taking advantage of the full lane width to let your ball roll in its normal way.

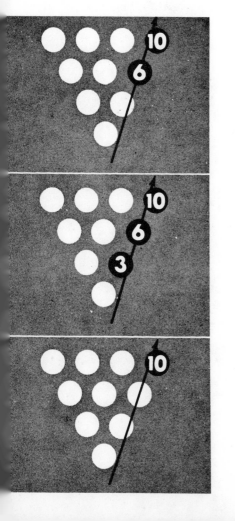

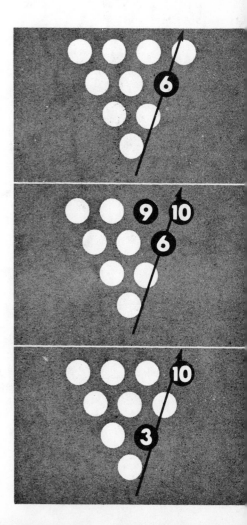

Converting the Splits

No bowler enjoys seeing a split come up, especially in an important match, but neither can he help but be thrilled when he manages to convert a difficult leave. To the beginner, every split looks difficult. Actually some are easier than some of the spare leaves illustrated on the preceding pages.

The general rule for converting spares applies in converting splits. Study your set-up, decide on the aiming point, and use the cross-alley technique. The following diagrams will help you to convert those "tough" ones.

The 4-5—Start at right center to roll cross-alley. Accuracy essential since distance between pins is less than two inches narrower than ball width.

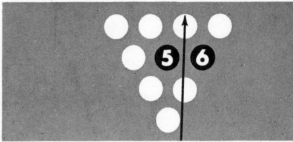

The 5-6—Shoot from the left of center to connect squa between pins. Make your aiming adjustment in the st rather than in your form or speed of delivery.

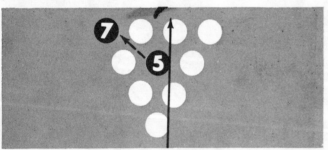

The 5-7—Start from just right of center to hit the 5-pin on its right side causing it to deflect into the 7-pin.

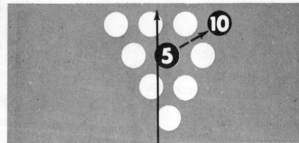

The 5-10—This shot calls for deflection of the 5-pin into 10-pin. This type of split also can be made by deflecting ball from pin to pin.

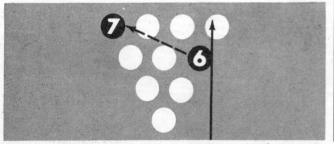

The 6-7—Difficult, but possible to hook into the 6-pin on its right side (from the left side of approach) causing it to skid across to the 7-pin.

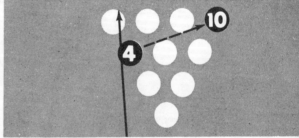

The 4-10—Even more difficult for right-handers. Aim to g the 4-pin on its left side to deflect it into the 10-pin.

Bowling Etiquette

Some sports, such as football and basketball, have definite rules that apply to the conduct of players. Other sports, like golf and bowling, have codes of good behavior. Codes are not written rules which an umpire or referee will enforce, but are unwritten standards of sportsmanship which every bowler should attempt to apply to the game. Observance of the code of etiquette, listed below, will make bowling more fun for you, as well as all the bowlers around you.

1. Be prepared to take your regular turn on the alley.

2. Remember, the player to your right has the right-of-way.

3. When a bowler, on the adjoining lane, is getting set for his delivery, respect his priority. Don't step in front of him to pick your ball off the rack.

4. Take your time, but do not waste everybody else's by useless posing or waiting, while standing in your starting position.

5. Remember to stay back of the foul line at all times, even if no one is calling fouls.

6. Confine "body-English" to your own lane. Do not cross over into the next approach.

7. Check your temper and your language with your coat.

8. Keep the game moving. After your ball hits the pins, walk directly to the back of the approach.

9. You should not use another player's ball, except with his permission.

10. Refrain from kidding your opponent when he is addressing the pins.

11. It is fun to be a winner, but it is a real challenge to be gracious in defeat.

12. Respect the equipment. Getting the ball out on the alley is good bowling, but "lofting" (dropping the ball) hurts your game and damages the alley bed.

13. Splits, misses, and taps are just as much a part of the game as strikes and spares. Don't blame the equipment, instead determine your faults and correct them.

Scoring

Scoring is easy. A game or line consists of 10 frames. Two balls are allowed in each frame, except when a bowler scores a strike. The markings used in scoring are shone in the diagram below.

1. A horizontal line, in the box, is used to indicate an "open" frame or "error," in which the bowler failed to convert a spare leave. That is, after the second ball was rolled, some pins remain standing. Count for the frame is the number of pins knocked down with the two balls. The number in front of the box represents pinfall for first ball.

2. An "X", in the box, denotes a strike, all 10 pins knocked down with the first ball. For a strike, you get 10 pins, plus total pinfall on next two balls.

3. A spare is marked, in the box, with a "/". This signifies that the bowler converted a spare, all pins were knocked down with two balls. For a spare, you get 10 pins plus pinfall on next ball thrown.

4. The circle indicates that the first ball left a split.

5. The circle with a diagonal slash through it shows that the bowler converted the split into a spare.

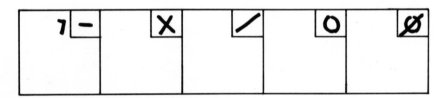

The following figures will give you practice and show you how to score a bowling game. Let us follow a bowler named Bill through his 10 frames and score along with him.

On the first ball Bill had 7 pins so a 7 was placed in front of the box. On his second ball Bill got two of the three pins standing for a total pinfall of 9 in the frame. A horizontal line indicates that he failed to convert the spare.

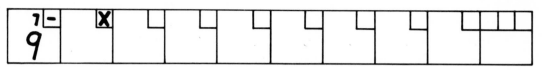

In his second frame Bill threw a strike and this was indicated by an X. No score was written in the box because Bill still had the pinfall coming on the next two balls to be thrown.

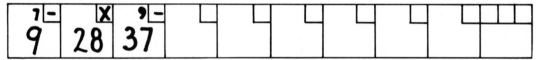

In the third frame Bill got a 9 with his first ball, and then missed the single pin for an error. His total of nine pins was added to the strike in frame 2 and *also* counted as the pinfall in frame 3 for a cumulative total of 37 for three frames.

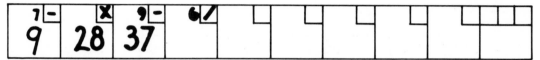

In frame 4 Bill started with a 6-pin count on the first ball, converted for a spare with his second. No total score was written in the frame as Bill had the count of the next ball to add to his spare.

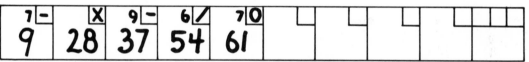

The first ball in the fifth frame knocked down 7 pins, but left a split. The 7 count was added to the previous frame's spare. Bill's second ball failed to get any pins so 7 was the total pinfall for the fifth frame, making the total 61.

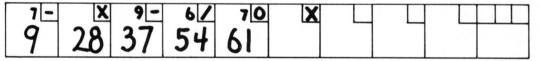

Bill picked up another strike in the sixth. Remember he had two more balls to count on this strike.

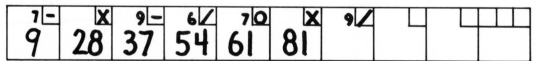

In the seventh Bill got 9 on the first ball, and converted the single pin leave into a spare. This gave him a 10-count to add to the previous strike for a total of 81 in the sixth. Because he got a spare, and had to add the pins on the next ball, he marked the spare but did not total the pins.

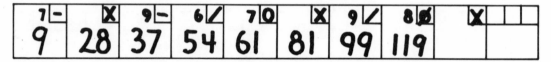

7 −		X	9 −	6 /	7 0	X	9 /	8 Ø		
9		28	37	54	61	81	99			

The eighth frame found Bill getting 8 pins with his first ball, leaving him with a split. He added the 8 pins to his seventh frame spare for a 99 total. With the second ball, Bill then converted the split into a spare.

7 −		X	9 −	6 /	7 0	X	9 /	8 Ø	X	
9		28	37	54	61	81	99	119		

The first ball in the ninth frame took all 10 pins — a strike. Ten pins were added to the eighth frame's spare and the score totaled 119. An X marked the strike and Bill had two more balls coming.

7 −		X	9 −	6 /	7 0	X	/	8 Ø	X	X −
9		28	37	54	61	81	99	119	148	167

Bill started the tenth with another strike and marked an X in the first box. The strike entitled him to two more balls in the tenth. On Bill's next roll he got 9 pins. The 9 and the 10 for the previous strike were added to the ninth frame where, you remember, Bill still was to get the pinfall from his strike and the next two balls, a total of 29 pins, and the ninth frame total was now 148.

Bill threw at the single pin leave and missed for an error. But the tenth frame strike and the 9 gave him a 19 total pinfall for the last frame. This, added to the accumulated score of 148 in the ninth, gave him a game score of 167.

If, at any time, Bill had fouled (gone over the foul line), the pinfall for that ball would not have counted and an "F" would have been marked, in front of the box, instead of the number of pins knocked down. If a foul occurs, on the first ball of a frame, the pins down do not count so they are reset and the bowler throws at the complete set-up with his second ball.

If the foul is on the second ball, the pins knocked down with that ball do not count. The pins that were downed with the first ball do count and an "F" is scored and the pins are set for the next bowler.

We have not covered the subject of "Body English" in this bowling section but it does seem to be an important maneuver with many bowlers as "Rusty," opposite page, shows to perfection.

Bibliography

American Bowling Congress and American Junior Bowling Congress. *Rules and Regulations of Bowling*. Milwaukee, Wisconsin: The Congress, latest edition.

Division of Girls and Women's Sports. *Official Bowling Guide*. Washington, D. C.: American Association for Health, Physical Education, and Recreation, latest edition.

National Duck Pin Bowling Congress and American Rubberband Duckpin Bowling Congress. *Rules and Regulations*. Washington, D. C.: The Congress, latest edition.

Women's International Bowling Congress. *Bowling Rules and Regulations*. Columbus, Ohio: The Congress, latest edition.

Carter, Don. *Ten Secrets of Bowling*. New York: The Viking Press, 1958.

Falcaro, Joe, and Goodman, Murray. *Bowling for All*, 3d. edition. New York: The Ronald Press Company, 1957.

Fraley, Oscar, and Yerkow, Charles. *Complete Handbook of Bowling*. Englewood Cliffs, N. J.: Prentice-Hall, Inc., 1958.

McMahon, Junie, and Goodman, Murray. *Modern Bowling Techniques*. New York: The Ronald Press Company, 1958.

Weinberg, Jack. *Duck Pin Bowling*. New York: The Ronald Press Company, 1954.

Wene, Sylvia. *Women's Bowling Guide*. New York: David McKay Company, 1959.

Wilman, Joe. *Better Bowling*. New York: The Ronald Press Company, 1953.

CANOEING

Ruth Schellberg

History and Growth

THE CANOE HAS BEEN an instrument of history. In various primitive forms it was used for transportation in many lands from recorded times. In fact, the changeless pack or saddle animal is the only mode of transportation comparable with the canoe. Explorers, prospectors, trappers, and missionaries ventured into unknown wildernesses with canoes. Barter and trade among the natives of many countries were possible because the craft could be navigated with a heavy cargo in streams as well as in open waters.

In the earliest of times on the continent of North America there were three kinds of native craft: the graceful birchbark canoe made on closely prescribed lines by the Indians of northeastern United States and eastern Canada; the heavy, unstable log dugouts evolved by the Indians of the South and West; and the skin and whalebone kayaks used by the Eskimos. The white man took as his model the birchbark canoe, and pioneers used this craft to penetrate the wilderness and push the frontiers westward.

Not until the latter part of the nineteenth century was the canoe used for sport and recreation as distinct from business. In England, a kayak-type decked canoe known as the Rob Roy was popular as a pleasure craft. This canoe, originally designed in 1865 by John Macgregor, a British barrister, was propelled by a double-ended paddle. Macgregor added sails to the craft and cruised throughout Europe and the Holy Land. Exponents of Macgregor and the Rob Roy founded the Royal Canoe Club, the first of many canoe clubs to champion the sport.

In Canada and the United States the Peterboro canoe far surpassed the Rob Roy in popularity. This was an all-wood open craft based on the design of the birchbark canoe, propelled by single-blade paddles. In 1871, some ardent American canoeists organized the New York Canoe Club, the first one in the United States still in existence. Because of the interest in cruising and racing, the American Canoe Association was organized in 1880 at Lake George, New York. To facilitate the holding of competitions between Canadians and Americans in both paddling and sailing, the Canadian Canoe Association appeared. Subse-quently, the American Canoe Association set up its national camp and regatta site at Sugar Island, Gananoque, Ontario, Canada. Today the Association's many members are organized in nine geographical divisions which hold meets and competitive events. Many local canoe clubs are affiliated with the ACA and conduct their activities under its rules.

Canoe trips into wilderness areas are "tops" in aquatic sport. Annually, sponsored by the Boy Scouts alone, thousands of young voyagers come from all states in the union to embark on trips into Superior National Forest and Canada's adjacent Quetico Provincial Park. In this roadless area, following trails blazed in fur-trading days, these canoeists paddle and portage through an endless chain of lakes camping in evergreen-birch forests where moose, deer, beaver, bear, loon, and porcupine may be observed and fishing is *par excellence*.

Juniors and seniors alike use canoes for leisurely pleasure, for camping and fishing trips; for paddling races with crews or for water slalom, white water races, and sailing races. Whether you run rapids, take cruises, or compete in racing events, canoeing means adventure and calls to all lovers of the out-of-doors.

Group of college girls portage through the dense forest country on the Minnesota-Canada border.

Breakfast is ready at campsite on canoe trip into the wild north country.

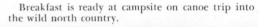

Canoes

Canoes are of numerous types, sizes, and construction. Though they are made primarily to be paddled, certain canoes can be rigged for sailing, equipped with an outboard motor for boating, or geared for racing. They ordinarily are made in lengths from 13 to 20 feet, and their ability to carry weights and to run safely in heavy water depends upon their length as well as their lines.

For all around pleasure the standard canoe, which is somewhat pointed at both ends, is best. The standard canoe comes in aluminum or wood. The aluminum canoe, smooth inside, is shaped from two pieces of aluminum held together by a keel. Air chambers are under the decks so that the canoe will right itself when overturned. This type canoe has bow and stern seats about 4 inches lower than similar craft to increase stability. In weight, the aluminum canoe varies from 45 pounds for a 13-foot craft to 86 pounds for an 18-foot canoe. The canvas-covered canoes have a light wood shell and ribs; in weight, from 50 pounds for a 13-foot craft to 90 pounds for an 18-foot type. An average two-man canoe is 16-feet in length with 14 to 16 inches draft or depth at the center thwart, and weighs 70 to 80 pounds. It can carry about a 600-pound load. Standard wood canoes come with or without seats. Representative pleasure canoes usually have cane-bottom seats in the bow and stern.

Though some canoes are made with a square stern for a motor attachment for boating, the standard canoe can take a motor with a side bracket, and is faster, lighter, and easier to paddle than the model with a square stern.

A sailing canoe is a fully decked craft equipped with a hiking seat. Rigged with a fore-and-aft sail, the sail area ranges from 40 to 60 square feet. It has watertight bulkheads in the bow and stern, weighs about 70 pounds, and is usually about 17 feet long.

The kayak, a popular racing craft, is paddled with a double paddle. It is a sharply pointed canoe and resembles a racing shell in shape. Since most of the craft has a deck covering, the cockpit is small. A folding-type kayak (foldboat) can be dismantled and folded into a bag. Its covering is canvas over a collapsible wooden frame.

Parts of a Standard Canoe. — Almost every part of a canoe is built in a curve to give the craft a maximum degree of rigidity and bracing strength and to permit maximum efficiency in passing through water. The main parts follow:

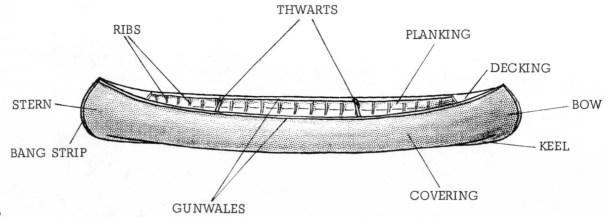

Keel — a strip which runs along the bottom in the center from bow to stern. The keel protects the bottom, makes it easier to paddle a straight course, and lessens side-slipping when paddling broadside to the wind or current.

Gunwales — two uppermost curved strips along each side from bow to stern.

Ribs — strips of wood from gunwale to gunwale at regular intervals and curved around the body of the canoe. These give strength and rigidity to the craft.

Planking — boards running lengthwise over the outside of the ribs.

Covering — canvas carefully fitted and stretched over the planking.

Thwarts — braces from gunwale to gunwale across the canoe to hold the gunwales apart and to maintain the shape of the canoe. These are used to lean against by kneeling paddlers and serve as a carrying beam for portaging. The front thwart, to allow space for the bow paddler, is farther from the front end than the rear thwart is from the stern. The center thwart is on the balance of the canoe.

Seats — caned bottoms placed bow and stern. These are unnecessary, except for pleasure paddling.

Decking — triangular wood wedges, both bow and stern, where the gunwales meet. Besides acting as a brace, they shed any spray or water which comes over the ends.

Bang Strip or Fender — a metal strip around the curved end of both bow and stern. This protects the canoe from impact or abrasion.

Cleats or Rings — arrangements for fastening a line to tie up the canoe.

Paddle and Cushion

Paddles are of two types: single-bladed for average canoeing, and double-bladed used almost invariably in kayaks. Both types are made of wood, the most common wood being spruce.

The lower third of the single-bladed paddle is a flat blade about 6 inches wide and generally rounded at the tip. The upper part is a round shaft (loom) about 2 inches in diameter. The grip flares somewhat at the top and is curved to fit the palm. Your paddle should be fitted to your own size and needs. It should be about 3 inches shorter than your height for stern paddling, and six inches shorter for bow work. Both bow and stern paddles should be of the same type and shape to give better balance in paddling.

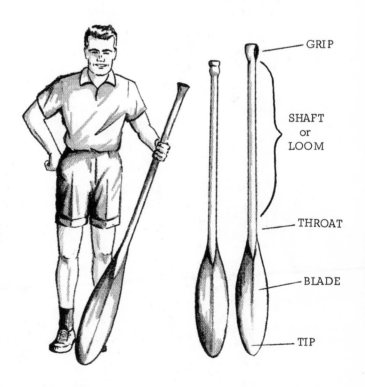

GRIP

SHAFT
or
LOOM

THROAT

BLADE

TIP

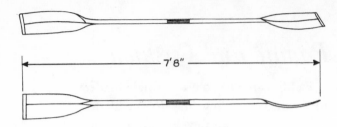

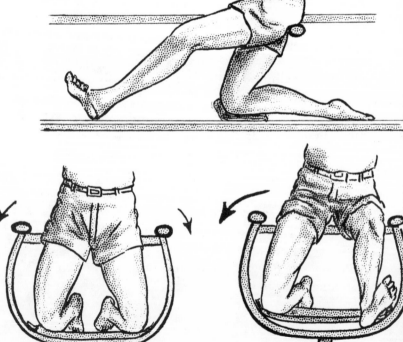

The double-bladed paddle is about 7 feet 8 inches in length with a blade located at each end. The planes of the blades are at right angles to each other to simplify feathering. The blade tip is usually straight like an oar rather than rounded like a single paddle. For ease in carrying, double paddles are made in two sections. When in use, the sections are joined by a ferrule at the middle of the shaft.

Since it is difficult to kneel on bare boards for any length of time, kneeling pads or a cushion are essential. Sponge rubber pads clipped to the knees are satisfactory; a pneumatic cushion is good. You can make a cushion by stuffing shaved or ground cork into a covering about 2 feet long. This piece of equipment protects your knees and serves as a life preserver as well.

Paddling Positions

The ideal position for paddling is on both knees. You kneel on the bottom of the canoe with knees spread about a foot apart. Rest a portion of your weight on the front edge of a seat or thwart, but keep most of the weight on your knees. This places the center of gravity lower in the canoe and, consequently, makes the canoe less shaky and wobbly.

Another paddling position is the single-kneeling position. You kneel on the knee of your paddling side and extend your other leg forward and toward its own side of the canoe, the heel and outside of the ball of your foot against the edge of the ribs to grip the canoe securely. When you change paddling sides, you reverse this single-kneeling position.

Canoe Safety

Canoeing is for swimmers only. If you are not a deep water swimmer learn swimming skills first.

Before paddling a canoe there are certain procedures which should be practiced to give one a feeling of "at-home-ness" in the craft.

Capsize. — Jump into the water maintaining contact with the canoe and propel it to shore.

Place hands on gunwales with head down and crouch ready to spring upward.

Keeping hands on gunwales vault up and sideways and when body arcs over release left hand, transfer right to nearer gunwale and land feet first in the water while keeping a hold of the canoe.

Swamping. — Seated on the floor of the canoe, alone or with one or two others, rock the canoe sideways taking in water at both sides until the canoe is gunwale-full. Try to stay in the canoe as it fills with water. If you should roll out crawl back in again. Hand paddle toward shore. The canoe will support you even when full of water.

Keep body flat on surface with elbow on bottom of canoe and right hand on gunwale, crawl and kick to draw canoe under you, then turn hips and sit down in canoe.

Sit in bottom of canoe with knees under thwart and legs spread out. Balance with hands on water.

Never leave your canoe in the event of capsize. Take it with you. Whether you cling to it or sit in it you have a good resting place if the distance to shore is greater than you think. This precaution has saved many lives.

Hand Paddling. — Kneeling in front of and facing the bow deck, hand-paddle your canoe crawl-stroke-fashion. A canoe is easily propelled by hand and loss of a paddle is not as serious as is generally thought.

Changing Positions. — Take these positions in the canoe:

1. Sit in the stern seat. Note how high the bow rides.

2. Kneel in front of stern seat with hips resting against it. Kneeling is better than sitting when the water is rough.

3. Kneel in front of the stern thwart, facing forward, with hips resting against it. This is the best position when paddling alone.

4. Sit on the floor of the canoe in front of the stern thwart. This is the passenger's position when there is a single passenger.

5. Sit in the bow seat.

6. Kneel in front of the bow seat with hips resting against it.

In changing positions keep your weight low in the canoe and centered. This can be done by bending forward to hold on to the gunwales and by stepping in the center of the canoe.

When there are several in the canoe only one person should move at a time. Others should be seated on the floor.

Fundamental Skills

Single-Blade Paddle Strokes

Each separate propulsion of the paddle is a stroke. You reach the paddle in the air, dip it into the water, and pull it through the water, manipulating it differently for varying desired effects.

Grip. — To hold the paddle, your upper hand grasps the top, fingers forward over the knob. Your lower hand slides down the shaft a short distance above the blade, thumb on the inside or outside of the shaft. Your upper hand holds the grip firmly, elbow in close to the body. This hand does the driving. Your lower hand grasps the shaft loosely so that you can rotate the paddle in steering. The lower arm is usually held rather straight. Keep your body erect so that you can apply the weight and driving power of your shoulders to the stroke as well as the pulling power of your lower arm.

Whether you are right- or left-handed you should learn to handle the paddle and execute all strokes equally well on both sides of the canoe.

Bow or Forward Stroke. — The bow stroke is used from any paddling position in the canoe. It is a straight-ahead stroke and not a steering stroke. For this stroke your upper hand, holding the paddle by the grip, is back within a few inches of your right shoulder. Your lower hand grasps the shaft near the blade, left arm straight.

Bow
Stroke

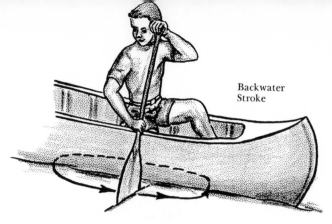

Backwater Stroke

From your kneeling position, reach forward with the lower hand and dip the paddle squarely in the water as close to the gunwale and as near the bow of the canoe as is comfortable. As you dip, push the top arm diagonally forward until it is out over the water; at the same time pull back to your hip with your lower arm. The course of the blade is parallel to the keel with your paddle perpendicular to the gunwale. The stroke ends when your lower hand is directly in line with your hip. (Any farther carrying back of the paddle is a waste of energy and a hindrance to the forward motion of the canoe.) At this point both lower and upper arms are straight.

To make the recovery, move your upper hand backward in an arc parallel to the gunwales. This slices the blade sideways out of the water. Twist it flat or parallel to the water, and swing it forward in a wide arc just an inch or two above the surface of the water. When the paddle gets as far forward as is comfortable for you, turn the blade quickly so that it is again perpendicular to the water, straighten your upper arm, and repeat the stroke.

In the recovery, feathering the paddle (holding the paddle parallel to the water) cuts down the wind resistance to the forward motion of the paddle and saves energy. This is particularly important on a windy day.

In tandem paddling, for safety in balance and for even distribution of power, paddlers should stroke on opposite sides of the canoe and in unison. The bow paddler sets the pace for the stern paddler to follow.

Backwater Stroke. — The motions of the backwater stroke are practically the reverse of those for the bow stroke, except that you do not keep your lower arm straight throughout. You use this stroke to propel the canoe backward, to check its headway, or to stop it. If a single paddler uses this stroke, the canoe has a tendency to turn toward the paddling side.

Start with the blade just at the water. Your lower hand holds the shaft opposite the hip, and your upper one grasps the handle over the water. Reach a comfortable distance back of your hip, keeping the blade of the paddle flat to the surface of the water. Push down and forward with the lower arm as the top arm bends and brings the grip of the paddle to your shoulder. Carry the paddle forward and parallel to the keel about as far as your lower arm can reach.

For the recovery, cut the blade out of the water by a slicing motion away from the canoe, and swing the blade in an arc to the stern.

To stop the canoe, dip your paddle deep into the water just a bit forward of your hip, with the blade facing flat against the direction of motion, and hold it rigid. If you need additional support to withstand the pressure, lock the thumb of your lower hand over the gunwale.

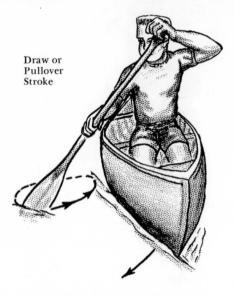

Draw or
Pullover
Stroke

Draw or Pullover Stroke. — The draw or pullover stroke is used to move the canoe toward the side on which the paddle is working. On the left side, the draw moves the canoe toward the left; on the right, the draw pulls the canoe toward the right. If you use the draw paddling solo in the middle of the canoe, the canoe moves broadside; if you use the draw at one end only, that end moves the more. When two paddlers execute the draw on opposite sides, the canoe pivots in a circle. The draw stroke will help you avoid snags and make a good landing at docks. Both bow and stern paddlers use this stroke.

To execute the draw, reach out with the paddle toward a point in the direction you intend to move the canoe. Swing the blade with your lower hand, flat side parallel to the keel of the canoe and keep the upper hand in front of your head, elbow bent and held high. Dip the paddle into the water and push outward with the upper hand as you pull in vertically to the canoe with the lower hand. This motion moves the canoe over.

Recover either over the surface of the water or underwater. An underwater recovery will steady your canoe in rough and choppy water. In this case, just before the blade reaches the side of the canoe, turn it sideways and feather outward to the beginning of your next stroke.

A diagonal draw, one not executed at right angles to the length of the canoe, can be either forward or toward the stern. When you are a bow paddler, you use the diagonal draw forward to pull the bow back on course should the bow swing away from the side on which you are paddling. You reach well out and forward and, dipping with the flat of the blade parallel to the course of the canoe, you draw with a sliding motion directly to the bow and then curve the blade into the regular bow stroke. This will not break your paddling rhythm. The diagonal draw toward the stern is used to move a standing canoe backward and sideways.

Pushover Stroke. — The pushover stroke makes the canoe move away from the paddling side. You can use this stroke from any paddling position in the canoe; it moves the part of the canoe from which it is executed.

Pushover
Stroke

The path of the paddle in the push-over stroke is opposite that used in the draw stroke. It is accomplished by a prying action using a point on the gunwale as the fulcrum. Both wrists are flexed and the inside edge of the paddle is turned backward as the paddle pries. Recovery is either by cutting the paddle back through the water or by lifting the paddle over the water.

When the canoe is standing, a bow paddler using a pushover and a stern paddler a draw, simultaneously, can move it sideways. To move a canoe at right angles in the opposite direction, the bow uses a draw and the stern a pushover.

J Stroke — A J stroke is so-called because the path of the blade through the water somewhat resembles the letter J. A stern paddler or a solo uses the J stroke to counteract the tendency of the bow of the canoe to swing away from the paddling side.

The J stroke is started in the same manner as the bow stroke. As the paddle blade approaches the hip, both wrists flex to turn the paddle in its backward course so that the inner edge is up. During the turn of the paddle there is outward pressure against the water as is needed to turn the bow toward the paddling side.

To exert exactly the right amount of outward pressure and hence to paddle in a straight course, a point of aim is necessary. When the canoe is on course, outward pressure has been sufficient and the blade is lifted from the water. Recover as in the bow stroke.

The first part of the J stroke tends to start the bow swinging away from your paddling side. The outward pressure during the turn at the end of the stroke counteracts further swinging of the bow and keeps the canoe on a straight path. The stroke is thus a combination of the bow stroke and the pushover.

Sweep Strokes. — You use sweep strokes to maneuver the canoe through turns to the left or to the right from any paddling position. To execute either a full, quarter, or reverse sweep, hold your paddle as nearly horizontal as possible, with about one-half to two-thirds of the blade submerged in the water, inner edge down and outer edge straight up. Slip your lower hand higher up on the shaft and reach to extend the radius of the arc as much as you can. Your upper hand and grip of the paddle travel waist high in an arc parallel to the surface of the water.

J Stroke

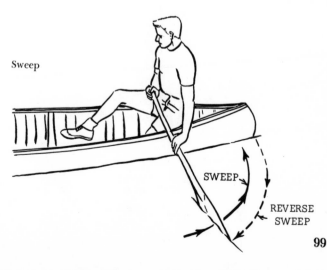

Sweep

SWEEP

REVERSE SWEEP

Quarter Sweep. — Both bow and stern paddlers use the quarter sweep. If in the bow and the canoe swings off course toward the side on which you are paddling, you can straighten the canoe by one or two quarter sweeps, matching the rhythm of your regular stroke. Dip your paddle edgewise in the water well ahead and close to the bow, and sweep outward away from the canoe through an arc of 45 degrees; this brings your paddle back to a point in line with your hips and forces the bow back on course. If in the stern, start the sweep at a point directly in line with your hips and sweep back to a point alongside the canoe.

Reverse Sweep. — To turn your canoe toward the paddling side, a reverse sweep is necessary. You execute this stroke in the opposite direction from the quarter sweep. Since its forward motion checks the headway of the canoe, you use it to turn or stop a canoe under little head-

way or to make a pivot turn. For a reverse sweep, hold your lower hand on the paddle near your hip and extend your upper hand forward and low. Dip the blade into the water vertically, well back and alongside the canoe. Push with your lower hand and pull with your upper hand to sweep the blade in a wide arc toward the bow. When the blade comes in line with your hip, your swing is completed. As in all sweep strokes, the wider your reach the greater your turn.

Full Sweep. — A full sweep is generally used when you handle a canoe alone. You are positioned about in the center of the canoe; hence you sweep in an arc of about 180 degrees to make a pivot turn away from the paddling side.

For a full sweep, start with your paddle edgewise in the water and as far ahead as possible. With your lower arm straight, upper hand close to the lower part of your chest, dip about one-half to two-thirds of the blade in the water. Sweep in a wide circle as far to the stern as you can and close to the canoe. Push forward with your upper hand and diagonally toward the stern. Keep your lower arm straight and pull in a flat arc toward the stern. In the recovery, feather forward just above the surface of the water and parallel to it, front of your blade down. A reverse full sweep causes the canoe to make a pivot turn towards your paddling side.

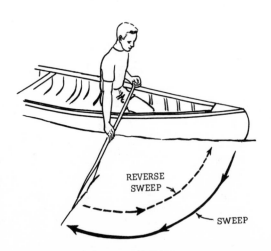

REVERSE SWEEP

SWEEP

FULL SWEEP

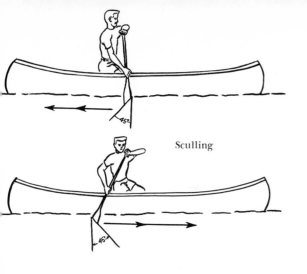

Sculling

Sculling.—Sculling draws the canoe continuously toward your paddling side. To scull you place the paddle vertically in the water slightly ahead of you, flat of the blade facing directly toward the canoe. Turn the paddle with your upper hand so that the rear edge of the blade moves outward until the flat of the blade (previously facing toward the canoe) faces exactly 45 degrees toward the stern. Then move the paddle, still in its vertical position, toward the stern and in a line exactly parallel with the keel. Your blade must not move in a circular path; therefore, hold its angular position firmly against the pressure of the water. To continue, your upper hand reverses the 45-degree setting of the blade so that the side which faced toward the stern now faces at the same angle toward the bow. Move it forward, parallel with the keel and to the point where you began. Repeat the movements and you are sculling. In both the backward and forward movements of this stroke, the water pressure is against the same side of the blade; thus your canoe is always drawn toward your paddling side.

Loading and Positioning

Weight has a definite effect upon the actions of your canoe, hence, you must never overload it. Always position your load as low as possible in the canoe to insure a low center of gravity, and center and balance it so that the canoe does not list. In loading gear from a dock, load from the middle toward the ends; unload in reverse order, ends to the middle.

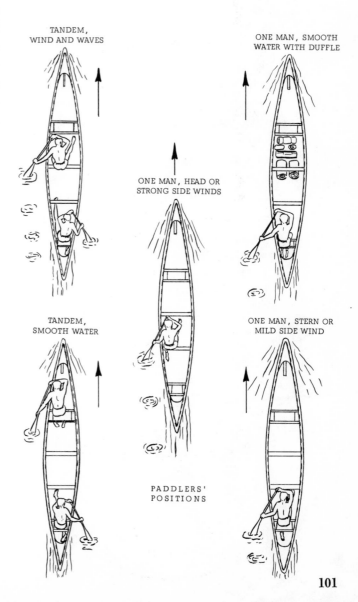

TANDEM,
WIND AND WAVES

ONE MAN, SMOOTH
WATER WITH DUFFLE

ONE MAN, HEAD OR
STRONG SIDE WINDS

ONE MAN, STERN OR
MILD SIDE WIND

TANDEM,
SMOOTH WATER

PADDLERS'
POSITIONS

When you paddle into the wind you can carry a heavier load in the bow, but, if your load is heavy your canoe may wallow and ship water. When you are going with the wind, you can keep the bow light; however, the stern must not get so low that waves come over it.

With two paddlers, the lighter paddler should be positioned at the bow and the heavier paddler at the stern. In rough weather and high wind, tandem paddlers have better control if they place themselves closer to the midsection of the canoe.

To board a canoe from a dock, crouch low and, keeping your weight on the dock, place your outside foot into the center of the craft. Then shift your weight from the dock to a position over the foot in the canoe, bringing your other foot into the canoe last. During this process, hold the gunwale nearer the dock with one hand. As you complete your entry, your hands should be grasping both gunwales.

In loading, positioning, and paddling, the stern paddler is in command; he directs all procedures. He is the last one to enter the canoe and the last one to get out.

Embarking from Dock

Fishing from a canoe requires special positioning. For trolling, the fisherman should sit facing the stern paddler either on the floor of the canoe or in the bow seat facing the stern paddler. If casting, the fisherman sitting in the bow seat may face either the bow or the stern.

To land a fish, either fisherman or paddler must quickly slip down to sit on the bottom of the canoe to stabilize it. The one landing the fish should be in a kneeling position.

Bibliography

American Camping Association. *Canoeing Standards and Graded Classifications.* Chicago: The Association, latest edition.

American Red Cross. *Canoeing.* Washington, D.C.: American National Red Cross, latest edition.

Claussen, W. Van B. *Canoeing.* New Brunswick, N.J.: Boy Scouts of America, 1952.

Elvedt, Ruth. *Canoeing A-Z.* Minneapolis: Burgess Publishing Company, 1953.

Handel, Carle W. *Canoe Camping.* New York: The Ronald Press Company, 1953.

Handel, Carle W. *Canoeing,* New York: The Ronald Press Company, 1956.

Pinkerton, Robert. *The Canoe: Its Selection, Care, and Use.* New York: The Macmillan Company, 1948.

Russell, M. *Starting Canoeing.* New York: John de Graff, Inc., 1959.

American Canoe Association. *Rules.* (single and double blade paddle races, water slalom, white water races, and sailing races). Jacksonville, Florida: Nathan L. Mallison, Commodore.

Jacques, Florence. *Canoe Country.* Minneapolis: University of Minnesota Press, 1938.

Rowlands, John J. *Cache Lake Country.* New York: W. W. Norton Co., Inc., 1947.

HANDBALL

Roy B. Moore

History and Growth

Since ancient days people have played games with a ball. Hard or soft, large or small, in all parts of the earth a ball has been thrown, batted, struck, kicked, pushed, rolled, or carried in hundreds of forms of play or games.

One of the oldest of these forms is the game in which a ball is batted by the hand against a wall — the forerunner of the modern game of handball. History records that this type of game was played by the young men in Ancient Rome using the marble walls of their elaborate public baths. As the Romans invaded other countries, the soldiers undoubtedly introduced their games throughout the Roman Empire.

Handball in its modern form began as a game called "fives", in Ireland, in the eleventh century. Here a hard leather ball was batted against walls in a game demanding speed, accuracy, and energy. Its popularity grew and spread to England, France, Italy, and Spain.

As early as the twelfth century players started to wear gloves or bind their hands in order to increase their striking power and to avoid injury. This was the forerunner of games using bats and rackets such as squash, tennis, and jai alai.

In Ireland and England handball or fives reached great heights of popularity from the sixteenth through the nineteenth centuries. The fives champion at Eton was looked upon as a real man of distinction in that distinguished school. When the great Irish champion, John Cavanaugh, died in the mid-nineteenth century his friend, William Hazlitt, wrote, "It may be said that there are things of more importance than striking a ball against a wall — there are things, indeed, which make more noise, and do as little good, such as making war and peace, making verses and blotting them, making speeches and answering them, making money and throwing it away.

But the game of fives is what no man despises who has ever played it. It is the best exercise for the body, and the best relaxation of the mind. . . ."

The first game was played in the United States in the 1840s when some of Ireland's best fives players migrated here. One of these immigrants, Phil Casey, has been called the father of handball in America. In 1882 he built the first handball court in Brooklyn. It was a huge four-wall court, 65 feet long and with a front wall 30 feet high. In 1887 Casey challenged the Irish Champion, John Lawlor, to an international match and won.

The game of handball grew in popularity and spread throughout the United States, especially through the efforts of several organizations. The Amateur Athletic Union has held tournaments since 1897 and has developed standards of participation. The Young Men's Christian Association has included handball in its physical education program since 1890 and also held regular district and national tourneys. The first four-wall rules were assembled by a YMCA handball committee and are used virtually unchanged today. The United States Handball Association, organized in 1951 by a group of handball enthusiasts, has done much to promote handball through its publication, *Ace*, national tournaments, exhibitions, research, and development of standards for facilities. The first intercollegiate tournament was inaugurated by the USHA in 1953.

Out of these promotions have come national champions who are able to take their places beside such greats of the past as John Cavanaugh and Phil Casey. In fact, a Handball Hall of Fame was established in 1952 by the Helms Athletic Foundation of Los Angeles.

Who is the best of the modern handball players? Some say it is Alfred Banuet of San Francisco who won the AAU singles championship in 1929, 1930 and 1931 before he lost his amateur standing. Joe Platak of Chicago may be the one since he won the championship nine times in eleven years (1935-45). It may be the supreme medal winner, Vic Hershkowitz of Brooklyn, who has won sixteen national championships, singles and doubles, on one-wall, three-wall and four-wall courts. In 1955 Hershkowitz was dethroned by Jimmy Jacobs of Los Angeles, below, who retained his championship in 1956, 1957, 1958 and made a comeback in 1960.

YMCAs and private athletic clubs, along with colleges, have provided most four-wall facilities since the beginning of the twentieth century. Interest in the sport has been country-wide wherever these organizations have been established.

Another form of handball is more localized and truly an American version of handball — the one-wall game. It originated about 1910 on Brighton Beach, New York City, where the hard sand and the smooth 15 feet high sides of a bulkhead furnished a perfect court, and a tennis or rubber ball substituted admirably for the hard leather ball, then used in the four-wall handball game. The popularity of the game resulted in the building of many one-wall courts, with standard specifications, on beaches, in parks, in playgrounds, at fire departments, and in school gymnasiums. Enthusiasm for the one-wall game is still extremely high in New York and vicinity. Its recreation possibilities for both sexes and all ages has caused other areas of the country to consider building courts. Certainly it has a far greater spectator potential than the four-wall court, because of its open sides.

The use of a softer ball in the one-wall game encouraged the development of an official "soft" ball for use in all handball games. Since 1919 the AAU has sponsored a four-wall softball tournament and in 1938 held its last hard ball tournament.

Handball is now played, in some form, in all parts of the United States. Like the early game of fives in Ireland, any modern form of the game requires precision, control, speed, endurance, alertness and the effective use of both hands. It is a decided challenge!

Equipment and Playing Area

Basically a game of handball can be played with a wall, a smooth ground surface, and a ball.

The simple way it started in ancient Rome and the one-wall game developed at the beginning of the twentieth century, on the beaches of New York, show that equipment and facilities can be simple. However, more formal games have been developed — four-, three-, and one-wall — in which a regulation ball, gloves, and a handball court are essentials.

Ball. — The official American standard ball is made of black rubber, inflated, about $1\frac{7}{8}$ inches in diameter and 2.3 ounces in weight. Rules require that this ball should rebound 62 to 65 inches from 100-inch drop at 68 degrees Fahrenheit.

Gloves. — Gloves are required for the four-wall game and are recommended for all types of games. They protect the hands and keep the ball free from perspiration. Use snug-fitting gloves of soft material — either cloth or leather. The best ones are made of pigskin, horsehide, or goatskin, with an adjustable wristband. Rules do not allow the fingers of the glove to be connected or webbed in any way. Illustration, below, shows top of a glove with holes for ventilation and adjustable wristband. Other view shows reinforced or padded palm.

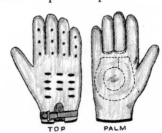

TOP   PALM

Costume. — According to rules, you must wear a white uniform during official competition. Choose a costume which will give you freedom of action and protection — a cotton jersey, shorts, wool sweat sox (wear two pairs to prevent sore feet), and rubber soled shoes, similar to basketball shoes, laced tightly. Low cut oxfords do not give enough support to the ankles. Sweat suits may be used during your warm-up period and removed during the game.

Court. — The four-wall and one-wall games are played on different sized courts. The three-wall court is the same size as the four-wall, with one of the side walls removed.

The four-wall court resembles a rectangular box — it has a front wall, two side walls, a back wall, and a ceiling. The size does vary but it is usually 20 feet wide, 20 feet high, and 40 feet long. The back wall need not extend to the ceiling but must be at least 10 feet high. A line, parallel with the front wall, divides the court equally into a front court and a back court. This line is called the *short line*. Five feet in front of the short line is another parallel line called the *service line*. The area between these two lines is called the *service zone*. The *service box* is in the service zone at each side-wall, formed by a line parallel to and 18 inches from the side wall. All lines are one and one-half inches wide.

A standard one-wall court measures 20 feet in width, 34 feet in length, with the wall 16 feet in height. The short line is 16 feet from the front wall. The service line is designated by a line or markers 9 feet behind the short line.

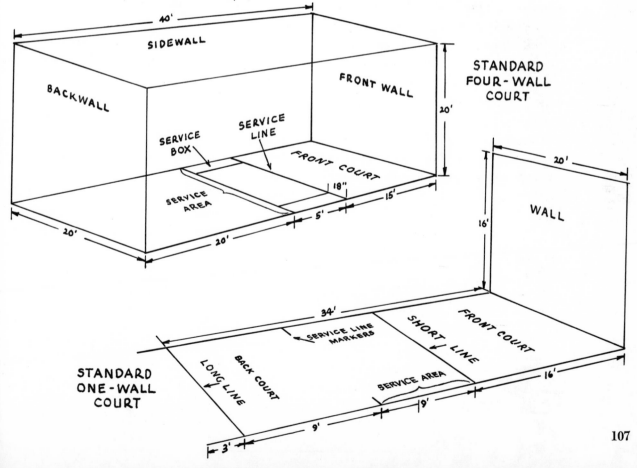

Fundamental Skills

To become a good handball player you must possess accuracy, endurance, and speed. To be an effective and efficient player you must be able to use an underhand, overhand, or sidearm stroke, with either hand, from any position.

Use of Hand and Ball.—There are three common methods of striking the ball. One is with your hand semicupped in a manner of shaking hands. You keep your fingers relatively close together and slightly bent (cupped), with your thumb in its natural position, and strike the ball on the cushion of your hand at the base of your fingers. You slide the ball off the palm between your thumb and index finger or off the base of your little finger. As you hit the ball, snap your wrist.

A second method of striking the ball is with the flat of your hand. With this method your fingers are close together,

your thumb parallel and right next to your index finger. Your wrist acts as a hinge as you slap the ball on the cushion of your hand; the ball then slides off the ends of your fingers.

A third method is with the fist. This speeds the ball past your opponent faster and is especially effective in making sharp-angle serves. The small, rough surface of the fist makes control of these shots difficult and beginners should master the first two methods before trying this fist or "punch" ball.

One of your hands will normally be weaker than the other. To develop strength in the weaker hand, use it in practice as much as possible. Play one hand against the other and practice hitting your shots over and over. For accuracy, at first try to hit the ball just before it reaches the top of its arc (1) on the rebound from the floor. Then try to pick up the ball at other levels: (2) — just after it leaves the wall; (3) — just after it rebounds from the floor. As you become more proficient you will learn to play a kill shot from (4).

FRONT
WALL

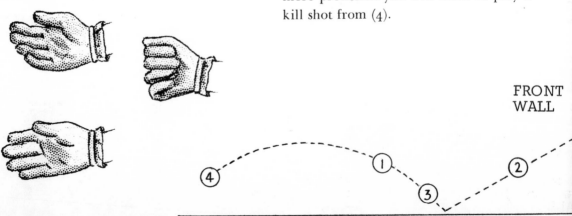

Ready
Position

Start
For
Underhand
Stroke

FRONT WALL

BALL

BALL

LEFT HANDED
SHOTS

RIGHT HANDED
SHOTS

BALL

BALL

Stance and Footwork. — The court position you try to obtain in order to be in a key spot for playing any shot is in the center just back of the short line for four-wall and a bit farther back for the one-wall game. Here you assume your stance, your key position. You face the front wall squarely, crouch a bit, arms away from your body, elbows half bent, and hands out in front and slightly to the sides. One foot should be a little in advance of the other, knees easy, weight forward on the balls of your feet. From your key position and with this stance, you can go to either side or forward or backward and you are set to execute any stroke.

To play the ball, shove off the floor with the foot to match the hand (see diagram below left) — left foot for left hand and right foot for right hand. Then strike the ball as you step forward with your other foot, shifting your weight into the ball. At the moment you strike, your toes should point toward the side wall or side line. The foot on the side of the play should always be behind the ball. When you run for the ball, your first steps in the direction of the play should be short ones to maintain balance; and the few just before you hit the ball should be short, also, to enable you to quickly swing through the ball. Never rush the ball. Wait for it to come to you so that you can get into the proper position to hit it. Exact timing of your play improves your speed and accuracy.

Basic Strokes

Underhand Strokes. — The underhand strokes are the most important ones to master to play a fast game. To stroke underhand you must have your hand lower than your elbow, with the elbow usually bent.

Full-arm Underhand Stroke. — The full-arm underhand stroke is your most effective weapon. In motion, it is similar to skipping a stone on the water. To execute a right-handed underhand stroke:

1. Face the right side wall or line with your left side and left foot toward the front wall, feet about 18 inches apart. Bend your knees slightly and crouch over a bit at the waist. Do not let your head drop forward.

2. Swing your right arm, elbow bent, back to about shoulder height. At the same time, rotate your waist to the right and shift your weight to the rear or right foot.

3. Snap the right arm forward and down, and hit the ball with the base of the fingers of a slightly cupped or flat hand (whichever you prefer) in front of your body at about knee height. Simultaneously, take a short step forward with the left foot to shift your weight to the front foot, and rotate your waist to the left. If you hit the ball above the knee, do not bend at the waist as much and use more wrist snap. Keep your eye on the ball.

4. Follow through by bringing your arm up across the front of your body, rotating your upper body to the left.

Your shoulders and arms should swing through naturally.

A left-handed stroke is made with your right foot advancing with the arm swing. With either hand, this is a stroke used when the ball can be played at or below knee level. It can be used to *pass* an opponent with a fast low rebound, to kill with a low shot to the front wall or corners, and to serve accurately.

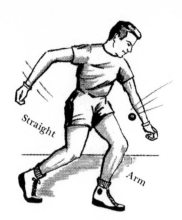

Straight Arm Under Hand Stroke

Straight-arm Underhand Stroke. — The straight-arm underhand stroke has a motion similar to a softball pitch. You use this stroke to hit balls close to the front wall or ones that you have to run forward to reach, or to kill a lobbed ball dropping directly off the wall in the front court. To execute this stroke right-handed: (see illustrations above).

1. Face the front wall, left foot in advance.

2. Bring your right arm straight back underhand as you shift your weight to your right or back leg.

3. Swing your arm straight forward from the shoulder and step forward with your left foot as you strike the ball. Bend your knees to conform to the height you intend to hit the ball.

4. Follow through with your arm in the direction you want the ball to go as you shift your weight to your left leg.

Underhand Serve. — The full-arm underhand stroke, right-handed or left-handed, is used almost exclusively on the serve. The problem is to coordinate and time the rebound of the ball with the execution of the stroke. The secret lies at the point of your elbow, which must lead your hand at the beginning of your stroke.

For a right-handed serve (see below), take your full-arm underhand stance in the service zone and hold the ball in your left hand at about knee level. Turn your head slightly to the right so that you can see any change your opponent might make in court position or stance. As you begin the backswing of your right arm, drop the ball lightly to the floor just in front of your left leg. With the forward swing of your right arm (and a diagonally forward step with your left foot) strike the ball as it rebounds from the floor and aim it to the front wall. Keep your eye on the ball at all times. Remember to stay within the service zone until your serve passes you on its return from the front wall.

If you have trouble getting enough power in your serve at the beginning, you may be using too straight an arm swing. So check your elbow. Pull it down and across in front of you so that your forearm whips through as you complete your arm motion. Practice of the underhand serve will bring power to your stroke. Only practice will teach you how to place each shot with a view of forcing your opponent to make a weak return.

Overhand Strokes. — The overhand strokes — bent-arm and full-arm — are good strokes for defensive play. The motion is similar to that of throwing a ball overhand: the bent-arm like a catcher's throw to a base and the full-arm like a ball thrown high in the air.

Bent-arm Overhand Stroke. — No stroke is more accurate than the bent-arm overhand stroke for shots in the vertical plane, especially for pass shots down the lane (space near the side wall or side line). You hit the ball shoulder high or higher with a cupped hand, snapping your wrist as you contact the ball. To execute a right-handed bent-arm shot (right):

1. Face the front wall, left foot about 18 inches ahead of the right, weight on the rear foot and right arm bent at a right angle. Keep your hand cocked behind your ear, elbow pointing forward.

2. Step forward to the front or left foot and throw your arm at the ball, hitting it slightly above shoulder level. You derive power from the straightening of your arm and the snapping of your wrist.

3. Follow through by shifting your weight to your left leg and allowing your arm to carry down and across in front of your body.

Full-arm Overhand Stroke. — The execution of the full-arm overhand stroke (above) is similar to the bent-arm, except that you extend your arm to begin the stroke and strike the ball at full arm's length over and slightly back of your head. You will have to bend your body back at the waist, and push your weight off your right leg. On your follow through your hand follows the ball in a rising rather than a declining plane. This is a good stroke to use for a soft lob serve or for playing a high bounding ball before it drops to the back wall or long line.

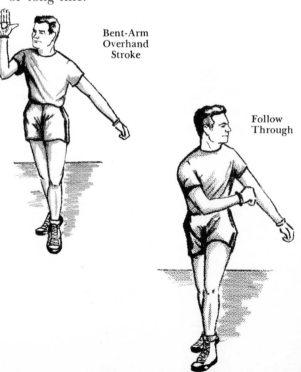

Bent-Arm
Overhand
Stroke

Follow
Through

Sidearm Stroke. — The motion and principles of the sidearm stroke are basically those for the full-arm underhand stroke, but since the ball is higher from the floor you hit it from an upright instead of a crouched position (left). Your arm swings through the ball in a plane parallel to the floor with your hand slightly cupped and your wrist flexible. This stroke will save you a step or two in getting to the ball. Use it to prevent balls from going past you. It is particularly effective for a kill shot and later on, for variation, try using it on your serve.

Basic Shots

Kill Shot. — A kill shot is played below knee level. The objective is for the ball to hit the front wall so low that its rebound (no more than 4 to 5 inches) is too close to the floor to be played. The kill shot is most effective when the ball comes off the front wall close to one of the side areas.

your hand rather flat, palm facing the floor. On contact, slide your hand over the top of the ball and strike the ball on the cushion of your hand, allowing the ball to slide off the ends of your fingers. Swing your hand through naturally on the follow through, your wrist serving as a hinge.

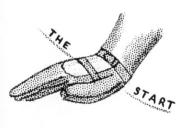

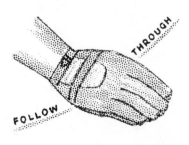

For the kill you use the full-arm underhand stroke, and you keep your body and knees bent forward as you play the ball low. Your wrist, which essentially guides all shots, points downward. Hold

Normally you kill the ball hard and utilize the shot when your opponent is back. Sometimes a soft kill, as a change of pace, will catch your opponent completely off guard.

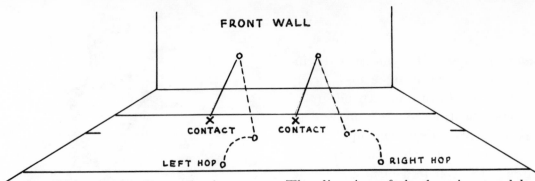

FRONT WALL

CONTACT   CONTACT

LEFT HOP   RIGHT HOP

Hop Shot. — A hop shot, or hook curve, is a ball which rebounds to the left or right as it strikes the floor directly from the front wall. Advanced players can cause the ball to take these angle hops by slicing the hand through the ball.

The direction of the hop is caused by the direction the ball slides off the hand — between the thumb and index finger for a left hop, and at the base of the little finger for a right hop. Its use by experts keeps their opponents off balance.

START

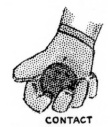

CONTACT

FOLLOW THROUGH

Left Hop Shot. — If you are right-handed, the ball on a left hop should bound toward you as it strikes the floor on the rebound from the front wall. To give the bounding ball this curve, start with a relaxed hand, palm turned toward the side area and away from your body.

With the palm of your hand facing away from you, slice your hand through the ball. Strike it at the base of your fingers, and slide it off between your thumb and index finger. In your follow through on a left hop your palm turns upward.

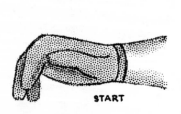

START

CONTACT

FOLLOW THROUGH

Right Hop Shot. — If you are right handed, the ball on a right hop should bound away from you as it strikes the floor on the rebound from the front wall. On this shot, cup your hand with the palm toward the floor. Bring your hand over the top of the ball and strike it on the cush-

ion, allowing the ball to slide off the base of your little finger. With this motion the palm of your cupped hand faces your body. On the follow through, brush your hand through with a natural swing of your wrist.

Back Wall Play. — Back wall play makes up to 20 to 35 per cent of the four-wall game. Timing and position are of utmost importance and much practice is required. In early play you will tend to stand too close to the wall. The speed, height, and angle of the ball as it hits the back wall will affect your position. Experience will make you a better judge.

When you decide to make a back-wall play, face the back wall near the probable spot of the rebound. Take the key stance position (ready position, page 109), your left foot slightly behind the right (for a right-handed shot). As the ball rebounds from the back or side wall, pivot on the right foot, the one nearer the wall, and step with the left foot toward the front right corner as you strike the ball with a full-arm underhand stroke. An extra step or two will increase your power.

It is of utmost importance to keep your eye on the ball as long as possible in making this play. The pictures of Vic Hershkowitz and Jimmy Jacobs, below, were taken through a glass back-wall. These national champions are watching the ball intently as they pivot on their right foot, take their stride with the left foot toward the front wall, and prepare to hit the ball with the right underarm stroke when it reaches knee level or below. Experts make exciting kills from this back-wall position.

If the ball is rebounding deeply into a corner and you cannot judge whether it will bounce to you from the side or back wall, face the corner directly so that you can pivot on either foot and play the ball with either hand.

Playing Strategy

The strategy of handball is to play to your opponent's weaknesses to keep him off balance with a variety of shots, and to attain and hold the strongest floor position for yourself. This calls for placement of your shots, according to plan.

A shot is the end result of a stroke. Any shot which your opponent cannot reach is a placement. The idea in handball is to score a placement on every shot. You acquire this skill only after diligent and long practice.

Most shots, except the kill, are made from the service position and thus are called service shots. Those described here are used as effectively during a rally as in putting the ball into play. Each shot — serve or placement — made from one side of the court has its counterpart on the other. Defensively all are played either on the rebound from the floor or on the volley or half-volley (played immediately after the ball strikes the floor).

Placing your shots so that they rebound just back of the short line, along either side line, or just short of the long line will keep you on the offensive.

Within these areas your opponent will have more difficulty returning your serves, and you will have more time to get to the key position for the rally. For shots to rebound within one foot from the short line, you must serve the ball very low, with speed and with a hop. Shots rebounding within a two-foot area from the side lines, especially cross-court shots, force your opponent out of position on his return. Serves rebounding within a distance of about three feet from the long line, especially if they are hopped, keep your opponent on the defensive from the start.

Adding a left or right hop to your shot is a difficult skill to master, and you should try hopping the ball only if you are familiar with the simpler fundamentals of the game. When correctly placed and when mixed with the right hop serve, the left hop results in many aces for you or many weak returns on the part of your opponent. The hop serves are equally effective along either side line and in mid-court. Remember, from outward appearances they seem identical; the difference occurs just as the ball strikes the floor.

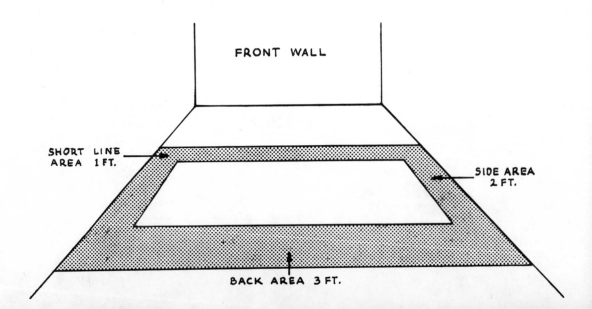

FRONT WALL

SHORT LINE
AREA 1 FT.

SIDE AREA
2 FT.

BACK AREA 3 FT.

Serves and Placements for Four-wall Handball

Although the basic skills are almost identical in one-wall and four-wall handball, there are some differences in serve placement and playing strategy because of the extra walls. In the descriptions which follow the directions given under the one-wall section (pages 118, 119), are not repeated.

Low Drive Serve. — This is executed in the same way, as described in one-wall, but you can add an extra difficulty to the receiver by causing the ball to hit the side wall and floor just back of the short line.

High Side Wall Lob Serve. — The presence of the side wall, in four-wall, makes it difficult for the receiver to return a hard offensive drive. This serve often drops dead in the far corner or is deadened by slightly touching the side wall during its slow high bounce.

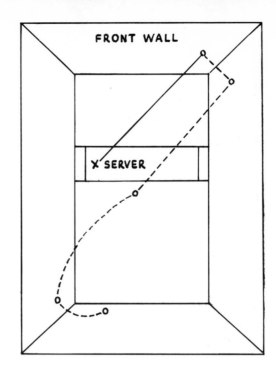

Sharp Angle Serve. — This is a serve made possible because of the extra walls (above). The server stands on one side of service zone and hits the ball at an angle so that it rebounds from the front wall to the side wall and to the floor, just back of the short line. If it is hit high enough, it may rebound to the back wall and corner behind the server.

Two-Wall Serve to Back Corner. — This is called the "run around" serve by handball players, and may be started from either side of the court (left). From the right side, the server stands close to the wall and uses an underhand stroke to serve the ball to the front wall about head high and 4 to 5 feet from the left side wall. The ball then rebounds to the left wall, floor, backwall, and possibly the right side wall before touching the floor again. The angle is not as sharp as the sharp angle serve and the two, when mixed, are very confusing to the receiver. His best choice, in defense, is to volley the ball up-court, or he can use a half-volley or wait until the ball hits the right wall in the corner.

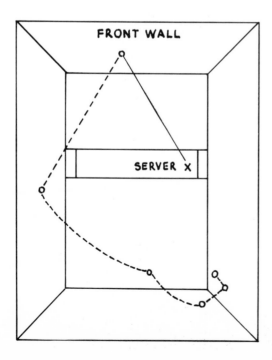

Serves and Placements for One-wall Handball

Low Drive Serve. — For the low drive serve you use a full-arm underhand stroke and play the ball below the waist, so that it rebounds from the wall low and just back of the short line. The effectiveness of this serve depends upon your skill and choice of placement. One placement is to either of the side lanes.

For this serve, you stand about three feet from the side line (below). Try to place the ball so it will rebound close to or on the side line and, if not returned, will drop in the back corner near the long line.

If you add a hop to the drive to the lanes the ball will go toward the outside. For a hop, take your stand about two feet from the side line in order to hide the ball from your opponent.

The best defense against serves rebounding near the side lines is to play the ball just as it rebounds. Then it cannot get to the back corner or over the sidelines.

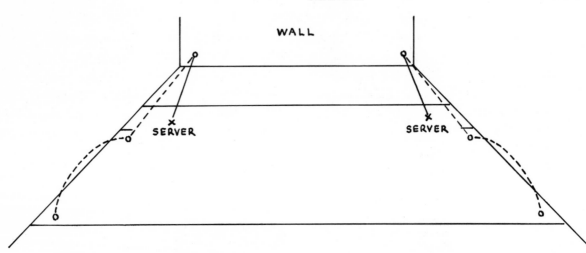

On a low drive serve from the center of the court you have several placement possibilities (right). Since your ball will be partially hidden from your opponent's view, if you play all shots with similar motions at the beginning your opponent will not know which angle to expect. Serves with an added left or right hop and directed to points 1 and 2 on the wall rebound toward the sidelines, as shown. Serves to points 3 and 4 can be made to hop both ways.

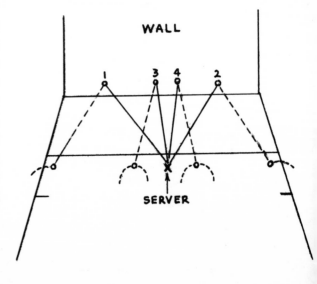

For cross-court shots you must serve a few feet in from the side lines. Serves from one side can be made to rebound short or deep on the opposite side and, with a hop added, will go toward the side line (right).

For any of these low drive serves you must concentrate on every ball you put in play. You want to put your opponent on defense from the start of the rally. If you have a variety of serves at your fingertips, you can keep your opponent guessing all the time.

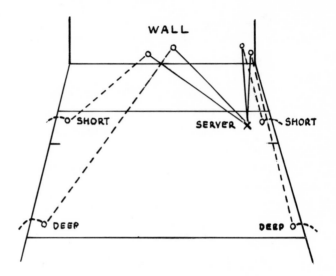

High Lob Serve. — The effectiveness of the high lob serve depends upon your ability to keep the ball close to the side line; therefore, this serve requires much practice. Using the straight-arm underhand stroke, you strike the ball about knee level and aim it about 10 feet above the floor and about 2 feet from the end of the wall (below). Stand about arm's length from the side line, facing the front wall; your arm swings in a plane parallel to the side line. On a good lob serve the ball should land just back of the short line, rebound fairly

high, and drop into the back corner. Try to keep it close to the side line throughout.

Use this shot to force your opponent to the back court with a resultant weak return. It is particularly good along the left side line if your opponent is right-handed, because, if he lets the ball rebound from the floor he has a difficult left-handed overhand return.

The best defense against this shot is a quick volley or half-volley — just before or just after the ball strikes the floor.

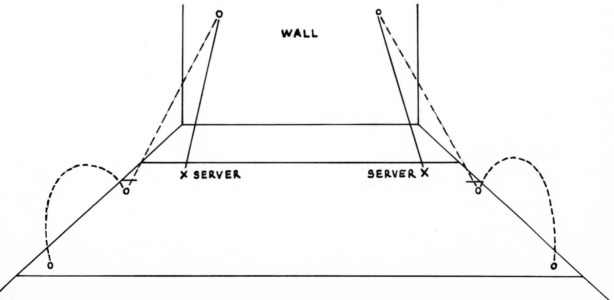

Singles and Doubles Play

Singles and Doubles Play. — The game strategy given for one-wall, previously, can be followed with success in the four-wall game. Sizing up the opponent and changing the pace by mixing high lobs, fast drives, and various angle shots to fit his weaknesses will mean more points for you. Wait for the opportunity to make the low kill shot to the bottom of the front wall using the corner kill. Maneuver for the "hole" or "well", located in the center of the court, and keep your opponent in the defensive positions — the side lanes or against the back wall. A well-placed lob to the back wall makes your opponent less effective. A two-wall placement into the back court is especially difficult to retrieve.

The ceiling crotch shot using a full-arm overhand stroke is an especially good one to use in four-wall to disrupt your opponent's strategy.

As in one-wall, partners in playing the doubles game should balance one another's strengths and weaknesses. By talking to each other during play ("I'll take it", "your ball"), a pattern of defense and offense can be worked out on a teamwork basis. Unlike the one-wall game "screening" is not legal as a strategy in four-wall doubles.

Kill Shots

There is more variety to the kill shots in four-wall than in one-wall handball. All of them are varieties of the five given below. Kills can come from the back wall position but are difficult for beginners to make and should be attempted when you have your opponent out of position.

The Straight Kill. — The ball is hit directly off the front wall back to the low part of the front wall without it touching the side walls. It is most effective when driven down the side line. This is the only one of the five kills described that can be used in one-wall handball. In four-wall it is often made from the back wall.

The Right Outside Corner Kill. — In this shot, play the ball to hit the right side wall near the front corner close to the floor. If you feint a straight kill it will fool the opponent into rushing to the wrong position at the front wall. (See A in drawing below.)

Left Outside Corner Kill. — This is played in the same way as the right inside corner kill. If you use your right hand, the arm is brought sharply across the front of the body. Either hand can be used in all of these corner kills. The dead english makes the shots very difficult for your opponent to reach. (See B in drawing.)

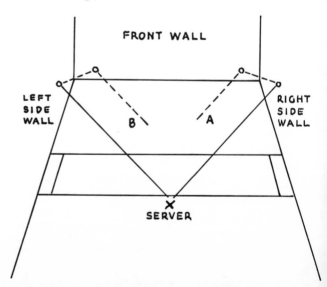

FRONT WALL

LEFT SIDE WALL

RIGHT SIDE WALL

B   A

X
SERVER

Right Inside Corner Kill. — This shot is made by the ball hitting the front wall, the right side wall, and the floor. Since this shot is generally attempted from farther out in the court it is generally not as effective as the outside corner kill. It is most successful when the ball rebounds from the front wall to the juncture of the side wall and floor. (See A in drawing.)

Left Inside Corner Kill. — This is identical to the right inside shot except it is driven to the left corner. The ball rebounds from the front wall to the left side wall, preferably at its juncture with the floor. (See B in drawing.)

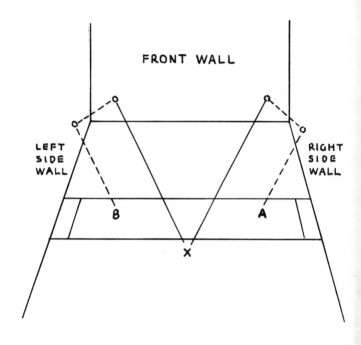

Rules and Scoring

Play is started by a service which consists of dropping the ball to the floor and, on the rebound, striking the ball with one hand so that it hits the front wall first. It then must rebound back of the short line, provided it is not hit on the fly (volleyed) by the receiver. The server may stand any place within the service zone on his serve. In the doubles game the partner of the server is restricted to a special position until the served ball passes the short line. In four-wall he stands in the service box with his back flat against the wall. In one-wall he stands outside the lines between the service line and the long line.

The receiver (or receivers) must be at least 5 feet back of the short line during the service in four-wall, and back of the service line in one-wall. The receiver may volley the service on the fly (before the ball strikes the floor) but must play it to the front wall after the first bounce. If successfully returned, each side plays the ball in turn until one of the players fails to make a return. If missed by the receiving side, a point is awarded the serving side (only the serving side may score), while a miss on the part of the serving side constitutes a *handout* (loss of serving turn). In doubles, the side starting each game is allowed one handout. When the server is out, the side is out. Thereafter during the game both partners serve in turn before loss of serve to the opponents.

During the service the server makes a *handout* by failing to cause the ball to hit the front wall before it hits the floor (or, in the case of four-walls, the side walls or ceiling), or by missing the ball entirely, or by allowing the ball to hit him after the front wall rebound. In doubles he is out if he serves out of turn.

Handouts can also be made by serving two illegal serves. Such serves are sometimes all called *shorts* but are often designated as *shorts, longs,* or *faults.* Aside from the rules involving the extra walls and the different court markings, illegal serves are the same for one-wall and four-wall handball. It is an illegal serve if:

(1) The ball rebounds correctly from the front wall but strikes the floor in front of the short line (short).

(2) The ball rebounds from the front wall to the ceiling or back wall (or behind long line in one-wall handball) before hitting the floor (short or long).

(3) The ball rebounds from the front wall and strikes both side walls before hitting the floor (short).

(4) The server steps beyond the service or short line while serving (fault).

(5) The server's partner, in doubles, is not in his designated area during the serve (fault).

(6) The server serves before opponents are ready (fault).

A *hinder* is accidental interference of an opponent or obstruction of the flight of the ball. When a hinder is called, no penalty occurs and the point is played over. It is the duty of the side that has played the ball to get out of the way of the opponents; however, sometimes this is not possible and a hinder follows.

A game in handball consists of 21 points, and a match means winning two of three games. Handball may be played by two, three, or four persons, the games known as singles, three-handed or cut-throat, and four-handed or doubles, respectively. The three-handed game is not an official game. In this game the server plays against the other two. He must play every other ball and must alternate his serve to the opponents. After he loses a rally (handout), the players rotate, with the one having played the left side of the court on defense moving in to serve. Each player keeps his own score.

Summary

So this is handball — a game that can be played for fun at every level of ability. You can play it as a recreational game with your family or friends — needing only a ball and a wall. On public playgrounds or private picnics, on beaches or in backyards, an old tennis ball and an invitation will soon start a rollicking game. Or, you can play at a more formal and skilled level, either one-wall or four-wall, in the organized programs of public and private groups. The thrill of successful aces, kills, placements, and teamwork at high level tournament competition is fun, too. Try it.

Bibliography

Phillips, B. E. *Handball—Its Play and Management.* New York: The Ronald Press Company, 1957.

Amateur Athletic Union. *Official Rules: Four-Wall and One-Wall Handball.* New York: Amateur Athletic Union, latest edition.

National YMCA Handball Committee. *Handball Rules.* New York: Young Men's Christian Association, latest edition.

United States Handball Association. *Handball Rules.* Washington, D. C.: The Association, latest edition.

FIGURE SKATING

Jack S. Wilson

Origin and
Early Growth

Skating has been a popular sport for hundreds of years — and has been enjoyed by young and old alike of varying ability. Boys and girls went out on frozen lakes and rivers even when they didn't have the fine skating equipment that we enjoy today. It is said the first ice skates were made out of bone — and that in ancient China the early skaters were able to glide over the ice by tying cornstalks to their feet.

It was in Holland that skating first really became popular. The many rivers and canals were frozen so long each year that people used ice skates as a means of transportation, because it was the easiest way to get around. The skates were made of wood and iron and strapped onto shoes. It is very difficult to imagine how people could glide over the ice using such bulky, awkward objects on their feet. Famous painters of the Thirteenth and Fourteenth Centuries have given us scenes showing the ice crowded with skaters out for their daily exercise enjoying skating with their friends and families. Some of these early skaters became quite good, even with the crude skates of those times, and competed against one another.

Skating races, at the time, were mostly over long distances. People soon became interested in the fancy marks and tracings they could make on the smooth ice surface. The interest grew and parties were organized to hold races and games where people could demonstrate their skills and compete against one another. People were really starting to enjoy the wonderful sport of ice skating.

By 1742, in Edinburgh, Scotland, the

first official skating club was formed. A little over one hundred years later, in 1849, the first skating club in America was formed in Philadelphia, Pennsylvania.

Naturally, the interest in this new sport spread from town to town, then from country to country and the passing of time has brought many amazing changes to skating. Modern indoor rinks have made skating a sport that is no longer dependent on the whims of Jack Frost. Modern mechanical methods of ice making and resurfacing provide us with ice as smooth as glass.

Constant study and experimenting have produced quality ice skates designed to give maximum support, long wear, comfort, and beauty — a far cry from the original bone and wooden blades strapped onto everyday shoes.

Out of the small neighborhood ice skating parties, have grown professional ice reviews that travel around the world creating a land of make believe on ice with beautiful costumes, lovely music, and graceful skating.

Yes, skating has certainly "grown up" from its original introduction. Today many towns and cities have a skating club where boys and girls start to skate and amateur skaters practice hours and hours to prepare for figure skating competitions. Huge carnivals are put on with all the members joining the fun and excitement.

It is a common sight to see little toddlers, school children of all ages, mothers and fathers, and grandmothers and grandfathers enjoying the wonderful, modern sport of ice skating.

Benefits of Ice Skating

Actually it would be almost impossible to list all the benefits a person can gain from this wonderful sport. The following list points out a few:

Exercise. — Skating offers a true workout to help us keep our physical fitness. It builds stamina and strong legs.

Character Building. — Skating, in its many forms, offers competition and the desire to perform. Sportsmanship, team play, and individual performance are everyday by-words.

Social Pleasure. — Skating is a social sport that helps you meet and enjoy new friends. It is one of the true family sports, one where the entire family from the youngest to the oldest can participate.

Recreation. — Skating is truly fun, a sport that offers many hours of pleasure to all.

Confidence. — Skating is a definite confidence builder, through performance, and a developer of poise and grace.

You won't glide like an expert at first, of course. However, it won't take long to enjoy the thrill of ice skating. First you will learn motion forward and backward. Then you will learn the stops. As you progress, you will want to try the turns — then jumps and spins. Each new trick will feel like a challenge, and each one you accomplish will feel like a great achievement, even though we all know the more advanced a skater you become the more difficult tricks you have to learn. Each step makes the next one seem easier. Ice skating is a challenge that offers great satisfaction and achievement.

Skating Equipment

The most important single factor in learning to ice skate is to have a proper fitting skate. A large percentage of our new skaters become discouraged by what they think, or are told, are "weak ankles." These skaters find themselves flopping all over, with their ankles almost on the ice, and, even though they try twice as hard, they become discouraged and give up trying to learn by saying, "Oh, well, I guess I just have weak ankles." In almost every case, the trouble is not in the ankles but with the fit of the skates.

The skate must be the right size — not a size or two larger with heavy socks making up the difference. The proper fitting of the skate, in the ankle and at the ball of the foot, determines how much support the skate will give you. This is the most important thing to remember.

A good fitting heeled boot will give you sufficient support to withstand the strain placed upon your arch while skating.

The steel blade attached to the boot is curved from toe to heel; only the center section (the flattest part) actually comes in contact with the ice. This curving of the blade is called the radius of the blade. The blade itself is hollow-ground. This means that a shallow concave-groove runs throughout its length, making two distinct cutting edges. These edges are the sides of the groove, called inside and outside edges, and correspond to the outside and inside of your foot. The diagram below exaggerates the groove, in the blade, to make it more noticeable.

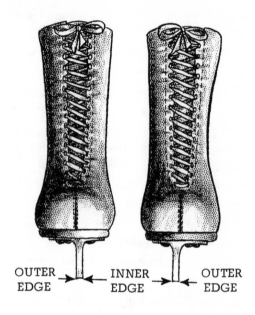

OUTER EDGE — INNER EDGE — OUTER EDGE

Selecting Skates. — When selecting your new ice skates, you must naturally place the utmost importance on the fit. The quality of the skate is also of great importance. Be sure the skate is of substantial quality; that there is life in the leather and that the skate will not "break down" after short usage. Price is of importance to everyone — yet many times you would be better off spending a few dollars more to secure a quality skate that will have a high trade-in value. Many skates will bring only a fraction of their original cost.

A FIGURE SKATE

BLADE

HEEL

BLADE ← FLAT SECTION →

TOE PICK

126

For example, sometimes skates costing $10-$14 might only be worth 10 per cent of their original cost on a trade-in. Yet, very fine skates costing $20 might bring a trade-in value of 35-40 per cent, when outgrown. So, in reality, the more expensive skates only cost you a couple of dollars more in the long run than the less expensive ones. Be sure to inquire about the trade-in value of your skates, when you make a purchase.

The three main types of skates, available to the public, are figure skates, hockey skates, and racing skates. The selection of the correct type is yours depending on what purpose you plan to use the skate for. Usually, the figure skate will give far greater support to the skater — and is generally recommended for beginning skaters. The greater support and blade radius makes it easier to do the various movements on the ice. However, all three types are used widely in recreational skating.

Clothing and Accessories. — Skaters should wear clothing that is comfortable and warm. Girls should have short dresses with full skirts to permit freedom of movement. Skating tights may be purchased, very reasonably — and offer this freedom of movement while providing warmth, at the same time. If slacks are preferred, avoid tight fitting ones that restrict ease of movement. For boys, regular trousers and sweaters look neatest and give most freedom of movement.

Skate guards are just about a necessity. They are made in all sizes and styles in plastic, wood, rubber, and leather. They fit on the blade of your skate and permit you to walk on your skates, without fear of dulling the blades. You can put your skates on at home, before going to the outside pond — and not have to worry about not lacing your skates properly, due to cold hands.

Lacing. — The proper lacing of the boot is very important. The service an ice skate gives you depends on proper lacing, just as the service a new car gives you is dependent on proper driving. The lacing should be loose around the toe of the skate. You should be able to put your finger under the lace with ease — in other words, they are not pulled tight. On a figure skate, generally, the bottom three eyelets should be left loose. This proper lacing, at the bottom, prevents the problem of "cold toes" by allowing free circulation.

The same principle applies at the top of the boot — the final three hooklets should be simply wrapped around with no effort to pull tight. If you have laced your skates properly you can put your finger down into the top with ease.

The proper lacing at the top helps to eliminate tiring, due to lack of circulation. However, in between the top three and bottom three, the laces should be pulled as tight as possible. This will give you the full support of the skate. The only part of lacing that supports you is at the ankle area where the boot curves. Be sure to remember to practice correct lacing, then you will always lace your skates properly by habit.

After tying a knot at the top, be sure to tuck in the ends for neatness and safety. Many an accident has been caused by tripping or catching the blade, due to forgetting this important safety tip.

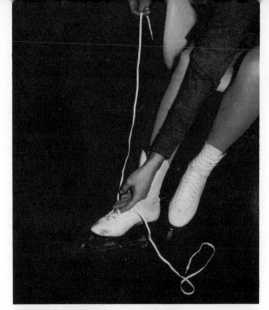

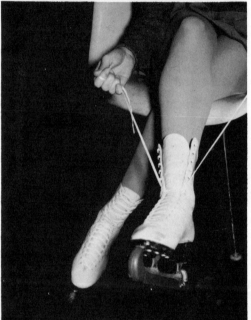

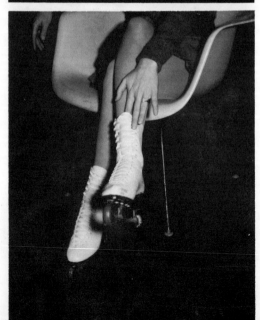

Basic Movements

On the Ice. — Now that we're on the ice, our first goal is movement and is done by developing a "skating stroke." This is the big secret of proper balance in skating. When we walk down the sidewalk, we simply get our motion by a stepping process of placing one foot in front of the other. This will get you moving on the ice, but it is very awkward. People who skate in this manner are generally called "toe skaters." In skating, you move by a skating stroke, or "the pushing to the side."

Keep your body erect, with arms out about waist high, bend your skating knee (the knee you will be putting your weight on), and push out. A long push will make you stretch out your free leg (the leg you have just pushed out with and not touching ice) until it is almost perfectly straight. So instead of a step-step-step, in skating we must remember to stroke, or push out to the side to get proper skating motion.

A good skating stroke will take a while to develop, so remember to practice and to train yourself to "push" not step. Next time, watch the skater who seems to float along the ice so easily and smoothly that it almost seems effortless, and study the stroke. This gracefulness is skating stroke and its development makes skating effortless and so much more fun.

Remember, *bend* that skating knee and *push out*.

Head erect

Body erect

Arms waist high

Free leg

Bend skating knee

Stops

It is sometimes easier to start skating than it is to stop. Most skaters prefer to use the stop they can do best. It is of extreme importance that you learn to stop quickly and safely, in order to avoid collisions with other skaters, holes in the ice, etc.

There are many ways of stopping just by making your skates act as a brake.

"Snowplow" Stop. — The easiest way to stop is called the "snowplow" stop.

When skating forward, simply bring your knees close together, toes in, heels out, and create a braking action by forcing your heels outward. From the picture, you can see how this stop was named. Remember, with both feet flat on the ice you slowly push your heels apart. Be careful not to lean too far forward. (Above.)

"T"-Stop. — The "snowplow" isn't very graceful, so you might prefer the "T"-stop. The "T" is formed by placing the stopping foot against the skating foot at right angles to it. Get the feeling of this stop by lightly dragging the stopping foot sideways on the ice behind the gliding foot. The transfer of weight to the stopping foot creates the braking action. The faster the pressure or transfer of weight is made to that foot, the quicker the stop will be. (Below, left.)

Hockey or Ski Stop. — The most popular stop, in skating, is called the hockey stop or ski stop. The skater swings his entire body to the left or right and keeps his feet flat on the ice. Any stop must be started with the blade flat so that both edges hit the ice — that's what causes the skid mark. (Below, right.)

Other stops are the front T-stop (opposite, right) and the one foot stop (above).

Practice Time. — In order to improve in skating, it is necessary that you practice and have a planned practice program for yourself. The earnest skater will practice the many turns and tricks that he has learned to do well. However, the majority of his time will be spent practicing the movements he is weak on. For example, if you are able to turn to the left easier than to the right, you should concentrate on turning to the right in practice.

Practice your strong points, but improve your weak points. You will soon discover that a planned practice program will pay off where it counts — in results. The old saying, "If at first you don't succeed — try, try again," certainly applies to ice skating. Don't be discouraged if your progress isn't as fast as you would like it to be — the true secret is in practice and more practice. Spend five minutes or so on each movement — then start over. You will find this type of practice more enjoyable. Yes, practice makes perfect.

Skating Tips. — Proper skate care is of the utmost importance. The blades should be sharpened, when needed, to insure good service. Polish should be used regularly for beauty and to protect the leather of your boot. A waterproofer should be applied regularly to the heel and sole of the boot, to prevent cracking and warping of the leather. This proper care will assure maximum trade-in value and give you longer service from your skates.

Many skaters take their skates out of the closet and discover that the blades have started to rust. You can help to prevent this by thoroughly drying the blades before putting them away, after use. Before storing your skates, at the end of the season, oil both blade and shoe.

When you get your skates, put your name, address, and telephone number inside *each* boot. Many a misplaced skate has been returned because the owner had the foresight to do this.

JOHN D. DOE
STREET & PHONE
CITY & STATE

Advanced Figure Skating

Figure skating is the sport of moving the body around a circle or semicircle, with a single stroke and with ease and poise while balanced on a skate. Although many skaters enjoy practicing figure skating maneuvers, competitive skaters follow rigid and well defined progressions in patterns, arranged in degrees of increasing difficulty. The skating patterns, called school figures, must be skated to the satisfaction of judges.

The International Skating Union has set up a series of tests which include required school figures, and skaters are not eligible for the next higher test until they have an acceptable rating in the test just finished. The Eighth Test, the highest, is known as the Gold Test. Before a skater can take the First Test he must show skill in a preliminary test which includes straight skating forward or backward, with correct takeoffs from one foot to another, and two school figures.

In a meet, the judges draw six required school figures, and all skaters must perform each of these in triple repetition. Certain figures must be skated with the right foot and then with the left. The judges award points for correct tracing (shape and proportion of the print on the ice, form (carriage and movements), triple repetitions of the figures, and sizes of the prints.

The circle is the basis of all required figures. Each figure consists of two or three circles whose tracings must be continuous except for a brief interruption for a change of feet. The aim is to make the radii of the circles and half circles of the figure about the same length, and to begin and end as near to a certain point as possible.

Circles vary in size, from 6 feet in diameter up; the larger the circle the more difficult it is to perform. For competitors, a measure for diameter is three times the height of the skater.

Lean, Edges and Carriage

Before you try to skate school figures you must be familiar with the effect of lean and edges, carry yourself well on skates, and know the fundamentals of plain skating. In ordinary skating you stroke in curves — aiming to each side rather than straight ahead. In figure skating you curve the strokes to a much higher degree — aiming to make a tracing or pattern on the ice. Either way you start from a standstill and must launch yourself on a proper edge in good form.

Lean and Edges. — The word "edge" in figure skating means not only the outside and inside skating edges of the figure-skate blade, but also the lean of the entire body, including the blade, to the right or to the left. The "lean" is in defiance of the law of gravity; therefore you can only lean while your body is in circular motion. The centrifugal force works against the force of gravity and keeps you from falling on the ice. The angle of your lean is proportional to the speed around a curve — the faster the speed the greater the lean. As you lean you maintain an erect body position, with your weight directly over the center of your skating foot.

The edges are named according to the foot and the edge of the blade included in your lean. Thus you have four edges: right outside (RO), right inside (RI), left outside (LO), and left inside (LI). Whether you skate forward (F) or backward (B) in a curve, the lean on RO and LI edges is to the right; on RI and LO edges, to the left. Examples of these abbreviations, which will be used later on, are:

ROF-LOF; Right Outer Forward-Left Outer Forward, ROIF-LIOF; Right Outer Inner Forward-Left Outer Inner Forward.

Skating on an edge, plus lean of your entire body, achieves a curve in the direction of the edge. If you go forward on your RO edge you curve clockwise; on your RI edge, counterclockwise.

The center section of the blade, the flattest section, provides you with the greatest stability in flight. Your aim is to try to skate forward on the back part of the flat section and backward on the forepart of the section. Then when you come to your turns, you will be all set to lift your weight onto the forepart of the blade for a forward turn and onto the back part for a backward turn.

Carriage and Form. — In skating the figures, keep your motion effortless, flowing, and graceful. Carry your head upright in a natural position, your body erect but leaning sideways, inward toward the circle you are making. Never bend forward or to the side from your hips. Keep your shoulders low, one leading ahead of the path of travel, the other following. Moving forward, the leading shoulder is in front of the body, the following, behind; moving backward, the leading shoulder is behind the body, the following in front. Hold your arms easily, away from the body, leading arm bowed in a graceful curve below waist level. Keep your palms parallel to the ice, fingers neither extended nor clenched. Your knee joint of your skating leg must be elastic or easy, because it comes into play in every curve.

Keep your free leg slightly bent either behind (following) or in front of (leading) the skating leg; the free foot never parallels the skating foot. Carry your free foot as near to the tracing you are making as possible, toe of the skate pointing downward and outward. Use your arms and free foot to help you execute your figure, but avoid any kind of exaggerated pose. Remember that your hip joint is the pivot of every change of edge. It supports every lean or turn in the position of your body.

Basic School Figures

A knowledge of how to perform the figures described here will enable you to pass the first test prescribed by the International Skating Union. These figures present the fundamentals of figure skating: the circle eights test control; the threes, confidence; and the serpentine or change of edge, rhythm. All these qualities are needed to a high degree if you intend to become an accomplished figure skater.

Circle Eights. — A "circle eight" is a figure made up of two circles of the same size, arranged so that they touch and are opposite each other. Thus they have a long center line which divides the eight vertically into four equal parts, and a cross line which forms a right angle with the center line and passes through the point of connection of the circles. In the diagrams within this chapter, right-foot circles, those skated on the right foot regardless of edge or direction, are represented by solid lines; left-foot circles by dashed lines. (The circles can be skated in just the opposite manner, but for ease of describing the methods and drawing them the above system is used.) The slashes on the circle divide them into thirds. The curves at the points of connection show where a foot change is made to take a new edge.

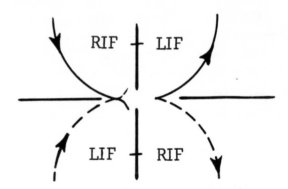

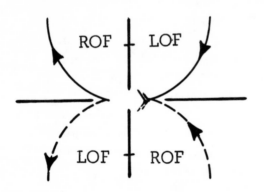

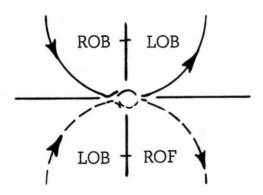

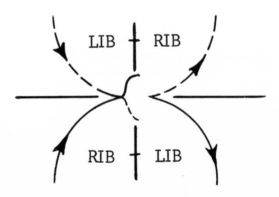

The ROF-LOF Circle Eight is the easiest figure to master. You skate the circles forward on the outer edges, the first circle on the right foot, clockwise; the second on the left, counterclockwise.

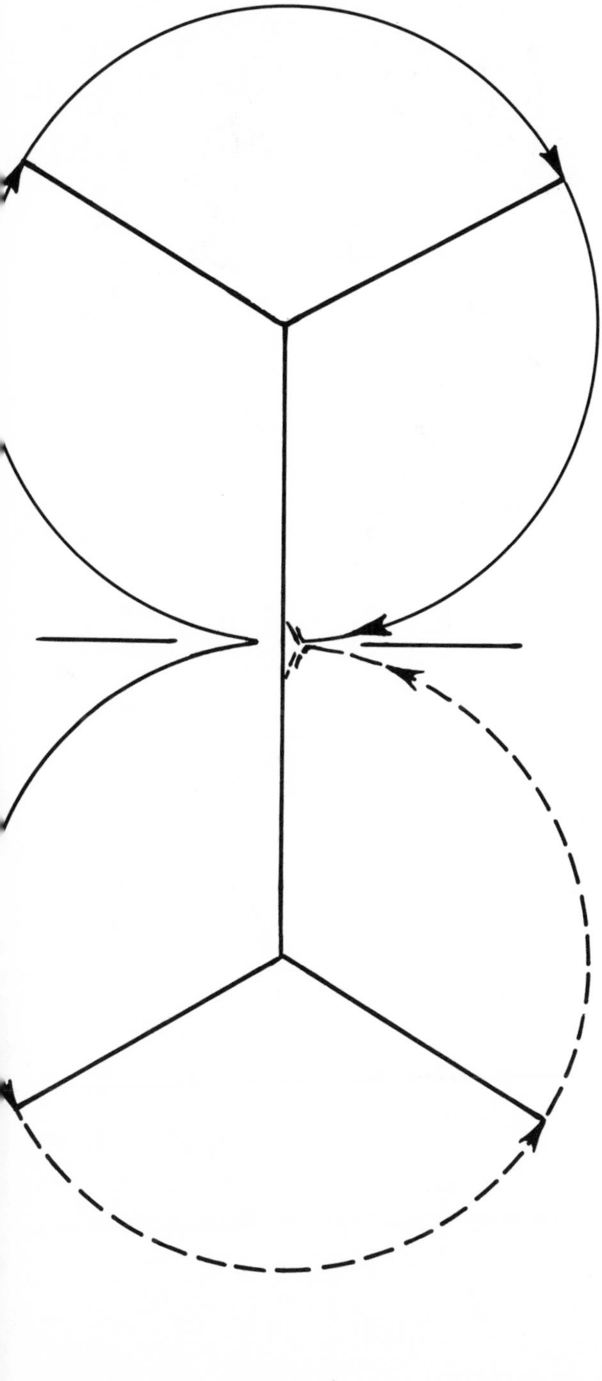

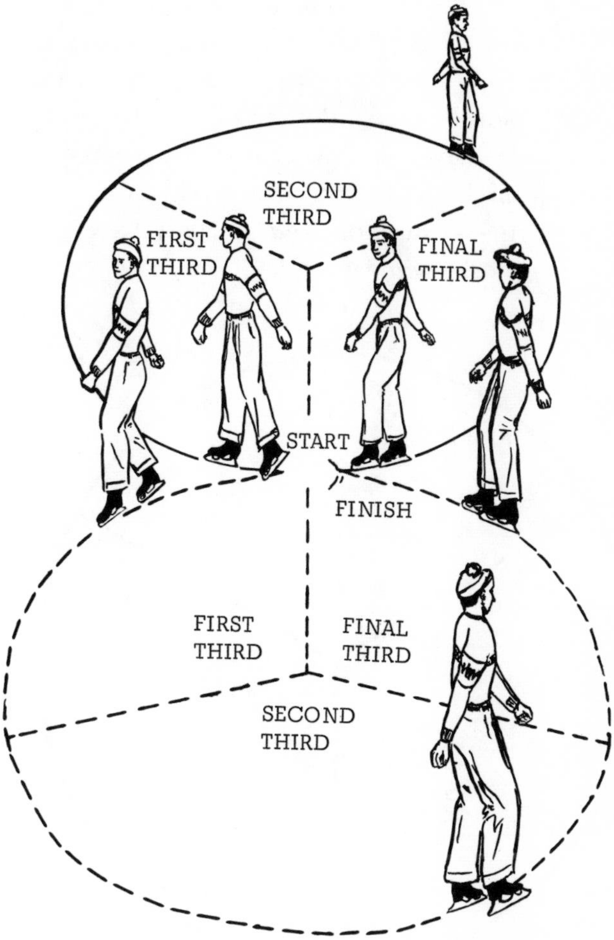

SECOND
THIRD

FIRST
THIRD

FINAL
THIRD

START

FINISH

FIRST
THIRD

FINAL
THIRD

SECOND
THIRD

The RIF-LIF Circle Eight is skated forward on the inside edge, right circle counterclockwise and left, clockwise. The balance on this edge is harder to maintain because you must skate somewhat on the inside of your foot.

The first figure to try skating backward is the ROB-LOB Circle Eight. This takes time to master. It is skated on the outside edge — the key edge in dance and free-style skating. You skate your first circle backward, counterclockwise, on the right foot; your second backward clockwise on your left.

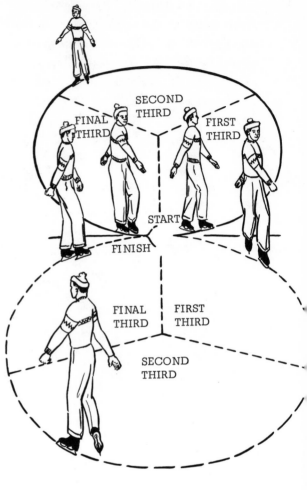

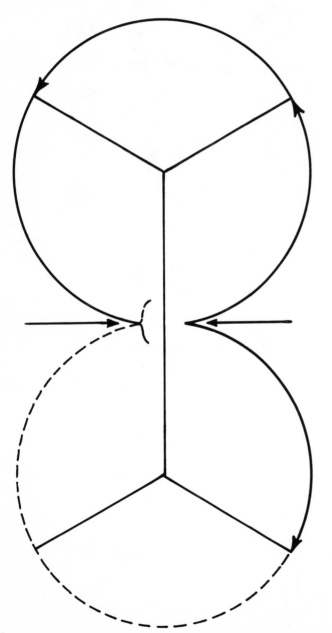

The RIB-LIB is the most difficult of the four circle eights. It is not only skated backward but also on the inside edge. Work on this figure only after you have the first three eights under control; it will take time to perform smoothly. You skate your first circle backward clockwise on the right foot; the second backward counterclockwise on your left. This figure is one required in the ISU Second Test; it has a higher difficulty rating than the other eights.

Serpentine. — A serpentine is a figure composed of three circles of equal size, arranged so that the long center line runs through all three centers dividing the circles into six equal parts. The serpentine has two cross lines. To skate a serpentine you push off from the starting position on one foot and trace a half circle plus a full circle; then you change to the other foot and skate a circle and a half.

The ROIF-LIOF Serpentine is skated forward and starts with the right foot. Your half circle is skated on the outside edge, clockwise on the right foot; your full circle on the inside edge, counterclockwise. Then you skate a half circle on the inside edge, clockwise on the left foot, and finish the figure with a full circle on the outside edge, counterclockwise on this foot.

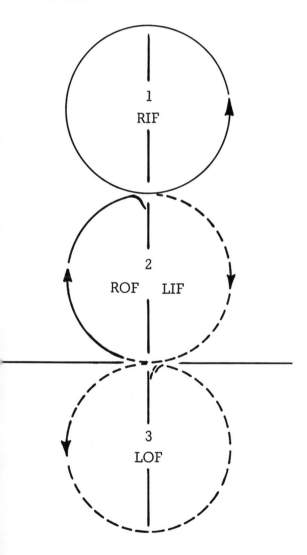

You will be familiar with the main part of the performance of a serpentine. It is actually a combination of ROF-LOF and RIF-LIF Circle Eights. The serpentine, however, requires more power to execute and better control of balance, because you have a one foot change of lean.

Threes. — Your next step in advancement from the basic circles is to the three turns. Performed on the circle eights, they are so called because the finished tracing of your figures looks like a 3. In the three turns you skate the first three on one foot and the second on the other. You make the three marks (arcs) on the circles by turning your body on the skating foot to the inside at the halfway point in the circle, changing either from forward to backward or backward to forward motion on the same foot; your body makes the turn. A three turn means changing the edge from outside to inside or inside to outside on each foot.

The ROF-LOF Three is made by skating a half circle clockwise forward right on your outside edge, making a turn at the halfway mark on the right foot and skating the remaining half of the circle clockwise backward right on your inside edge. Then you skate a half circle counterclockwise forward left on the outside edge, make a turn at the halfway mark on the left foot and skate the remaining half of the second circle counterclockwise backward left on the inside edge.

The RIF-LOB Three is an inside forward three skated on the right foot, followed by an outside backward three skated on the left. You start with a half circle counterclockwise forward right on the inside edge, turn on the right foot, then skate a half circle counterclockwise backward right on the outside edge. The second circle you skate clockwise, a half circle backward left on the outside edge, turn on the left foot, and then skate a half circle forward on the inside edge.

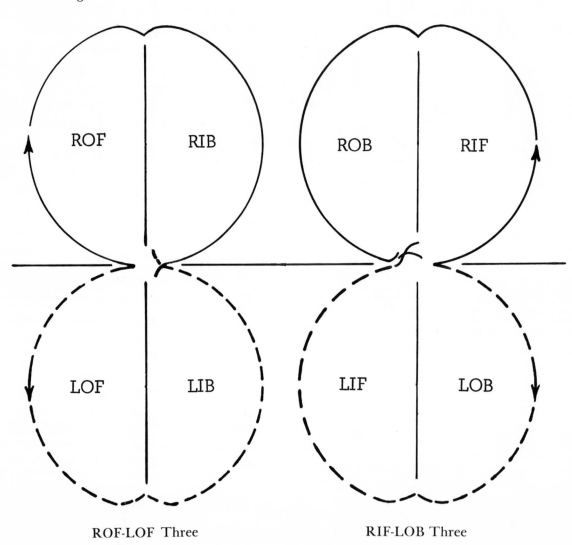

ROF-LOF Three   RIF-LOB Three

138

Double-Three. — A "double-three" is made in much the same way as the plain three, except that you have two changes of edge in each circle on the same foot. Since your turn occurs at the one-third mark on the circle instead of the half-circle mark, you have less time to prepare for it. Your turning movement is continuous throughout the whole figure. In other words, coming out of one three is the same thing as gradual preparation for the next.

In the ROF-LOF Double-Three you skate the first circle clockwise right. You start forward on the outside edge, change to the inside back edge at the one-third mark, and change back to the outside forward edge at the two-thirds mark. The second circle is skated counterclockwise left. You skate forward on the outside edge, change to the inside back edge at the one-third mark, change back to the outside forward edge at the two-thirds mark, and hold this position through the final third. This figure, like the RIB-LIB Circle Eight, appears in the Second Test of the ISU; however, it has a lower difficulty rating than the eight.

ROF-LOF Double-Three

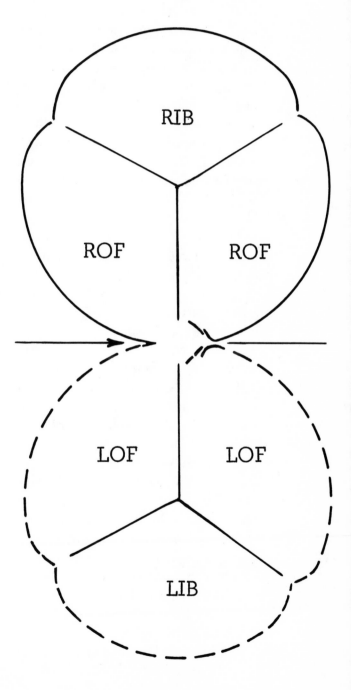

Starts and Pushoffs

The starting point for circle eights and threes is the point of connection of the two circles; in the serpentine, of the center and lower circles.

Right Outside Forward. — To start a ROF circle, place your feet at right angles to each other, heel of the right foot against the instep of the left. Turn your back squarely toward the center of the circle to be skated, and hold your shoulders and hips parallel to the line of connection of the circles. Look directly away from the circle, head erect, arms to the sides. Now, change your weight to the right foot, keeping your left foot resting on the ice on the inside edge of the blade for balance.

To push off into the circle, bend your right knee and place your body in motion on the right outside edge by a push of your left leg against the ice on the forward part of the blade. Do not bend your left leg at the knee. Your aim is to push with enough force to carry you around the circumference of the circle and back to the starting point. Skate your first third on an inward lean, right shoulder and arm well forward, hips parallel to the arc of the circle. Your right hip leads on the inside; your back is toward the circle. Keep your body erect, in a straight line from head to blade. Carry your free left leg back, toe slightly out. You use this start, pushoff, and body position in the first third of the circle for these figures:

        ROF-LOF Circle Eight
        ROIF-LIOF Serpentine
        ROF-LOF Three
        ROF-LOF Double-Three

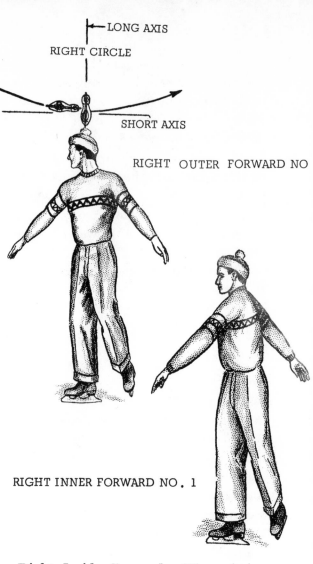

RIGHT CIRCLE

LONG AXIS

SHORT AXIS

RIGHT OUTER FORWARD NO

RIGHT INNER FORWARD NO. 1

Right Inside Forward. — The relative position of the feet for the RIF start is the same as the ROF start. Your body, however, faces the circle squarely, and your pushoff is onto the right inside edge. For the first third of this circle you skate on an inward lean, left shoulder and arm leading, hips parallel to the arc of the circle, right hip leading. Your head faces forward in the direction of flight over your leading left shoulder, and you carry your free left foot on the inside of the circle, toe turned slightly out. Use this start, pushoff, and body position in the first third of RIF-LIF Circle Eight and RIF-LOB Three.

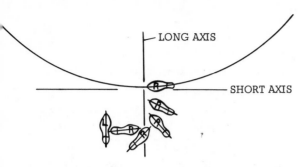

LONG AXIS

SHORT AXIS

Right Outside Back. — The difficulties you face in your backward starts are twofold: getting into a true edge position immediately after your pushoff and obtaining enough speed to carry you in flight. Turning solves these problems. You use turn to swing you into the start rather than beginning from a standstill. So, for the ROB start, first face the circle you will inscribe; stand a distance of about the width of your hips from the short cross line, facing the long center line — your feet exactly reversed from the position for the ROF start.

Get a firm hold on the ice with the forward inside part of the blade of your left foot. Your object is to coil up and unwind to get speed or force for your takeoff. Bend both knees; then lift your right foot from the ice as you make an 180-degree turn with your body to the left. This turn reverses the right foot; you can place it directly over the starting point on the circle on the outside edge of the blade, your heel pointing in the direction to start the backward circle. Through a continuous motion and powerful thrust from your left leg you will get a good pushoff. The left hip comes around immediately on the outside in assuming the outside edge position.

From the pushoff your back is turned toward the circle on the inward lean, hips parallel to the arc of the circle, left hip leading. Your left shoulder and arm lead backward into the figure along the circle on the outside, head turned over the left shoulder, facing backward in the direction of flight. At the pushoff bring your left foot back to the skating foot on the outside of the circle with a quick movement of the leg, and then let it out behind in the direction of flight. Use this start, pushoff, and body position for the first two-thirds of the ROB-LOB Circle Eight.

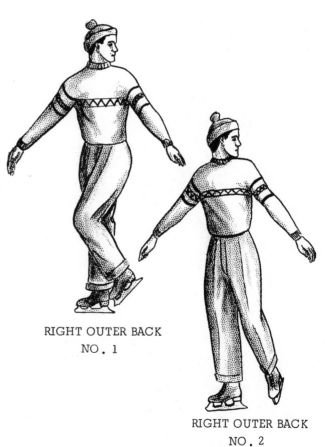

RIGHT OUTER BACK
NO. 1

RIGHT OUTER BACK
NO. 2

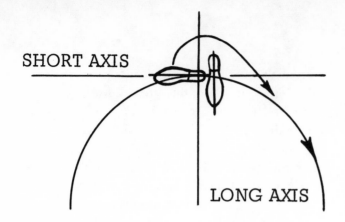

SHORT AXIS

LONG AXIS

Right Inside Back. — For the RIB start, stand directly over the starting point with your feet in the same position as for the ROF start. Turn your back to the circle; point your right foot along the line of connection in the direction of flight.

RIGHT INNER BACK NO. 1

On the pushoff from your left foot, pick up your right foot and place it back as your body turns back into the figure. Make your pushoff onto the right inside back edge on the heel of your skate, hips parallel to the arc of the circle, left hip leading into the figure on the inside, body facing the circle. Carry the left shoulder and arm forward on the inside, right arm behind, head facing the starting point. The free left foot trails in front over your right on the outside of the circle. Use this start and body position for the first two-thirds of the RIB-LIB Circle Eight.

Edges

Once you have mastered your starts and pushoffs you are ready to tackle your edges. Consider now that your circle is divided into thirds. You cover a third of the circumference in your starting position; you then continue on to trace the remaining parts. You skate each figure three times. Watch your tracings and continually try to improve them.

ROF-LOF Circle Eight. — As you complete the first third around in your position at the finish of your ROF start — left arm, shoulder, and leg well back — unwind the body in the direction you are skating. During the second third, slowly bring the free left leg forward. Then reverse the shoulders and arms gradually during the final third, ending the circle with your left arm and free leg forward over the print, right arm back, eyes looking forward in the direction of travel. Keep in mind that, in general, sinking down on the skating knee shortens the radius of the circle, makes a sharper curve; rising up on this knee lengthens the radius, makes more of a straight line than a curve.

To complete the eight, you skate a second circle forward on your left foot. Bring your feet together just before you reach the long center line, turn the right foot into the circle just skated, sink on the right knee, and push off onto your left outside edge. Because the right side of your body is back, rotate forward. In the second third, bring your free right foot forward, and during the final third bring your right arm forward.

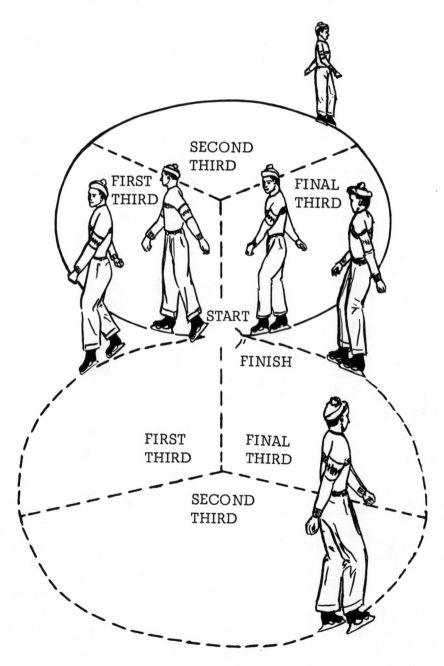

RIF-LIF Circle Eight — One third around in your position at the finish of your RIF start — left arm and shoulder leading, right arm extended behind, left leg trailing and turned — begin a turning of arms and shoulders in one direction, free left leg and hip in the opposite direction. Toward the end of the circle, complete the turning with the right arm and shoulder leading, and the free foot forward. The left foot passes the right at about the halfway mark. As it passes, your body faces straight ahead; your right hand is slightly in front because of the bend in the right elbow.

To complete the eight you skate a second circle forward on your left foot. Bring your feet together just before you reach the long center line, turn your right foot into the new circle to be skated, sink on the right knee, and push off onto your left inside edge. For the first third of this circle, your right arm and shoulder are forward, left arm and right free leg are back. In the second third, bring your left arm forward and keep it over the tracing, your right arm back. In the final third, bring your free leg forward. Keep a definite lean on the skating edge to the end of each circle.

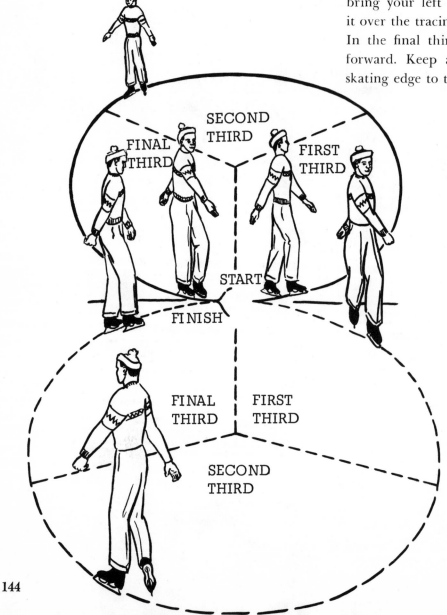

SECOND THIRD

FINAL THIRD

FIRST THIRD

START

FINISH

FINAL THIRD

FIRST THIRD

SECOND THIRD

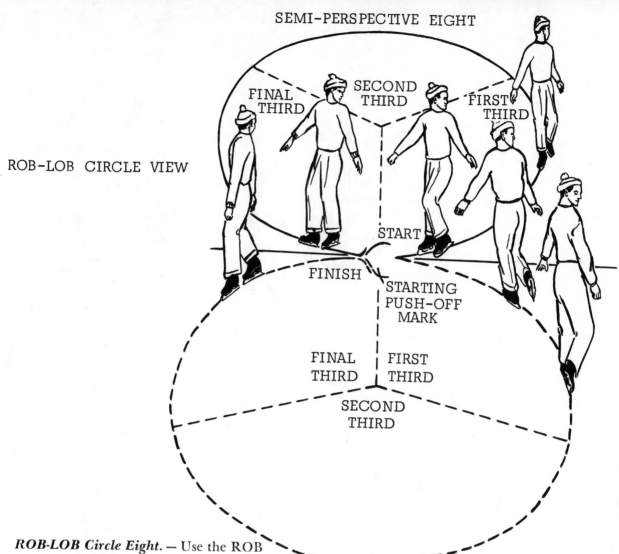

SEMI-PERSPECTIVE EIGHT

ROB-LOB CIRCLE VIEW

FINAL THIRD

SECOND THIRD

FIRST THIRD

START

FINISH

STARTING PUSH-OFF MARK

FINAL THIRD

FIRST THIRD

SECOND THIRD

ROB-LOB Circle Eight. — Use the ROB start for this figure and keep it, with the left free foot leading about a foot behind the right heel for two thirds of the circle. Look back over your left shoulder to see the print — down past the left hip over the left foot. Carry your right arm in front of your body, your left arm back over your left leg. During the final third, even up your shoulders and arms; draw the free foot back by the side of your skating foot and look into the circle.

Bend the skating foot deeply for the pushoff into the second circle. Your right hip comes around immediately on the outside in assuming the left outer edge position. Skate the first third of the second circle with your free right foot behind your left and over the tracing, right hip leading. Look back over your right shoulder to see the print. Turn your body to the right as you enter the second third, right arm extended back over your right leg and left forward. To complete the figure, even up your shoulders and arms, and draw your free foot back by your skating foot.

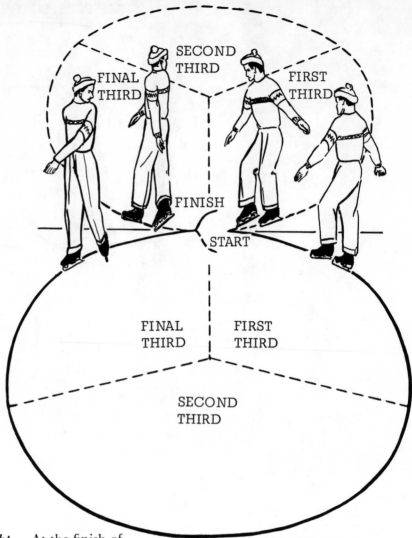

RIB-LIB Circle Eight. — At the finish of the RIB start, your head faces back to the starting point, left shoulder and arm carried forward on the inside, right arm behind. Before the end of the first third of the circle, turn your head to view the print down over your left hip and leg, and carry your leg over your skating foot to the outside. Entering your final third of the first circle, bring your free left foot back behind your skating heel; once back, keep the hip, knee, and toe turned out. This is the only change in body position around the circle. Your head now faces down to the starting point. As your circle is completed your right foot runs slightly into the new circle, and your knee bends for a pushoff on the left foot. You reverse your entire body, making the change from RIB to LIB edge, which gives additional thrust to the pushoff.

Now your right hip leads on the inside; your body faces toward the new circle, right shoulder and arm forward on the inside and head again facing back to the starting point. Keep this position to the end of the figure, except for passing the free right foot behind the skating heel, eyes looking over your right shoulder to the starting point.

ROIF-LIOF Serpentine. — Once having learned the four edges, you are ready to advance to the change of edge. This is a maneuver where you rock your skate to change edges without turning your body.

Use the ROF start for this serpentine, and execute your first half circle on the ROF edge, bringing your free left leg forward during this half. To make an almost instantaneous change to the RIF edge, swing your free leg back and reverse your shoulder and arms to bring your left arm forward. Skate the full circle on this edge, reversing your shoulders and arms to bring your right arm forward in the second third of the circle, and your left leg forward in the final third.

Place the left foot down on the ice just at the long center line, and push off on the inside edge of the blade to skate a half of the center circle on this edge. During this half, reverse the shoulders and arms to bring the left arm forward, and then bring the free right leg forward. Just before reaching the long center line, swing the right arm forward and right foot back in one movement to change the edge from LIF to LOF. Make the final full circle on the left outside edge, bringing the right leg forward during the final third. Repeat the figure by merely placing your right foot on the ice and pushing off once again on your ROF edge.

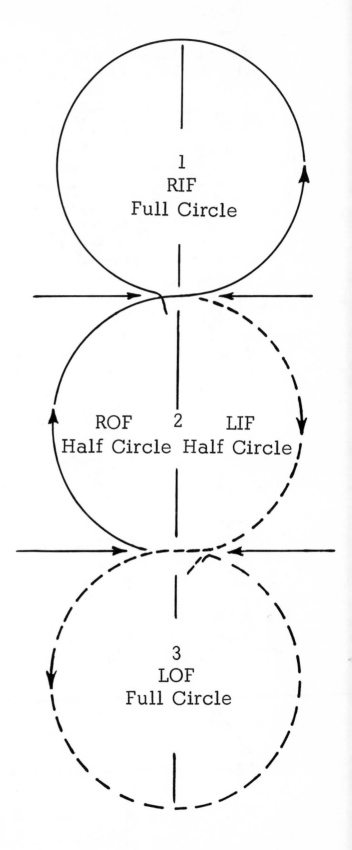

1
RIF
Full Circle

ROF   2   LIF
Half Circle   Half Circle

3
LOF
Full Circle

ROF-LOF Three. — To make the threes in this figure you change edge from outside forward to inside back, the first on the right foot and the second on the left.

Skate your first third of the circle using your ROF start and skating position, keeping your free left foot turned to the outside as it trails. In your second third, draw your left foot in close to your skating foot, left knee pointing in front of your right calf and toe out. About the halfway mark, draw your left hip through to the inside, and turn your shoulders and arms inward; bring your left shoulder and arm around to and through a position parallel to the circumference. Your head faces inward, looking down at your skating foot.

Now, quickly and precisely turn your skating foot, heel first, in the direction of flight; during this forward turn your edge changes from ROF to RIB. You have to lift your weight up onto the forepart of the blade and then drop back — heel to toe and back again—to cause your body to rise and fall during the turn. Lifting up and over this way leaves a mark on the ice the width of the blade, a stamp of a good three. Hold your free foot close and still during the turn.

As you assume the new edge in completing the turn, you counteract the inward turn of the body which starts the change by a quick move of the shoulders and arms to bring both left and right arm back; your left is behind and on the outside of the circle and your right is in front of your body, pointing into the circle. This countermove is called checking. By checking, you prevent the body from turning too far inward and curling in on the last half of the circle.

On the RIB edge let the free left foot out behind, pointing the toe first in the direction of the starting point, and shift your head backward toward the starting point. Coming to the long center line, your right foot runs into the new circle as you bend the right knee to push off on the left foot.

Make your three in the left foot circle in exactly the same way as in the right, but reverse your body positions and movements. Your edge change at the halfway mark is from LOF to LIB. To make your lean in this second circle, thrust your head slightly over your leading left shoulder.

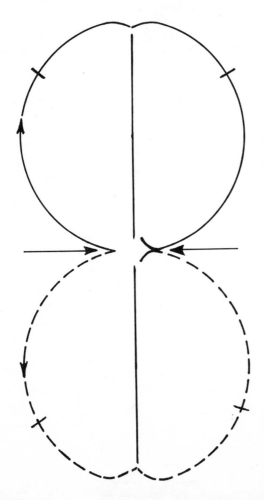

RIF-LOB Three. — This figure is an inside forward three skated on the right foot, plus an outside back three on the left.

Skate your first third of the circle using your RIF start and skating position, free left foot behind on the inside, toe out. Reverse your shoulders and arms in the second third, right arm forward; and draw your free foot close to the skating foot, toe out and heel behind the skating heel. Just before the forward turn, drop your right shoulder. With the left shoulder and hip, lift your weight to the front part of the blade and over in the turn, drawing your hip through as closely as possible. In the turn your edge changes from RIF to ROB.

Coming out of the turn, check your shoulders and arms in the parallel position with your left arm in front and the right behind along the circumference. Shift your head back over the forward left shoulder on the outside and look ahead in the direction of flight. Let your left foot extend behind. Complete the final third evening up your shoulders and arms.

Push off into the left circle, changing your edge from ROB to LOB, and skate the first third of your left foot circle with your right arm behind and right free foot trailing. As you near the turn, draw your free foot in close to your skating foot, right arch against the skating heel. In this backward turn, lift your weight onto the back part of the blade and over to the outside. Your edge changes from LOB to LIF.

Coming out of the backward turn, again check your shoulder and arms in the parallel position, and carry your

right foot in front. Hold this position for the final third of the circle. To repeat the figure your body completely reverses in pushing off into the right foot circle.

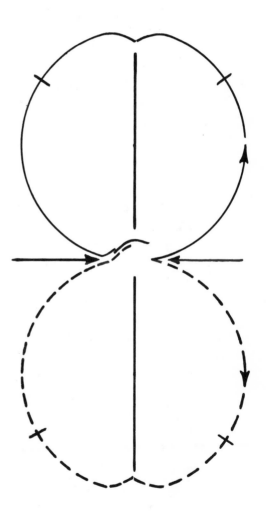

ROF-LOF Double-three. — In this double-three figure you make your turns at the thirds of the circles rather than at the halves; hence you have less time to prepare for them than you had for the plain threes.

Start the figure in your ROF skating position, but draw your left free foot in close to your skating foot much sooner than you did for the plain three, keeping the toe to the outside. Make your change to the RIB edge. In so doing, turn your free foot slightly in as you finish the turn and hold it close behind the skating foot through the change from inside back to outside forward at the two-thirds mark. Skate your final third, left foot and right arm forward, left arm back.

To start your second circle forward left on the outside edge, your body makes a complete reversal. In this circle you first make a forward turn, from LOF to LIB, and then a backward turn, from LIB to LOF. In this latter turn, come up to the two-thirds mark with your right knee bent and right foot drawn back to your skating foot. Make your three with a backward turn and come out with your free right foot and left arm forward, right arm back. Hold this position back to the starting point.

In this double-three you get a better lean if you carry your skating foot shoulder lower than your other shoulder. Keep your head over your skating foot throughout; do not push it ahead in the direction of flight between turns. Draw your free hip high over to the outside in making the change. Your big-gest problem is to control your twisting between turns. Try to travel slowly into the second turn with only a slight turning of your shoulders and arms in nearing the turn. This position may prevent over turning.

In checking your tracings of the double-three, remember that the short lines of the three marks should cut across at the center of the circle. If they do, your marks are in the right position along the circumference of the circle.

Taking a New Edge

A figure must be made in one continuous set of motions, rather than in circles skated separately with a pause between. Therefore, you must learn how to change feet smoothly as you go from circle to circle. The mechanics of the left executions are the same as for the right, but the relative body positions and motions in movement on the left foot are exactly opposite to those on the right.

When taking a new edge, you leave a double-track mark on the ice just before crossing the long center line of the figure. When going from an outside edge circle to any other edge, the track curves into the circle just skated; from an inside edge circle, the track curves into the new circle to be skated. The tracks for the edge changes are shown on all previous diagrams of the figures. The lines show the path the first foot takes in changing from one circle to let the other foot take its place on the short cross line to skate another circle in the figure.

Skating as a Profession

The skater who wishes to make a living as a professional skater would most likely do so with one of the many spectacular ice shows.

Show skaters earn an above average salary and also have the opportunity to see the world for today's ice shows not only tour the United States but play in South America, the Far East, and most of Europe.

Just as in any profession, it takes a lot of hard work and patience to get to the top.

Many of the stars of the ice shows are skaters who have won many important championships and are able to start right out with feature billing and an exceptional salary as a result of having already made a name for themselves. However, many skaters have been able to work themselves up from the line to a feature spot on the program.

Yes, skating has something to offer everyone. Those who enjoy it as a wonderful form of fun and exercise as a family or individually. The skater who gains recognition and satisfaction in competing against others. Those who through natural ability and years of practice and hard work earn national and world fame. And, the many who combine their skills and talents with others to bring entertainment to the public in the fine and beautiful productions presented by numerous ice shows.

A Future in Skating

Many young skaters have developed a sincere interest in this wonderful and challenging sport and wonder what sort of future skating can offer them.

Skating is a very competitive sport and contests on the city, state, sectional, and national levels offer an opportunity to everyone who is willing to spend hours in practice and hard work to perfect their abilities.

The reward for all this hard work comes in the thrill and personal satisfaction one feels after winning a trophy. There are also other compensating factors such as learning sportsmanship, developing new friends, and gaining recognition.

What Is Competition?

Figure skating competitions are just like contests in other competitive sports where individual competes against individual rather than team against team.

Competition is divided into two distinct parts, Compulsory Figures and Free Skating, which are judged and graded on performance.

The Compulsory Figures consist of the performance of tracings of the required figures which are composed of circles, curves, change of edge, turns, etc.

Free Skating is the performance of unspecified movements to music chosen by the skater. Skating is done during a prescribed period and the skater is graded on the contents of the skating program and the manner of the performance.

The Compulsory Figures total 6o percent of your grade and the Free Skating makes up the other 4o percent.

Competitions are classified as follows:

a. Club competitions.
b. Inter-club championships.
c. Sub-sectional championships.
d. Sectional championships.
e. National championships.
f. International championships.
g. North American championships.
h. Olympics.
i. Championships of the world.

In order to enter competition a skater must be an amateur and a member of a skating club that is a member of the United States Figure Skating Association, and he must be currently registered with the Association.

A skater may go as far as he or she wishes as long as he or she can qualify for the events they wish to compete in.

A perfect example of skaters reaching the goals they have set for themselves was seen when David Jenkins and Carol Heiss on Olympic Gold Medals in figure skating for the United States in the Winter Olympic Games at Squaw Valley, California in 1960.

Boys and girls have fun putting on a "western theme" ice show.

Bibliography

Button, Dick. *Dick Button on Skates*. Englewood Cliffs, N. J.: Prentice Hall, Inc., 1955.

Henie, Sonya. *Wings on My Feet*. Englewood Cliffs, N. J.: Prentice Hall, Inc., 1940.

Jones, Ernest. *Elements of Figure Skating*. New York: The Macmillan Company, 1952.

Lussi, Gustave, and Richards, Maurice. *Championship Figure Skating*. New York: The Ronald Press Company, 1951. *The Girls' Book of Skating*. New York: Roy Publishers, 1960.

Scott, Barbara Ann, and Kirby, Michael. *Skating for Beginners*. New York: Alfred Knopf, Inc., 1953.

United States Figure Skating Association, Boston, Mass. *Evaluation of Errors in Figures*, 1955. *How to Organize and Conduct Competition*, 1955. *Ice Dances*, 1948. *USFSA Rulebook*, latest edition.

Richardson, T. D. *Complete Figure Skater*. Hollywood, Florida: Transatlantic Arts, 1952.

SQUAW VALLEY, CALIFORNIA, U.S.A.

Scene of the 1960 World Winter Olympic Games

The 8th Winter Olympics, the biggest and most expensive in history, were held at the site of a former ski resort on the California-Nevada line. This little-used and poorly equipped winter area was transformed into a 640-acre of bustling activity (above), specifically constructed to accommodate 30 entrant nations and their 800 athletes who competed in 27 events. From February 18 to February 28, Squaw Valley, U.S.A., was the center of the world, tribute indeed to the international interest in sports. The U.S.S.R. team winner in the unofficial point total, captured six events and tied for first place in a seventh. The United States won three events, and staged the biggest upset in the 36-year history of the Winter Games by taking the Ice Hockey championship.

The Olympic Torch (left) was ignited at the opening ceremonies and remained aglow for the duration of the Games. A symbol of peace among all nations, the torch lights up the Tower of Nations design.

154

Figure and
Speed Skating

Carol Heiss of Ozone Park, New York, a 20-year-old New York University student, displays the form which helped her win the gold medal in the women's figure skating event. It was a memorable triumph for Carol who had lost the 1956 Olympic figure skating competition by a slender margin.

David Jenkins of Colorado Springs, Colorado, used his fancy whirling free-skating style to achieve victory in the men's figure skating event. The Western Reserve University medical student had to come from behind to gain the necessary points for his victory.

There was hardly any doubt about the pair skating supremacy of Canada's Barbara Wagner and Bob Paul. Performing the difficult lifts and the dangerous spins and twists as one, they were indeed a pair of perfectionists dance-skating to one of their country's two victories.

Norway's Knut Johannesen shattered the world record for the 10,000 meter speed skating race which he won in 15:46.6, 46 seconds faster than the old previous mark for this distance.

Russia's Lydia Skoblikova was the only woman to win two gold medals. The 21-year-old anatomy student set a world mark in the 1500-meter speed skating race and also captured the 3000-meter event.

U.S. Team Wins Hockey Title Undefeated in Five Games

All Olympic champions — and all smiles. The U.S. hockey team celebrates (right) its triumph of winning the title with a 9-4 victory over Czechoslovakia.

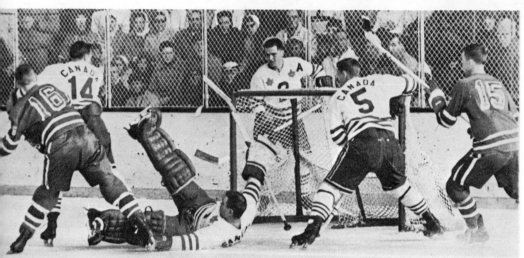

On their way to the Olympic ice hockey title, the U.S. team first stunned the favored Canadians. Paul Johnson (above) has just shoved in the winning goal as the Canadian goalie loses his footing.

The Americans came from behind to beat Russia (right) in their dramatic hockey struggle. Bill Christian, far right, has just rapped home the winning score as the capacity crowd lets out a mighty roar.

Following their mighty triumph over the U.S.S.R., the U.S. had to beat Czechoslovakia the following day to take their title. The Czechs were determined to upset the Yanks, but even body checks like this failed to halt the U.S. ice stars.

Ski Jumping

Holger Karlsson, Sweden's human snowbird, is captured by the photographer as his nose all but hugs the tips of his skis in a jumping event.

The huge ski jump was Squaw Valley's main attraction. Daily, the wingless fliers glided through the air, all eyes on them as they attempted to establish new records. The United States managed to capture but three silver medals in all ski events.

Slaloms

Penny Pitou, who learned to ski on the hills of New Hampshire, came close twice but still couldn't earn a gold medal. Penny was second in the downhill and had to settle for another silver medal in the giant slalom.

Betsy Snite, a San Francisco model-secretary, skidding through a gate, was just a trifle too slow navigating the turns in the ladies slalom and finished second, 3.3 seconds behind Anne Heggtveit of Canada.

157

Downhill and
Cross Country

Germany's Heidi Biebl was slow getting started in the downhill event. Later, she overtook Penny Pitou to win her gold medal by one second.

Marija Gusakova was favored to take the ladies 10-kilometer cross country and didn't disappoint, crossing the finish line in a six-mile event which was monopolized by the U.S.S.R.

The first official winner of the 8th Winter Games was Sweden's Sixten Jernberg, rounding a check point in the 30-kilometer cross country event. Regarded as the world's greatest cross-country skier, Jernberg also won a gold medal in the 1956 Games.

SKIING

Ruth Schellberg

History and Growth

Long before skiing became a sport, it was a method of transportation in snow-bound countries in Central Asia and Northern Europe. The ancients improvised a ski from tree branches, large bones, or skins. Not until the beginning of the Christian era were skis construced of wood. During those times travelers used skis over seven feet long to give them better support on unbroken snow, and carried a long pole for steering or propelling. Hunters and trappers pulled sleds on these long wooden blades. Later, during the Battle of Oslo in Norway in 1200 A.D., Swedish scouts used blades about three feet long to spy on the enemy camped in deep snow. In the centuries which followed, many Scandinavian troops were equipped with either skis or snowshoes.

The history of the sport indicates that skiing is of Norwegian origin. For example, slalom is an old Norse word meaning sled-track, skijoring originates from *kjoring* meaning driving, and telemark and christiana (the original name for the city of Oslo) both mean turn. The first official ski competition in jumping and cross-country racing was held near Oslo in 1862, and it was in Oslo that the Christiana Skiklub was founded in 1887. Norwegian immigrants introduced skiing to the United States during the middle of the nineteenth century. The Scandinavians founded the first ski clubs in this country in Berlin, New Hampshire, in 1872; in Altoona, Pennsylvania, in 1885; and in Red Wing, Minnesota, in 1886. The National Ski Association originated in 1904 at Ishpeming, Michigan, with 17 charter members, all from the Middle West.

During the 1920s ski enthusiasts in some 75 clubs located in the northern part of the Midwest, upper New England, and northern New York State numbered about 4000. The Winter Olympics held at Lake Placid, New York, in 1932, interested so many spectators in the sport that from then on the growth of the sport was remarkable. It was boosted in popularity by the coming of ski tows and ski trails built throughout the country, by the ski train, and by bus and ski resorts. Today the National Ski Association of America has more than 400 clubs and 50,000 members. It has, through its six separate divisional associations, aided considerably in transforming skiing as an unknown sport into a national pastime, participated in by an army of over three million ski fans. Through the direction of the Federation Internationale de Ski, the first worldwide ruling body for skiing founded in 1924, came competition on a universal scale and the addition of the sport to the Olympic program. Following the organization of FIS, the first Winter Olympic Games were held at Chamonix, France, in 1924, under the supervision of an International Olympic Committee. Since then the Winter Olympic Games have been held regularly in connection with the traditional games.

Skiing is not a sport which can be quickly learned by anyone; the average person needs a series of lessons to start him off. Also, it is not an inexpensive sport. It is, however, one of the most enjoyable of recreational sports. While excellent physical condition is necessary for fast skiing on big slopes, the sport is still one that, if properly learned, may be enjoyed by all ages.

Description of the Sport

For the average person, skiing means progress on level ground or downhill, purely for recreation, no competition involved. For the trained competitor, skiing includes downhill, cross-country, slalom racing, and jumping.

In downhill skiing the contestants compete against time, one skier at a time taking the run. Motive power is supplied by gravity, and a premium is placed on speed. Downhill skiing demands great control, including the ability to turn and stop at will in order to travel the marked (flagged) trails on which these races are run. The skier selects his own way down the course, attempting to choose the fastest way to get to a finish line.

The slalom is downhill racing against time through a number of flag combinations called gates, H's, flushes, or corridors. These are set at various positions on a serpentine zigzag course. Some are parallel to the fall line (closed gate); others perpendicular (open gate). The skier must go through the latter sideways to the slope instead of descending vertically. The skier choosing the wrong way through the gates penalizes himself by losing speed. The premium in the slalom is on style and speed. No gate may be less than 9½ feet wide, and the distance from one gate to another not less than 2½ feet. The courses for women cannot exceed 40 gates; those for men usually have between 55 and 60 gates, depending upon the terrain. For the giant slalom the course is much longer, the vertical drop at least 1000 feet. For this race there must be at least 20 sets of flags set a minimum distance of 13 feet apart. Standard skis can be used in all downhill racing.

Cross-country racing demands stamina and courage, the course providing a test of the competitor's strength, endurance, technique, and tactical knowledge. On natural terrain, one-third of the course is uphill, one-third downhill, one-third on the flat or rolling country. An average cross-country course is from 8 to 12 miles. Cross-country skis are light weight, narrow, with bindings which permit easy raising of the heel and toe.

In ski jumping the skier travels a steep slope of the side of the hill, at the end of which he takes off into the air, leaping at the same time, trying to land as far down the slope as possible. In jumping, form counts equally with distance in importance, and jumps of several hundred feet are common. Length of jumps depends upon the height and size of the hill and run, snow conditions, and ability of the jumper. The winner is decided by a point system, points being voted for distance, courage, control, and form or gracefulness. In jumping, no poles are permitted. Jumping skis are heavy, with two or three grooves on the underside instead of one.

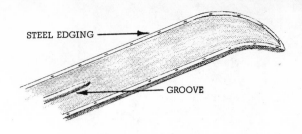

Equipment

You must pay particular attention to your equipment, since the proper kind is of utmost importance in this sport.

Ski. — The best skis are made from hickory. Good skis are available from maple, ash, metal, or even glass. All skis should be from straight-grained wood. You can check this by seeing that the grain does not run off the edge through the length of the ski. It must have an equal arch (camber) of the running surface for spring and flexibility, and an equal upturn (shovel) of the front of the ski. The shovel helps the ski float on the surface of the snow, and presses out a track wide enough for the rest of the ski to pass without drag on the edges. If your skis are too limber, the middle bears all the weight; if they are too stiff, the ends dig into the snow.

On the underside of the ski a groove about ⅜ of an inch wide runs from the shovel to the tail. This groove helps to keep the skis running straight. The underside is also edged with steel bands from close to the tip to close to the tail. These edges help in turning and maneuvering, especially when the snow is hard.

For general purposes your ski should be no longer than the distance between the base of your fingers, arm extended overhead, and the ground, ski standing upright. However, shorter skis are easier to handle than longer ones.

When not using your skis, store them in a cool, dry place. Bind them together with a leather strap or a set of straps, placing a small block of wood in the middle to hold the camber in the skis. After using your skis, stand them on their tips for a short time. This allows the water to run off completely. Before storing, clean the old wax from the bottoms of your skis, and cover them with a coat of linseed oil. During the season, cover the top surface with varnish to fill the nicks and scrapes.

Bindings. — Bindings attach the ski to the boot and are designed to prevent the foot from moving sideways.

They are also designed to release the boots from the bindings when the skier has a fall which twists the ski. This prevents the skier from fracturing his legs or feet.

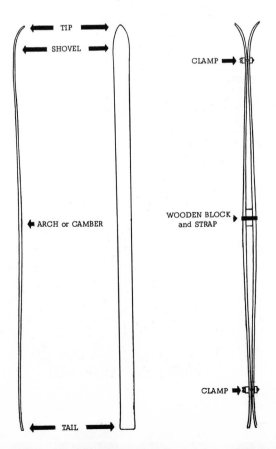

Double Spring toe release presses curved plate against piece on toe of boot and lets boot roll or lift out.

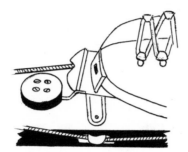

Single spring toe release has tongue fitting into a notch in front of metal plate. As ski twists away during a slow fall the pressure causes tongue to give until it snaps and releases boot.

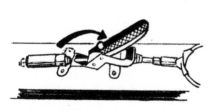

Front throw levers flip up under pressure and allow boot heel to lift free. A skier, standing in his bindings, should be held in place so well that he can lean as far forward as 30 degrees without losing his balance or loosening his skis.

Remember a skier controls his turns by proper swinging of his body, and properly attached and adjusted bindings let him do this.

Boots. — Your boots are the most important items in your ski wardrobe. You cannot ski well unless you have a comfortable fit which permits movement of your toes. You must feel no undue pressure on the front of your ankles when you lean forward from the ankles. Your heels must have no free play in the boots when you rise on your toes. Your ankles and insteps must feel securely held in place. When you select your boots, fit them over two pairs of wool socks.

A ski boot has a thick leather sole, stiffened with a steel shank between its layers to prevent buckling or twisting, and surfaced with a layer of corrugated rubber to prevent slipping. The boot heel generally has two notches, the lower one for a rigid binding of the heel spring

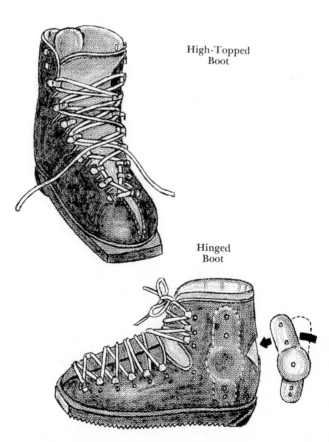

High-Topped Boot

Hinged Boot

for downhill skiing, and the higher one for cross-country adjustment. The inside of the boot and the tongue should be lined and well padded, the boot toe roomy. The uppers should be of high grade leather, stiff yet pliable enough to allow freedom of the ankle. Some boots come with a metal hinge sewn into the leather at the ankles, or with steel-braced leather sections above the ankle which prevent the boot from bending sideways as the leather ages and softens. If you need additional support, use a leather ankle strap over your instep and around your ankle. Your lacing edges must fit well when you lace your boot. If they are too close you cannot obtain a tight fit if the leather stretches; too widely-separated laces invite snow into your boot. Some boots have back lacings to fit the back tightly at the heel.

Keep shoe trees in your boots, especially when they are wet and drying. Polish your boots frequently with a wax-base shoe polish. Use a coat of linseed oil on the soles each season, but never use oil of any kind on the uppers.

Poles. — Ski poles, one carried in each hand, are used for pushing, for climbing, and for balancing, never for stopping. The shaft of the ski pole is of metal or cane; the point at the bottom is bent to assure a grip on ice or hard snow. The snow ring, made of metal or wood with a leather lacing, keeps the pole from sinking deeply into the snow. The leather handgrip at the top has a strap which goes over the wrist. When the grip is taken, the heel of the hand rests upon the strap, permitting a loose grip with the fingers when pushing. A leather top-

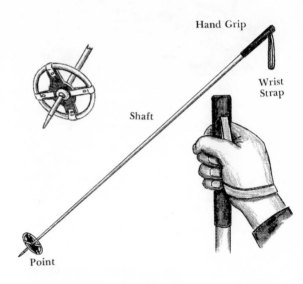

dressing will keep your handgrips and wrist straps soft and pliable.

Ski poles should be light in weight and balanced. For the best length, your pole should come to a point halfway between your elbow and armpit.

Wax. — Ski wax applied to the running surface of the ski gives varying traction and slipperiness, depending upon whether the snow is wet or dry, new or old, icy or crusty, and upon the temperature. A base wax protects the skis against moisture and wear; a running or surface wax should be applied over a base wax. As a general rule a hard, smooth wax is good for powder or dry snow and low temperature, and a soft, thick wax for damp or wet snow and warm temperature. When you wax your skis, first make sure they are cooled to the outside temperature.

Costume and Accessories. — Your ski wardrobe includes underclothing, socks, pants, jackets and windbreakers, shirts and sweaters, gloves and mittens, caps and knitted headbands, and sun goggles.

Choose underclothing for warmth and snug fit, although allow for freedom of movement. Long-sleeved, ankle-length garments of light wool or soft knitted fabrics are best. Since proper socks prevent blistered or cold and numb feet, wear a light inner pair under a heavy outer pair, with the outer pair about a half size larger. Wear your socks inside your ski pants so that they cannot pick up snow to melt into your boots.

Select pants, jackets, and windbreakers of smooth, hard fabrics which are weatherproof, windproof, water-repellent, and snow-resistant. Snow clings to soft wool or bulky materials and wets them too quickly. Choose pants that are zippered as buttons pull off easily, and be sure the bottoms have a webbing or elastic for under the foot to hold the pant leg down. Get jackets and windbreakers full enough to allow for several layers underneath. The sleeves should be long enough to stay under gloves or mittens and tight enough at the wrist to keep snow out of the sleeves; the waist should be long enough to cover the hips. Choose shirts and sweaters of light-weight wool or flannel. It is better to have two or three light-weight sweaters than one heavy one, then you can regulate your body temperature by removing one or more of them.

Two pairs of gloves or mittens are better than one. The under one should be of soft wool; the outer one of windbreaker material or leather. If the glove has a long cuff you can pull this over the jacket wrist band. You will need a cap or headband to protect you against the snow and wind, and unbreakable sun goggles to protect against the glare of the snow.

Fundamental Skills

Before you can handle yourself on the ski slopes you must first learn how to carry your equipment, walk, turn around, climb, and get up after a tumble.

Terms. — The following are some of the terms used in skiing and their meanings:

Fall Line. Gravity line down the slope or path a ball would take in rolling down a hill.

Stem. Stemming refers to the spreading of one or both skis out at the heels.

Rotation and Counter-Rotation. Counter-rotation is similar to drawing the hand back ready to strike. In skiing it means swinging the upper or outside shoulder back, usually at the same time the opposite (downhill) ski is stemmed. This movement, in preparation for the turn, makes it possible to get some body swing before the body lunges forward into the turn. Rotation is swinging or turning the body in the direction of the turn and, at the same time, pressing forward with the knees to crouch low.

Theory of Turning. All ski turns are based on the same principle of weight shift and center of gravity. A weighted ski travels faster than an unweighted ski. Since the outside ski must cover more ground on the turn your weight should be on that ski.

Carrying Skis and Poles. — To carry your skis, strap them together at each end and swing them to one shoulder, tips high, bindings just back of the shoulder. Rest them in your cupped hand, arm extended downward and relaxed. Carry your poles in the other hand, either low or over the shoulder. In the latter case, place them under the tips of your skis in a V-shaped position. In this manner it is easy to balance the skis.

Putting on Skis. — Lay your skis in front of you on level ground. Place one foot on the ski. Straps which secure ski to boot, when safety bindings release, are on the outside of each boot. This helps you distinguish between right and left ski. Snap the lever down to tighten the cable. Do the same for the other foot. When both skis are on, check your bindings by leaning forward, bending the ankles as far forward as you can. If your bindings are not holding your boots firmly you must have them adjusted so that they will.

Holding the Poles. — A proper grasp is necessary for good action with the poles. Take your poles and pass your hands upward through the wrist straps. Grip the pole with the loop between the thumb and index finger. The loop falls around your hand. The end of the pole protrudes a little above your fist. You balance the pole lightly in your fingers.

Walking on the Level. — In walking on the level you never raise the skis. You slide them forward with a gliding motion, keeping the weight solidly planted on one ski as you slide the other. You swing your arms alternately with the leg movement, and push with each pole to

aid the walking. Set the pole which you bring forward, its point toward the rear, in the snow about opposite the binding of the leading ski. Lean on it a bit to keep the ski from slipping back, and continue to push on it as your other foot and hand come forward. (Below, 168.)

Turning. — Once you can glide or walk about on your skis you will want to know how to change your direction. You do this by either a step turn or a kick turn.

Step Turn. — The step turn is the easier turn to learn. With your skis parallel and both poles in the snow a few inches to the front and side of each foot, lean upon your poles in front and step the heels of your skis around, fan fashion,

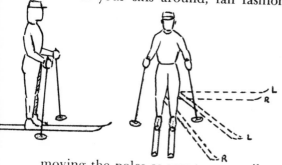

moving the poles as you turn, until you face in the desired direction. Do this slowly at first — your skis are long and they will cross in front or in back very easily. Once you get the feel of fanning one ski and bringing the other up parallel, you can increase the speed of the turn.

Kick Turn. — The kick turn (below) is quicker and more practical than the step turn. In a kick turn you use three points of support. You stand either on your two skis and steady yourself on one pole, or stand on one ski and steady yourself with both poles. The poles are actively used as supports. To make this turn always start with your skis parallel. To turn to the right, twist your upper body to the right and place the right pole a few inches behind the end of the left ski, and the left pole a few inches in front of the tip of the left ski. Kick your right foot upward, and let the tail of the right ski rest on the snow near the tip of the left ski. Your weight is now on your left ski, balanced by the poles. Let your right ski drop to the snow, facing in the opposite direction and parallel to the left ski. Change your weight to the right ski, pick up the left ski a little so that it clears the right one, and swing it around slowly until it parallels the right ski. At the same time with this movement, swing the left pole around and place it in the snow on the outside of the left ski. When you become more familiar with these motions you will eliminate some of them. Your kick turn made quickly becomes a step around with one foot around one pole. Practice this turn both to the right and to the left. Later on, when you do a kick turn on a slope, the level position of your skis at the beginning and at the end is still necessary. On a slope, however, start the turn with the uphill ski in order to get a little higher.

Climbing. — To climb (above) a gentle slope you edge your skis into the hill, that is, you turn your knees so that the uphill edges of both skis press into the snow, and you use your walking step to move diagonally upward. A strong push with the opposite pole helps the climbing. If you need a more secure hold, lift and stamp your forward ski down hard. For steeper slopes you should use either the side step or the herringbone.

Side Step. — Short, steep grades can best be climbed with the side step (below). This is a sideways alternating step, with your skis placed directly across the fall line (right angles to the slope). You press your knees toward the slope, while lean-ing your upper body toward the down-hill slide, the main weight on your lower ski. By bending your knees you control the edges, permitting them to grip firmly into the snow. Pick up or push the uphill ski forward about a foot; then move the lower ski up parallel to it. Move the left pole with the left ski and the right pole with the right to control your balance. Place the uphill pole at least a foot above the binding. Never lift both poles at the same time. To keep from slipping back down the hill, push firmly on your lower pole and cant (set at an angle), the uphill edges.

Less tiring than the side step is the half side step, in which you combine stepping to the side with a forward stride. You hold your skis level or point-ing slightly uphill. To climb diagonally upward a push from your lower pole is required.

Herringbone. — For short stretches and for hard rather than soft snow you climb herringbone style (below). Facing the slope, angle your skis out to the sides, rear ends close together, and edge them into the hill. Press your knees forward and toward the hill to give the inside

edges a good hold. Keep both poles behind, and lean on them to stop you from slipping back. Keep the palms of your hands on the top of the poles. Now, lift one ski and angle it forward and up the hill; at the same time move the pole on the opposite side forward, resting your weight on the ski and pole not being moved. Thus, as your left leg swings ahead the right pole goes forward, so that the left pole and right leg support much of your weight. You make a track in the snow which looks like a herringbone weave in a piece of cloth.

Getting up from a Fall. — If a tumble seems to be coming, try to fall away from the skis, backward and to the uphill side of a slope, keeping the poles to the rear and out of the way. Never use your poles, arms, or knees to break a fall. To get up from level ground, bring your skis parallel, draw your knees to your chest, and push up to one knee. With both poles together, one hand near the grip and the other near the snow ring, push to a stand keeping the weight forward.

If you fall on a hill you may find it more difficult to get up. First you swing your skis downhill and across (horizontal to) the fall line — or roll over on your shoulders until you have both skis on the downhill side and across the fall line. Then you pull your skis parallel to each other and close to your body. Shift your weight forward over your toes and stand. Use your poles, if you need to, to help lift you up. (below, left).

Downhill Skiing Techniques. — The secret of good skiing skill is in coordinating your own body motions and the natural forces propelling the skis. Gravity pulls your skis to the line of least resistance, downhill, and it takes only a slight slope for them to travel at high speed. So you must learn how to control your speed.

Downhill Running Position.—A straight downhill run is called a schuss (below); the body position in relation to the skis is called the schussing position. To attain this position, stand comfortably on skis which are parallel and close together, one ski a few inches in advance of the other.

Keeping your heels flat against your skis, press your knees forward from the ankles. Bend your upper body comfortably forward and keep your center of weight forward. Advance your arms, with slightly bent elbows, and hold the poles low and pointing backward. In this position, try to run down a gentle slope, using your snowplow to stop.

You will discover that proper forward lean controls your skiing. This forward body position, known as *vorlage,* is a forward lean from the ankles, not from the waist. The amount of lean necessary changes according to the grade of the slope. The steeper the slope the more vorlage; the flatter the slope, the more upright you can be. But you must never lean backward with the weight on your heels. If you lean backward or are too upright your skis will shoot out from under you. If you come to a steep drop on the slope, relax and lean forward with it by pressing your knees well forward; if you suddenly come upon a level spot, shift your weight back a bit. If you hit a bump, give with it by bending your knees and leaning a bit forward. Just stand easily upon the natural spring of your knees, ankles, and bindings. Watch the snow ahead and anticipate as much as possible, and you will be able to handle a downhill run.

Traversing. — When a run is any direction other than directly downhill it is called a traverse (below). When you traverse you run down diagonally across a slope, with your skis parallel and close together and in your downhill running position. Normally you keep the upper ski a few inches ahead of the lower or downhill ski; in deep snow or rough ground you advance the upper ski farther to act as a stabilizer to the body. As you traverse, keep your weight centered on both skis; but if the slope is steep, put your weight on the lower ski. You must edge or tilt your skis toward the hill. To get the proper edge, press your knees toward the slope and at the same time lean your body down the hill. Relax your arms and carry your poles pointing backward. The chief mistake in traversing is leaning toward the slope; this forces you into a wide ski position. Then it is impossible to edge properly as well as to weight the lower ski.

Sideslipping. — Sideslipping (skidding) is a good movement on steep slopes and a big help in swing turning and edge control (above). To sideslip you start in an upright traversing position, upper body facing downhill. Sink a bit (relax your ankles), press your knees forward, and incline your upper body downhill. Instead of running straight ahead you will skid down the fall line, because you have reduced the bite of the edges. Your skis ride almost flat on the snow. The steeper the slope and the smoother the snow, the more you edge and the more you lean outward. A decided turning of your knees downhill reduces the grip of your edges and you slide faster. On the other hand, a turning of your knees toward the slope slows the sliding movement or, more turning, brings it to a stop. When you start to traverse again you make a more forward lean.

Swinging Uphill. — Swinging uphill means turning out of a traverse and toward the upslope (above right). This is a good way to come to a stop. From a traverse position a slight turning of the body is necessary for the first turning toward the slope; momentum brings

about the rest. First counterrotate with the downhill shoulder behind the ski ends, and then turn your heels toward the downhill side and press your knees forward and inward. The turning pressure of your heels, with the help of counterrotation, swings you to a sudden stop.

If your downward movement is harder, your turning force of the heels will be stronger because of greater pressure. This is especially important when your momentum is less or the resistance of the snow to turning is greater. The greater your speed the more you must use your uphill edges during the swing. The more the edges are to grip, and the more your knees, well pressed forward, are turned toward the slope, the more you lean your upper body outward. This outward leaning brings about a strong weighting of your lower ski.

Turning. — In turning, the inside ski is always the one in the direction of the turn; the outside ski the one toward the outside of the turn. All parts of your body take the same relation to any turn. Thus you have an inside and outside shoulder, an inside and outside knee.

Therefore, if you make a turn to the right your right ski is the inside ski; in a turn to the left, your right ski is the outside ski.

The snowplow, snowplow turn, and stem turn are skills you must learn before tackling stem swinging. The snowplow teaches you to turn your skis by leg action only. The snowplow turn requires weight changing which is needed in all swings and turns across the fall line. The stem turn teaches you the effect of change of edges through the part turning of one ski by leg action.

forces the edges to bite the snow. If you tip the ankles either outward or inward your skis will cross in front. The braking control you have over your speed is adjusted by the amount of pressure you apply on the front part of the skis, and by the width of the plow you form. You get the greatest braking effect by the widest possible ski angle, along with strong edging and weighting on your heels. Keep your poles pointed back as you snowplow, elbows bent, and each hand out in front of the hip on that side.

Snowplow. — The snowplow is exactly what the name suggests — a plowing of the snow with the tails of your skis pushed out. You push your skis out by turning your heels outward. By spreading your weight evenly along the running surface of both skis and edging with the inner edges, a braking action follows. To snowplow hold the tips of your skis close together, bend your ankles, and push your knees forward. This position

Snowplow Turn. — A snowplow turn is a change of direction run throughout in the snowplow position. To turn to the right from the normal plow position, lean your body sideways and outward to the left, bringing back the left shoulder a little. At the same time, shove the left knee forward and inward and press the left heel outward. This one-sided knee bend position shifts your weight to the outside ski which thus receives a strong turning force toward the outside. Bring your weight back to both skis for a regular snowplow. Repeat the movements on the other side to turn to the left. Remember that when all your weight is on one ski you have to follow the line of the weighted ski. Complete each turn with an easy flowing motion. To go from one snowplow turn to another, begin the shift of weight for the next turn before the end of the turn then being made.

Now start to traverse in your normal downhill running position. When you come to the spot where you want to turn, lift upward (momentarily unweighting your skis) and forward at the same time, forcing your skis into the snowplow. Unweighting the skis at the moment of the lift makes them slide easily into the snowplow position. Once in position make your turn. Then let your skis run together and continue the traverse.

Stem Turn. — The stem turn starts from a traverse with skis parallel, continues through the direction-changing but not too wide a snowplow, and ends with a traverse in the opposite direction, skis parallel. Begin the stem turn from a slow traverse, with your body erect and most of your weight on your lower ski. Push your unweighted upper ski out to a stem position (half a plow), tips of both skis together. Keep your stemmed ski on its inside edge. While stemming, turn your body toward the upslope, in other words, turn opposite to the direction of the intended turn. Give your stemmed ski some weight, and a downhill turning of the skis starts. As in the snowplow turn,

you now turn and lean your body outward and, at the same time, push the outside (stemmed) knee forward and inward. Because of the lowering of the body and forward push of your knee, your heel turns outward still more and your outside ski takes the weight as you swing around the turn. Meanwhile your upper or outside shoulder stays back, already in the position for the opposite traverse. As soon as your outside ski, which has now become the lower ski, has almost reached the direction of the traverse, you change the edging of the unweighted inner ski from the inside to the outside edge, and pull it alongside the weighted ski for the traverse.

On a steep slope or on breakable crust, rather than outward stemming at the beginning of the turn by sliding the ski over the snow, lift your ski into the desired angle. And your final pulling together, too, is done by lifting.

Swinging Downhill. — Every downhill swing is a change of direction which continues across the fall line. You make the swing either with the help of an angling outward of the outside ski or with parallel skis. In the first case you make a stem swing; in the second, a pure swing.

Stem Swing. — A stem swing (above), often called a stem christiana, is a swing turn in which you stem the outer ski to start the change of direction. Though based on the fundamental principles of the stem turn, it requires more speed to make. In the stem swing you close the open skis quicker and by force, rather than letting them run together as in the stem turn.

From an erect traverse position, stem your unweighted ski out but bring its tip back a little. As you stem, turn your body toward the slope to bring about a turning opposite to the direction in which you are going to swing. Now lift, turn and swing, and edge your skis for the new direction, changing your weight to the outside ski. You may sideslip a bit

as you bring your skis around. Your body leans to the outside, with your outside shoulder left behind, your knees into the slope.

With the change of weight, you shift the edge of the unweighted inside ski from the inside to the outside edge and draw the ski alongside. Your body sinks while the heels turn outward, which increases the turning force of the weight shifting. The skis, now parallel, carry the swing through, driven by momentum and steered by controlled heel pressure.

With speed, smooth snow, and a steep slope, you have to increase the amount of edging to prevent too much drifting off to the side after crossing the fall line. The more you have to edge the more you press your knees forward and toward the inside of the turn, and the more you incline your body toward the outside as a countermovement.

If you are going to continue on with a traverse, your body goes into the traverse position toward the end of your swing. If you want to stop, you rise to an erect position after the finish of your turn.

Pure Swing. — The pure swing, sometimes called the parallel swing, is your final goal in ski running. If you can make a pure swing well you can run steadily over every kind of snow and ground. This swing is a change of direction made from beginning to end with parallel skis — an unweighting of both skis to allow the turning force of both legs to come into play.

You start the pure swing from an upright traverse position. In a continuous movement, lift up and forward to unweight the ski ends so you can turn your heels toward the outside; then immediately after the unweighting you crouch, weighting the skis again, and push your knees decidedly toward the inside of the turn to strengthen the turning pressure of your heels. This heel pressure, together with the momentum which acts as a turning force, furnishes the motive power of the swing. As you lift up and forward your inside shoulder is back; your outside arm partly in front. Your crouch is a downward and forward motion coupled with a counterrotation to change the edges of your skis.

From the start your body leans outward, a countermovement to the leg action. After crossing the fall line your knees, in order to increase the grip of the edges, press toward the inside of the turn as your body leans toward the outside, weighting the outside ski.

Your body rises before the end of the swing to come into the regular traverse position. If, however, you intend to make a quick stop, your body rises after the end of the swing.

Bibliography

Austrian Association of Professional Ski Teachers (trans. by Roland Palmedo). *The New Official Austrian Ski System, From Walking to Wedeln*. New York: A. S. Barnes and Company, 1958.

Bourdon, Robert. *Modern Skiing*. Philadelphia: J. B. Lippincott Co., 1953.

Brown, Conrad. *Skiing for Beginners*. New York: Charles Schribner's Sons, 1951.

Georg, Hans. *Modern Ski Systems*. New York: Hastings House, 1954.

Iselin, Fred, and Spectorsky, A. E. *New Invitation to Skiing*. New York: Simon and Shuster, 1958.

Kramer, Franz. *Ski the New Way*. New York: Sterling, 1959.

Lunn, Peter. *A Skiing Primer*. 2nd edition. Hollywood, Florida: Transatlantic Arts, Inc., 1951.

O'Rear, John and Frankie. *Skiing Illustrated: A Guide for the Young Skier*. New York: A. S. Barnes and Company, 1956.

Division for Girls and Women's Sports. *Winter Sports and Outing Activities Guide*. Washington, D.C.: American Association for Health, Physical Education, and Recreation, latest edition.

Federation Internationale de Ski. *International Competition Rules*. Milwaukee, Wisconsin: National Ski Association, latest edition.

National Collegiate Athletic Association. *Official Skiing Rules — Downhill, Slalom, Cross-Country, Jumping*. New York: The Association, latest edition.

National Ski Association of America. *National Downhill and Slalom Rules*. Milwaukee, Wisconsin: The Association, latest edition.

TABLE
TENNIS

Robert D. Johnson

Origin and Growth

Today city, intercity, state, sectional and national table tennis tournaments and championships are held every year. Thousands of spectators watch the final rounds of the competitions. Table tennis is a big-time sport now in the United States, controlled by the United States Table Tennis Association which was founded in 1933. It is also a world-wide sport, with world championships under the guidance of the International Table Tennis Federation for the Swaythling Cup for the victorious men's team and Marcel Corbillon Cup for the women's team. Some of the fifteen million players today may be surprised to learn that just about the turn of the century table tennis was a fad, a parlor game for the fashionables and aristocrats!

Table tennis was developed about 1890 by Parker Brothers, a sports equipment manufacturing concern, who sold it somewhat as a "toy" under the name Indoor Tennis. It was played with small wooden bats and a firm light ball covered with knitted web. The small net which accompanied the game could be set up either across a dining room table or, if the game was played on the floor, between the backs of chairs. Because the game was not too popular in the United States, Parkers exported the equipment for Indoor Tennis to Hamley Bros., their English agents in London.

The British took to the game readily. One Englishman interested Hamley Bros. in replacing the webbed ball with a celluloid ball he designed in an effort to improve the game. And in 1902 Hamley's came out with bats with a studded rubber surface instead of the old wood and sandpaper bats. Though officially still called Indoor Tennis, Hamley's named the game Ping Pong — the ping for the sound when the bat hit the ball and the pong for the noise when ball hit table. Parker Brothers patented this name both in United States and England.

Under its new name and improved equipment, the game was reintroduced to the United States — but though many people had fun playing the game, Ping Pong was treated as a fad. About 1910 it lost its vogue both here and abroad.

In 1920 groups in Europe, including England, revived the game under the trade-marked name of Ping Pong. When difficulties arose over this proprietary name, the British substituted the name Table Tennis and organized the English Table Tennis Association. At a meeting in Berlin in 1926, rules and equipment were standardized and the International Table Tennis Federation was created. Today this Federation includes about thirty-five national associations.

In 1930 in the United States enthusiastic players formed the American Ping Pong Association. This group staged a national tournament in 1931. Game manufacturers, alert to the demand for equipment, marketed the game under the name of Table Tennis. In 1933 a new organization — the United States Table Tennis Association — became a rival of the American Ping Pong Association. But it was not long before the two groups merged, dropped the words ping pong, and firmly established the game under the governing organization of the USTTA. This Association regulates the rules, publishes a monthly magazine, and sends the best American players to compete in amateur and world championship tournaments in Europe.

Table tennis is one of the finest, fastest, most spectacular, and difficult of sports. It is a game which can be enjoyed the first time anyone plays it, since it requires little skill to have fun with the ball. For the swift and agile athlete, it is a thrilling scientific game which requires amazing dexterity and endurance. Hardly a club of any description, school, or church is without a table, rackets, and balls; and in the majority of homes at some time or another this question will arise: "Where shall we put the table tennis table?" This game has earned a place for itself as one of America's most popular sports.

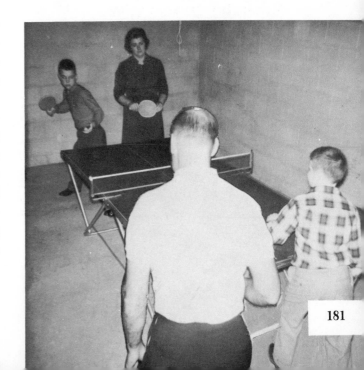

Equipment and Playing Area

Table tennis equipment is inexpensive compared with that required for other sports. Therefore you want to be sure to purchase the best.

Table. — The table — either folding or stationary type — should be sturdy and of standard size. The better-type table is constructed of ¾ inch thick, fine plywood. A standard table is 9 feet by 5 feet, with the playing surface 30 inches above the floor. A white line, ⅛ to ¼ inch wide, runs lengthwise down the center of the surface, and divides the table into two parts (for doubles). A white line, ½ to ¾ inch wide, runs around each edge — the line along each 9-foot side called the side line, and the line along each 5-foot side, the end line. The surface should be stained, not painted, a dark green or other non-reflecting color. You should have from 10 to 12 feet of free space (runback) behind the ends of the table and, where there are several tables, 5 feet between tables.

Net and Supports. — A net divides the playing surface into two courts of equal size. The net is suspended at each side by an upright post, and should extend several inches beyond the side. Along its entire length the upper part is 6 inches above the table's surface; the lower part close to the playing surface.

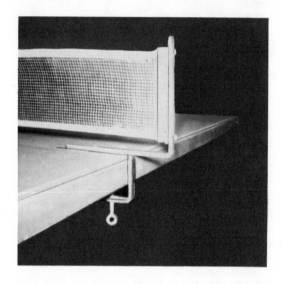

Costume. — For championship play tennis shoes are best, and clothing which permits freedom of action. Select white woolen socks, snug-fitting to prevent blisters from sudden starts, stops, and changes of direction.

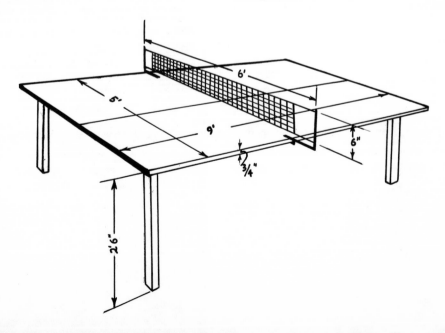

Racket. — The racket may be of any size, shape, or weight; however, expert players recommend a 3, 4, or 5-ply racket weighing from 5 to 6 ounces. Its surface must be dark-colored and non-reflecting, and its blade usually of wood, flat and rigid. The covering of the blade is generally of plain, ordinary pimpled rubber. The rubber pips prolong contact with the ball, permit more control and spin, and do not betray the speed of the shot by the sound. The handle is about 4 inches long, usually of wood and sometimes covered with leather.

How to Play the Game

Singles. — The ball is put in play by the server releasing the ball and hitting it onto the table on his side of the net and on the first bounce goes over the net hitting anywhere on the opponent's court. You and your opponent continue to hit the ball, playing it directly over the net, until one of you knocks the ball into the net, or off the table, or misses hitting the ball before it takes a second bounce.

Ball. — The ball is small, celluloid, round, white in color, and restricted by rule as to size and weight. It is fragile yet very tough to break unless stepped upon if left on the floor. When buying, be sure to rely upon USTTA approved standardization ball which has a uniform bounce. If it is dropped from a height of 12 inches upon a ¾ inch plywood table, it should bounce 8 to 9 inches.

Doubles. — In doubles play, the serve must be made from the right-hand court into the opponent's right-hand court and the players on each side must alternate shots until each rally is completed.

The starting position of partners is similar to the starting position in tennis but as partners must alternate shots in returning the ball, positions are taken as in singles after the first serve with the man who has just played the ball getting completely out of the way either to the side or rear of his partner as soon as he hits the return.

The rules for singles apply also for doubles with a few exceptions. Probably the greatest difference is in the serve. In doubles the mid-court line or center line which divides the table lengthwise creates a right and left-hand court on each side of the net. A good serve in doubles not only must be served as in singles but also must touch the server's right-half court, and then pass over the net and touch the receiver's right-half court. (A ball touching the center line is considered good.)

The side having first serve shall decide which partner serves and then the receiving side picks the receiver.

Each server shall serve five points. At the end of each five points the person receiving becomes the server, and the partner of the previous server becomes the receiver.

The order of play in doubles is different than in most net games. Partners must alternate returning the ball instead of either one making the return. Otherwise the small playing area would make it possible for the better player on each side merely to play singles in a doubles match.

In the last game of a match, or in a one-game match, the team that served first has the right to change their order of receiving or that of their opponents, at the score of ten.

Scoring

A point is scored by the side which makes the last successful return prior to the end of a rally. An unsuccessful return occurs when the ball is missed, hit off the table, into the net, or onto your own half of the court on the return. Failure to make a good serve also scores a point against you unless it is a "let." A let is declared:

a. If the ball while being served should, in passing over the net, touch either it or its supports — if the serve is otherwise good or is volleyed by the receiver.

b. If the serve is delivered when the receiver is not ready. (If the receiver strikes at the ball he shall be considered ready.)

c. If a player is prevented from making a good serve or good return due to an accident not under his control.

d. If a player loses a point under Law 13 due to an accident not under his control.*

A point is also scored against a player if any part of his person, clothing or racket, either touches the net or its supports, or moves the playing surface while the ball is in play. Touching the playing surface with the free hand while the ball is in play counts a point against you, as does also being struck by a returned ball

* United States Table Tennis Association: The
Laws of Table Tennis, page 2.

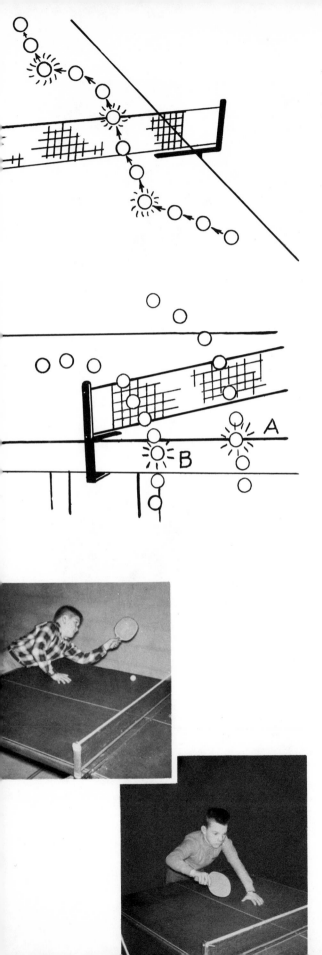

before it bounces on your side of the net, provided it has not yet passed over the end or side lines.

In either singles or doubles, each player serves five consecutive times before the serve changes. The first player or team to reach 21 points wins the game. If the score is tied at 20-20 the service changes after each rally until one side gains a two-point advantage, 22-20, 23-21, 24-22, etc. The player serving first in a match receives first in the second game. Players shall change ends of the court following each game in a match. If it is a one-game match or in the final game of a match of more than one game, players shall change ends as soon as either player scores 10 points.

An edge ball is good if it is ruled that it hit on the top edge and bad if it hits the side edge. In the latter case it is a point against the player who hit it.

In cases where players fail to change ends, and it is discovered, they shall change ends as soon as the error is discovered unless the game is completed, in which case it shall be overlooked. Points scored before the mistake is discovered are always counted.

In the event that a receiver acts as server out of his turn, points scored are counted. However, as soon as the mistake is noticed, the serve is returned to the correct person to serve out the balance of his points. If two were incorrectly served, he serves three to fill out his order. If all five have been served before the mistake is discovered, the error is ignored and the serve is carried on in the same order as if the sequence had been continuous.

Fundamental Skills

Grip. — Learning the proper grip on the racket is most important, as it is largely your wrist action that allows you to put your racket through the motions that produce extra power, quick change of direction, and various spins on the ball.

Good wrist action is the element of surprise for your entire game, serving, defense or attack, and can be impaired or limited with an improper grip on the racket.

Arm motion can easily "telegraph" your thinking to your opponent, while a quick flick or twist of the wrist is much harder to detect. Often you can purposely "telegraph" a message, with body and arm action, to your opponent leading him into a certain defensive position and then cross him up completely with a quick wrist action just before your racket contacts the ball.

Remember, proper grip assures maximum wrist action on any shot angle.

Things to remember: —

1. Do not grip racket too tightly — but relax.

2. Hold the wrist firm.

3. Face somewhat to the sides in forehand and backhand shots as one does in tennis.

4. Regularly check thumb and index finger to be sure they are in proper position on the racket.

Forehand Grip. — In the forehand grip, the short handle of the racket is gripped very close to the blade, with the blade itself partially held in the hand, and the forefinger and thumb bracing opposite sides of the blade. The index finger is used behind the blade for support.

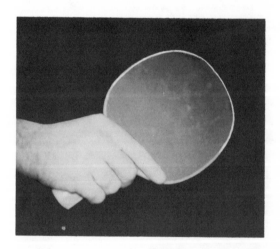

Backhand Grip. — The grip is the same as for the forehand, except that the thumb is now used on the left side or in back of the racket blade.

The Serve. — The choice of ends and of who will serve and receive is decided by chance. The winner may choose the court he wishes or to be either server or receiver. The loser has second choice. If the winner chooses a certain end of the court, the loser may choose either to serve or receive; if the winner makes the latter choice the loser may have his choice of courts. The winner may require his opponent to make first choice.

The ball is put in play either by a toss in the air or by dropping the hand away from the ball. The fingers must be straight and together, the thumb free, and no pinching or cupping of the ball is permitted.

The ball is struck by the racket below the wrist so that it bounces once in the server's court, passes over the net, and touches the receiver's court fairly. If the ball is missed completely by the server it counts as a point against him. A net serve is a let if otherwise good or if volleyed by the receiver.

Points to remember. —

1. Do not serve the ball too high, but keep it low and fast.

2. Do not "telegraph" your serve.

3. Learn to give the ball side spin on the serve.

4. Serve deep into opponent's court.

5. Always aim for good placement.

Position of Server. — The server must be in a position so that at the moment of impact both racket and ball are behind his end line and within the boundaries of the sidelines. At no time shall the serving hand, ball, and racket be in simultaneous contact. Failure to observe any of these restrictions on the serve results in award of a point to the opponent.

While learning to serve it is recommended that the player take up a position directly back of the center line about a foot from the table, facing slightly to the right with the left foot forward (for a right-hander, reverse if left-handed). The ball shall be struck not too far above table height and in such a way as to bounce deep into the opponent's court. This will keep the ball low and make it more difficult to return.

Footwork and Stance. — Proper stance and footwork in serving is just as important in learning table tennis skills as it is in tennis, badminton, or any sport skill where one must be constantly alert.

A good beginner's stance in serving the ball is a position about 1½ to 2 feet directly behind the center line of his court. Face slightly to the right side with the feet well apart, and the left foot forward (for a right handed player).

Types of Serves

There are four basic types of serve: forehand chop, backhand chop, forehand topspin, and backhand topspin. You execute each one similarly to the ordinary chops and drives, by bringing your racket either under or over the ball. You must keep your eyes on the ball from the start of your stroke to the end of your follow through.

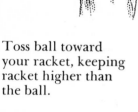

Rule says you must keep hand flat.

Toss ball toward your racket, keeping racket higher than the ball.

Bring racket around back-underside of ball to apply backspin.

Hit ball with center of racket face.

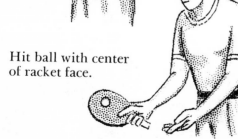

Chop Serves. — Both the forehand and backhand chop serves are relatively slow serves. Use these against defensive players because these serves do not permit heavily chopped returns.

It is more difficult to execute a forehand chop serve than a forehand chop stroke because the ball has no forward speed. You are chopping a "soft" ball. The only way to gain chop (spin) is by a vigorous use of your wrist. For the forehand chop serve keep the racket face higher than the ball. Toss the ball toward the racket, bring the racket around the back underside of the ball, apply backspin, and hit the ball with the center of the racket face. Tilt your racket back at about a 45-degree angle. Keep your wrist loose as you pass well under the ball with your racket. Follow through, arm and racket extended in the direction of your ball.

Follow through with arm and racket in direction of ball.

Keep wrist loose as you pass racket well under ball.

Ball lays in palm of
flat hand.

In the backhand chop serve, due to
stroking across your body, you can get
little wrist action and consequently little
chop. Pass the racket slightly under the
ball to produce a little backspin. Use
this serve to place the ball just over the
net. Your opponent will be forced to
give you a high return which you can
smash.

Toss ball up slightly
to meet racket.

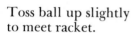

Aim at a chosen
spot on table.

Tilt racket blade back
at about a 45° angle.

Keep eyes on ball,
follow through, and get
set for return.

Chop down and under
ball with racket.

Topspin Serves. — Both forehand and backhand topspin serves are made in the same manner as the forehand and backhand drives pictured on pages following. The only difference being, in serving you throw the ball into the air and bring the racket over it. It is hard to conceal the direction of your service and the amount of topspin; but it is possible to do so if you don't release the ball until the moment of contact with the racket. Your two hands will almost touch as you make contact on the topspin serves. You will appear to be throwing the ball into the racket at the same time as you throw the racket into the ball.

Sidespin Serves. — After becoming more skilled in the game, you may want to add to your variety of serves, giving you more change of pace and ability to keep your opponent guessing.

Serves with sidespin at varying speeds are deceptive because the ball goes off on an angle. To produce sidespin, keep your wrist loose and draw your racket across the ball from one side to the other in conjunction with your regular chop or topspin movement. Drawing your racket across the ball to the right makes the ball angle from right to left; to the left, the ball angles from left to right. If you control the amount and type of sidespin you can more readily anticipate the direction of your opponent's return.

When using spin serves, you should observe closely the results that spin on the ball will bring when coming in contact with your opponent's racket on the return. You should always watch carefully your opponent's arm and wrist

movements and racket position to determine whether he has read your serve correctly and will choose to counteract the spin on the ball with a chop return, a push return with racket angled correctly; or will your spin serve go unread, spin off his open-faced racket, and in which direction.

Returning the Serve. — In returning the serve the receiver should aim at the spot on the table where the serve originated. If the server hit down on his serve (chops), hit up on the return and vice versa. The return should attempt to reverse the direction of the spin put on the ball by the server. The same rule is

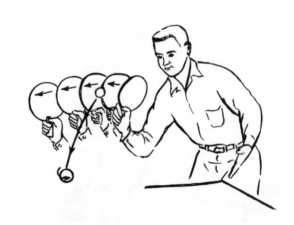

true in all play as well as on the return of the serve. Advanced players may be able to return a drive with a drive, or a chop with a chop, but, in general, the above rule is best for all, even the experts.

A good stance position in receiving is about 2 feet directly in back of the center line of the court. The feet are spaced well apart, the knees slightly bent, and the body bent slightly forward. From this position one can quickly step forward, backward, or to the side to effect either a backhand or forehand shot. After the shot is made again, recover to this position for the next return.

For a forehand or backhand return, the feet should be placed, at the moment of contact of racket with ball, so that they are perpendicular to the line of flight of the ball. The feet are well spread to shift weight from rear to fore foot in delivering a shot. This is effective body-weight follow-through. In going after a ball for an effective shot, remember to face it as you play it. Also remember to return to midcourt quickly after the shot is made. Keep your eye on the ball.

Common faults in stance, court position, and footwork. —

1. *Knee straight, flat-footed position.* Correction. More body crouch, shifting weight as a boxer does, until you have the feel of weight forward ready to move in any direction as needed.

2. *Failing to return to "On Guard" position after each return.* Correction. Have someone watch you and continually remind you when you are out of position. Mark your "On Guard" position on the floor with chalk and practice trying to return to the exact spot after each return.

3. *Failing to move into correct position to play each shot.* Correction. Volley with someone, concentrate on getting into proper position for each shot. Be sure you face the ball each time you play it.

4. *Interfering with partner's play in doubles.* Correction. Immediately after returning your shot get completely out of the line of play by stepping out to the side and getting behind your partner ready to step in for the following shot after his return. Each partner plays position just as in singles on his return.

Table Tennis Strokes

The Half Volley. — If any shot is easy this is it. As the ball bounces, meet it with the paddle and push it back over the net. The paddle can be turned slightly to either side at the moment of contact to add deception by angling the shot. It is mostly a defensive shot although it has a limited use on the offense.

The Drives

After the Half Volley or Push Stroke, with variations, you are ready to attempt the Drives.

The Forehand and Backhand Drives are considered basic strokes but they add speed and zip to your game and require more skill in mastering. Due to the fact that you are adding body motion and much more arm motion to your stroke, when driving, creates a need for a finer degree of timing in hitting the ball over the net into fair territory.

After mastering the drive strokes and moving on to faster varieties, you will soon realize that Table Tennis is a game of split second timing and adept body coordination.

Forehand Drive. — Assume proper position, eyes on the ball with the body at about a 45° angle to the net. The racket is held low and angled forward. Hit forward and upward so top spin is applied to the ball. Contact is made just before or at the height of the bounce. Play this shot on deep or high bouncing returns. Be sure your weight shifts from back foot to front foot in order to put power into this stroke.

Backhand Drive. — The backhand drive might be described as the reverse of the forehand drive. The backswing is shorter because the arm crosses the body and the wrist is used to a greater extent. Usually the thumb is shifted a little higher up the back of the blade in order to give more support and power to this shot.

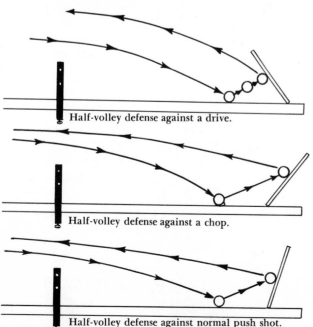

Half-volley defense against a drive.

Half-volley defense against a chop.

Half-volley defense against normal push shot.

192

Forehand Drive

Backhand Drive

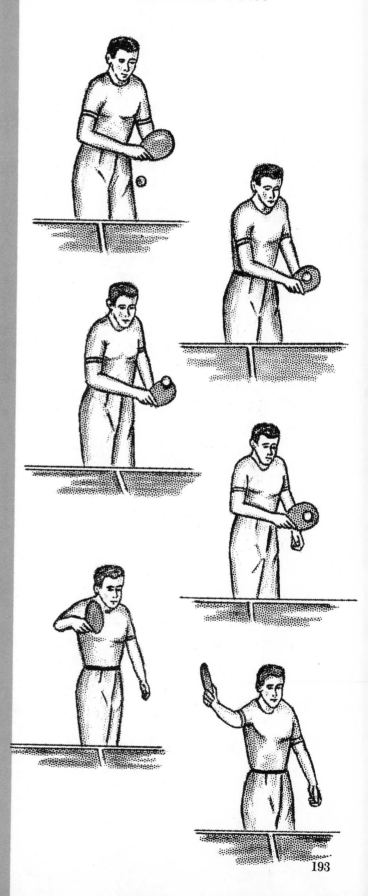

The Chops

Forehand Chop. — This is primarily a defensive stroke. It is executed like a hatchet chopping motion. The stroke starts from shoulder height and hitting forward and downward, the top of the racket blade is tilted back away from the ball. Finish the stroke with the arm almost fully extended in front of you. Cutting with the blade down behind and under the ball gives the ball a back spin as it leaves the face of the racket. This stroke should be executed with considerable speed, making it very difficult to return.

The stroke starts shoulder high.

Tilt racket back at about 45° ang

Backhand Chop. — For this shot the racket must be tilted, and is the reverse of the forehand chop except that it is a shorter stroke and calls for the stronger use of the forearm and wrist. The stroke is started at about chin height and ends at about waist height. This shot requires a great deal of practice.

Arm reaches across in front of body making stroke shorter.

Racket tilted back, wrist firm.

Stroke forward
and downward.

Blade contacts ball
on under back side.

Ball takes on backspin
when leaving racket.

Eyes on the ball,
follow through.

Meet ball at maximum
height of its bounce.

Master control
before power.

Put firmness and zip
into down slicing stroke.

Good follow through
brings you back to
a return position.

Smash Shot. — This shot is exactly what its name implies. It is used on an opponent's high bouncing return, the higher the better. Hit the ball straight forward and down over the net without spin. Use the smash only as a set-up shot when a good opportunity presents itself. Play it accurately with plenty of forceful body and arm action.

The smash is a "kill" point shot. Keep your eyes on the ball until contact, take careful aim, and place your shot just over the net.

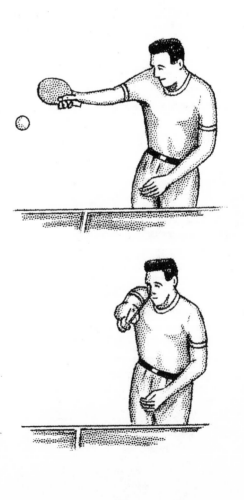

196

Drop Shot. — This is an excellent change-of-pace shot which can gain many points for you if used with some deception. It works best off an opponent's chop return that falls a foot or two over your side of the net. With body and arm motion, fake a drive or smash shot, keeping your opponent back away from the table. Then suddenly stop your driving arm motion just before your racket is to make contact with the ball, letting the ball hit your dead racket, tilted just enough to drop the ball over the net. Try to contact the ball before it bounces more than six inches above the table.

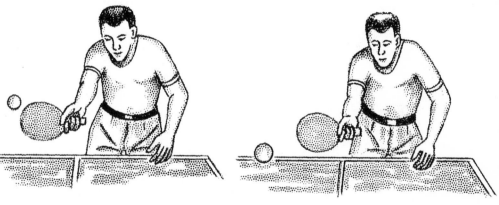

Spin. — Table tennis is a game of spin. Because of the lightness of the ball it is practically impossible in play to keep it from rotating on its own axis in one direction or another. Spin prevents a ball from rebounding normally and from following a straight arc. To become a top-flight player, you must know what effect this spinning motion has on the ball so you can use it to advantage, and you must know how to recognize the kind of spin your opponent is using in order to counteract it. Three types of spins are explained on the next page.

Topspin or overspin is rotation upward; the top of the ball spins forward in the direction of its flight. With topspin the ball dives forward and down and bounces high. The more topspin the higher the bounce. When the ball hits a receiver's racket, it crawls up on it. If your opponent starts his racket low, brings it up and forward, ending his stroke over his head, he is using topspin; you counteract with an underspin shot.

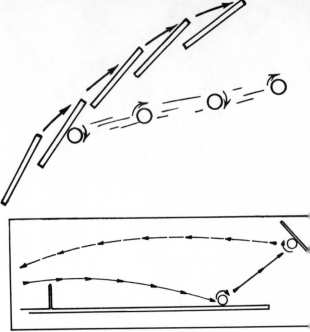

Counteract topspin by slanting of racket face forward.

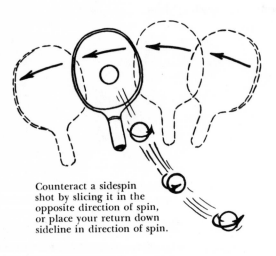

Counteract a sidespin shot by slicing it in the opposite direction of spin, or place your return down sideline in direction of spin.

With sidespin the ball rotates horizontally or sideways, one direction or the other. Sidespin is actually halfway between backspin and topspin. To impart sidespin you slice at the ball — sweep across it with the blade of your racket in a vertical position.

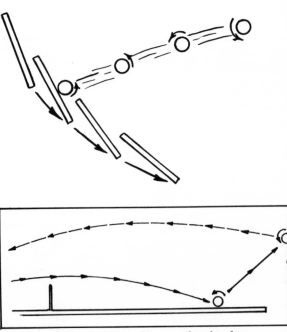

Backspin or underspin is rotation of the ball on its own axis, downward; its top moves toward the one who serves it, its bottom, away. With backspin the ball follows a flatter trajectory. When it hits the table it bounces abruptly; when it hits a receiver's racket it shoots downward. If your opponent starts his racket up high and comes down and under the ball, he is using underspin; you counteract with a topspin shot.

Counteract backspin by slanting top of racket face back.

Strategy

Singles. — Probably the best defensive, as well as offensive game, is similar to tennis — rely upon opponent to commit an error. Concentrate in returning the ball safely to the opponent's court. Mix the speed of the returns. Try different shots and study opponent's weakness or strong points. Size them up quickly and play to his weakness. Keep the opponent guessing. Avoid giving opponent set shots. Keep the ball in play.

Doubles. — Essentially strategy in doubles play is the same as for that of singles play. In doubles play there is more ground to cover, the court is wider, and partners must alternate each shot. Alternating each shot makes the doubles type of play actually a singles game. Offensive strategy, therefore, is keeping the opponents running and off balance as in lawn tennis. Do not drift into a slow deliberate game but mix the type of shots and tempo of the game.

If one wins the toss at the start of the game, it is good strategy to take the choice of first receiving. This causes the opponents to determine who is to serve first and the receivers can then choose wisely as to who is to receive, since the same player must receive from the same opponent throughout the game. Keep eye on the ball. Learn to react with "lightning" speed as to choice of shot to make on each shot and each situation of the game. Use cross-court angling shots. Keep opponents off balance. Constantly strive for a versatile attack and defense in a deceptive manner so that opponents cannot guess your shots in advance.

Coleman Clark, former national champion, lists two simple rules that are basic to all Table Tennis play, "Keep the ball in play, and keep the other fellow guessing." If these two points are kept constantly in mind and applied to your competitive play, your game should improve tremendously.

Safety. — 1. The floor should have a non-slip surface, and some type of gym shoes should be worn.

2. Be sure there are no posts or equipment close by which might cause injuries.

Social Values. — It is one of the best of the home rumpus-room games for the entire family. One of the reasons for its popularity is that all ages, both sexes, from junior to grandma can play the game the year round. It can be played both indoors and outdoors.

Bibliography

American Association for Health, Physical Education, and Recreation: *Physical Education for High School Students.* Washington 6, D. C., American Association for Health, Physical Education and Recreation.

Armbruster, David A.: *Basic Skills in Sports.* St. Louis, The C. V. Mosby Co., 1953.

Cartland, Douglas: *Table Tennis Illustrated.* New York, The Ronald Press Company, 1953.

Clark, Coleman: *Table Tennis.* New York, Prentice-Hall, Inc., 1942.

Purves, Jay: *Table Tennis.* New York, A. S. Barnes and Company, 1942.

United States Table Tennis Association: *The Laws of Table Tennis.* Newark, Delaware. The Association, latest edition.

VOLLEYBALL

Clem Thompson

Origin and
Growth

VOLLEYBALL WAS INVENTED by an American, William G. Morgan, at the YMCA in Holyoke, Massachusetts in 1895.

The game was developed for business men who wanted a game of mild physical activity.

Mr. Morgan stretched a tennis net across an indoor court, used an inflated basketball bladder for a ball, and specified that the ball had to be volleyed back and forth over the net during the play. For many years the game was confined to Morgan's gymnasium; but in time it spread throughout New England cities, eventually being played outdoors as well as indoors.

The amazing growth in popularity of volleyball has been the result of several factors: the interest and backing of the YMCA, playgrounds, and schools; the simplicity of the rules; the ease with which the game can be set up for outdoor recreation, with a net, ball, and level surface.

Another factor is that it appeals to both the skilled and unskilled; the young and old. It is one of our most popular co-recreational sports. With slight rule modifications it can be played with four to one-hundred players at the same time on the same court.

Volleyball had been introduced to some foreign lands as a direct result of World War I. But during World War II the American troops carried the game all over the world. Wherever they were and whenever they could, the servicemen improvised a net, secured a ball, and played the game for diversion. Eyewitnesses and participants from other countries caught on to the rules and ways of play, and in no time the game made great strides as an international sport. The International Volleyball Federation, founded in 1947 with a membership of less than 30 countries, doubled its membership in 15 years.

Because volleyball started within the confines of a YMCA gymnasium, this organization ruled the game during its early growth, wrote up its first set of rules and, in 1922, arranged for the first national championship. With the help of the Y, the United States Volleyball Association was founded in 1928, conducting its first championship in 1929. Now this Association governs the game through 16 regional organizations. Tournaments on the state, regional, and national levels are sponsored by the Amateur Athletic Union, the YMCA, and colleges and universities. On the competitive, interscholastic basis it is being played by more and more high schools, colleges, and universities. State sponsored high school volleyball tournaments are being held in New York, Pennsylvania, and Wisconsin. Divisional tournaments are conducted for championships in the Veterans YMCA group, the Women's organization, the Armed Forces group, and the Turners.

Hollywood YMCA Stars . . . National YMCA Champions and National Open runner-up.

Volleyball, rated as one of the fastest moving games in the world, is now a feature of the Pan American and Olympic Games. It is a major sport in 25 nations.

The popularity of volleyball stems from the fact that the game can be enjoyed in simple and informal or fast and competitive play. Either way it is a vigorous game which develops body strength, agility, and coordination. It requires jumping, stretching, lunging. The actions call for quick starts and stops, quick thinking, and immediate response.

It has been estimated that more than ten million men and over a half million women play volleyball in the United States. Volleyball ranks as the fifth recreational sport and the sixth competitive sport in our country.

Gene Selznick, star player of the U.S.A. team, puts one away in match against France.

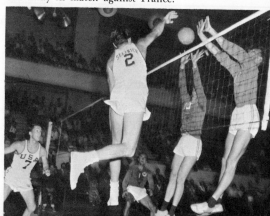

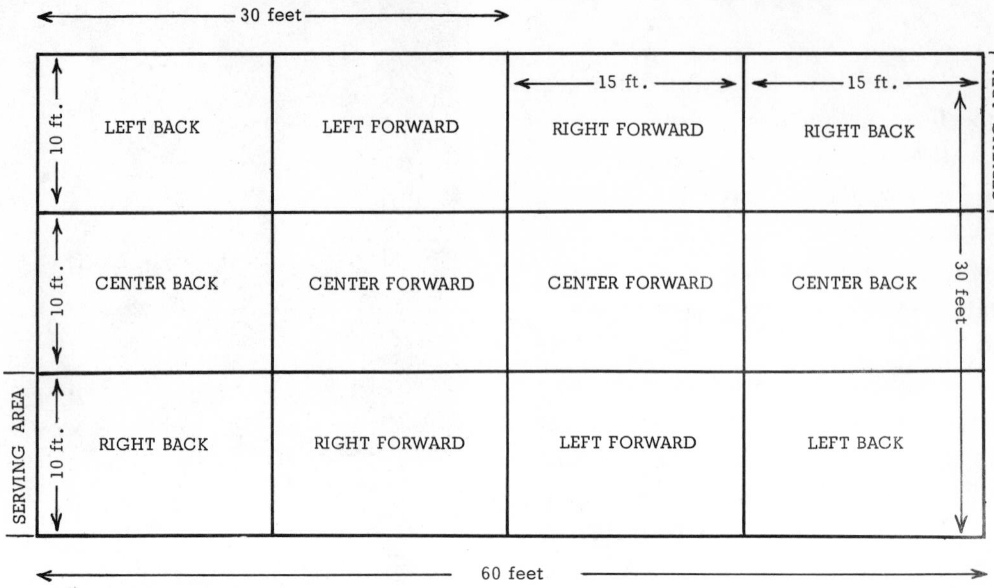

		← 15 ft. →	← 15 ft. →	
10 ft. ↕ LEFT BACK	LEFT FORWARD	RIGHT FORWARD	RIGHT BACK	SERVING AREA
10 ft. ↕ CENTER BACK	CENTER FORWARD	CENTER FORWARD	CENTER BACK	30 feet
SERVING AREA — 10 ft. ↕ RIGHT BACK	RIGHT FORWARD	LEFT FORWARD	LEFT BACK	

60 feet

Playing Area & Ball

Volleyball is played on a rectangular court 60 feet long and 30 feet wide, bounded by lines 2 inches wide. Those lines on the long sides of the court are called side lines; those on the short sides, end lines. A center line divides the court into two equal playing areas. Seven and a half feet from and parallel to the center line, from side line to side line, are spiking lines. Back of each end line and between the side lines is a serving area 6 feet in depth. A net 3 feet wide and 32 feet long, stretched across the court over the center line, separates the playing area. The top of the net is 8 feet from the floor (official); high school boys and girls play with a net 7 feet 6 inches from the floor. Junior high school boys and girls play with the net at 7 feet.

The game requires an inflated leather or rubber ball 25 to 27 inches in circumference and 9 to 10 pounds in weight, with an air pressure of about 7 pounds.

Rules & Scoring

Men's Rules. — A volleyball team consists of six players who position themselves at the start of the game in areas of the court as shown in the diagram: three back positions — right, center, and left; three forward positions — right, center, and left. No player consistently plays one position during a game, since a clockwise rotation system is followed after an exchange of serve.

The team that wins the toss of a coin has the choice of serve or court. To start the game the player in the right back position moves to the serving area. He puts the ball into play by hitting it with his hand, fist, or arm over the net into the opponents' court. All players may move from their starting areas once the ball is served. A served ball is dead if it touches the server's court, player, or net, or goes under the net or out of bounds.

Once legally over the net the ball must be volleyed back and forth — never permitted to touch the playing surface. In volleying, a player may not contact or reach over the net, make successive contacts of the ball, or play it twice in succession; and a team may not play the ball more than three times before it crosses the net to the opponents.

The server continues to serve until his team makes an error, commits a foul, or completes the game. When the serving team makes an error, side out is declared and the serve goes to the opponents. Before the opponents serve, each player on that team rotates one position clockwise, and the player rotating from right-forward position to right-back position is the next server.

A game consists of 15 points so long as the team first making 15 has a 2-point advantage. An official tournament game may be a combination of 15 points and 8 minutes of ball-in-play time. The game is over if a team has 15 points with a 2-point advantage before the time expires or, at the end of 8 minutes regardless of score, if one team has a 2-point advantage. Only the team serving can score, earning one point if the opponents make an error or commit a foul. No points are scored on a side out; rather, the serve is forfeited. A match consists of two games out of three.

Big Spring, Texas, High School team. First High School to enter a national tournament.

Girls' Rules. — In recent years the rules for boy's and girl's volleyball have become more and more similar. Some of the most important rule differences include: an assist in the serve is optional for the girls, a served ball which hits the net before entering the opponent's court is a "let" ball and is served again. A girl may hit a ball twice in succession, three players may play it and hit the ball a maximum of six times. As stated previously the net is 7 feet 6 inches.

Boy's and girl's rules are the same in size of court, scoring of points and side out, number of players, rotation, and general net play.

Co-Recreational Rules. — Slight modifications in the volleyball rules help make it one of our most popular co-recreational sports. Three boys and three girls in alternate positions make up a team. One serve is permitted. If the ball is played by more than one player on the team, one of the players must be a girl. Other rules followed can be either the official men's or girls' rules. But as has been indicated before, these differences are very minor and do not materially affect the game.

Monessen High School, Pennsylvania Interscholastic Athletic Association Champions.

Team Fundamentals

Volleyball requires team play in passing the ball from one player to another. The rules allow for three passes (hits) on each side of the net. This procedure of passing the ball three times before it goes over the net requires skill and makes the game of volleyball interesting and challenging.

To help you understand these playing procedures we shall designate the player who first receives the ball as No. 1; the player to whom he passes the ball as No. 2 (Set-Up), and the third player to receive the ball and hit it over the net as No. 3 (Spiker).

Any player who receives the ball may send it over the net without passing to a teammate; however, the 1-2-3 combination affords real team play and strategy.

In volleyball the players maintain a two-line playing formation, front and back. On receiving the serve the three front-line players are about 12 feet from the net; the backs, from 15 to 20 feet. Players with less skill will play closer to the net. On general defensive play this formation draws nearer the net, depending upon the location of the attacking play. The players on the back line get the ball forward to the forward line; these players in turn hit it over the net.

For point making, it is best for two players to work as a unit and remain as a pair through all play. The assignments for the pair are to set the ball up and spike it over the net. Through all play, when his partner (spiker) is at net position, the set-up player goes after the ball and sets it up in the air; his partner jumps up and bats it (spikes it) over the net.

As the team members rotate, the set-up player of a pair is either in the center-forward or right-forward position when his partner is at the net, because in rotation the set-passer precedes the spiker. In good team play the set-up on the front line gets the second ball and his spiker the third. It is up to the spiker to outwit the opposition by placing the ball in open spaces or by driving it through the defensive lineup.

Because of the rotation system in volleyball, every player must learn all fundamentals and techniques — serving, receiving and passing, receiving and setting, receiving and spiking — because at one time or another each serves, plays every position on the court, and functions as Number 1, 2, or 3 player on his own side of the court. Because the correct execution of one element of the game is so dependent upon its relationship to others, it is somewhat difficult, in explanation, to isolate the fundamentals of volleyball from team play.

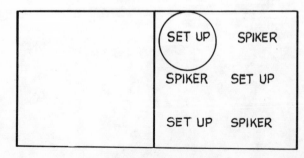

Ball Handling and Passing

In volleyball you play (pass) the ball with the inside fleshy part of your fingers in order to direct it. You cup your hands and fingers and spread your fingers like a claw, so that the finger and thumb tips touch the ball. Better control of the ball is obtained when it is hit with the fingers and thumbs. You also play the ball with elbows wide apart and to the side, which further insures better ball control.

The player who receives an oncoming ball from the opponents immediately becomes both the receiver (Number 1) and the passer. His objective is to pass the ball to his set-up (Number 2). The teammate getting the ball from his Number 1 immediately becomes both the set-up and passer. His objective is to pass the ball to his spiker (Number 3). The best and most accurate pass to use is the chest pass. Whether the ball comes high, low, or to the side, receiver or set-up should make every effort to get directly underneath the ball for the chest pass. The fundamentals for the set-up's forward set pass and over-the-head set pass are basically those for the chest pass.

Of course, when hitting low balls, there are times when the passer has to use the one-handed dig pass or the underhand pass. But regardless of the kind of pass executed, the passer must reduce the spin and speed of the ball to give the player at the net ample opportunity to complete the play. Number 1 must direct his pass upward about 15 feet and toward his set-up, to give the latter time to get into position to set the ball to the spiker. Number 2 must know the skill and ability of his spiker for a proper placement of the set pass.

Chest Pass. — By far the most common pass in volleyball is the chest pass. It is simply a forward and upward batting motion as you straighten your arms and thrust your fingers forward to meet the ball. This pass is most effective if your legs, body, arms, and fingers function coordinately and continuously.

To be ready for the oncoming ball, advance one foot forward for a steady base. Bend your knees slightly, tilt your body forward with the weight on the balls of your feet, and bring your hands up to chest position. You must raise your elbows sideways so that your upper arms are almost straight to the side. Keep your thumbs in and pointing downward and slightly forward, fingers flexed and spread. When the ball is almost to you, bring your hands back like a spring.

Your wrists tilt the hands only far enough to meet the flight angle of the ball.

Your wrists and fingers at contact are stiff; you hit the ball with your fingertips. To give the ball extra control and force, your hands and fingers snap forward ahead of your arms. Your wrists and fingers control the ball; your arms and body add the power.

If the ball comes high over your head, bend back at the waist to meet it; if it comes low in front, drop to a knee to get under it. Both these situations require quick movements in order to properly play the ball; regardless, the two-handed chest pass is the best pass to use in either case.

You will use the chest pass in a volleyball game but to improve your skill

The series of pictures on this page show Mel Spejcher, National AAU Champ, in perfect chest-pass action.

more rapidly volley the ball against the wall of the garage, house or gymnasium.

Another effective way to learn to pass the volleyball better is to play with a partner passing the ball back and forth to each other from varying distances. A few minutes of practice of this type each day will greatly improve your skill.

Forward Set Pass. — The set-up (generally number 2 man), uses the forward set pass when he is close to the net. He passes the ball near the net so that his spiker can smash it into the opponents' court. The mechanics for this pass are based on those for the chest pass; the stance, however, is different.

Preparatory to the pass, spread your feet comfortably apart, both feet parallel to the net. Keep your weight evenly distributed on the balls of your feet and your knees slightly flexed. Contact the ball in front of your face, and project it upward to a designated spot along the net in front of your spiker. As you pass it, turn your palms outward from your face. You raise your body upward as you straighten your legs. Release the ball without jumping, thus increasing your accuracy.

Over-the-head Set Pass. — When the set-up is in the center-forward position near the net, with a spiker at each end area, the over-the-head pass keeps the opponents guessing from which side of the court the spike will come.

Footwork and delivery for this pass are similar to the forward set pass. Just before the final contact with the ball, you snap your wrists and extend your arms upward and backward. As you pass the ball backward, your head tilts back and your back arches. Accuracy and power depend upon coordination of all the movements.

HIGH SET

MEDIUM ARC SET

PARALLEL NET SET

Placement of Set Passes. — In team play the set-up and spiker work together. Each knows how the other plays. The set-up must know how high and at what distance from the net the spiker plays his best ball. And the spiker must know about where his set-up will place the ball along the net. These conditions are altered, of course, by the position of the set-up in relation to the net.

The set-up has three choices of passes to set the ball for his spiker; but in each case his one objective is to place the ball in front of the spiker. His first choice is a high set; he hits the ball into the air about 12 feet high so that it comes down within 6 inches to 2 feet of the net. This high set is the easiest for the spiker to smash but most difficult to get by the opponents.

The set-up's second choice is a medium-arc set; he places the ball halfway between himself and the end of the net, passing the ball about 6 feet above the net. His third choice is a parallel-net set; he passes the ball parallel to the net and about 6 feet above it so that it comes down near the end of the net. With either of these two set passes the spiker has more opportunity to vary the placement of his spike, but both require plenty of spiking skill to handle.

It must be remembered that when you are learning to play volleyball your skill in passing the ball accurately and high should improve each time you practice or play. Also, individuals who become good spikers have to spend considerable time practicing this skill.

Dig Pass. — Dig Pass is the name given to a pass where the player has to return a low ball to the extreme right, left, or front. It is a very difficult pass to control.

To make this pass you lunge forward in a crouched position. The hand is closed and the ball is met in an upward movement with the heel and cushion of the hand. To make the ball ascend higher, snap your wrist at the completion of the stroke.

The series of pictures above and right show Howie Gould, National AAU champion, in top form while making a one-hand dig pass.

Edith Conrad, outstanding among women players, below, shows perfect form and balance while making the two-hand dig pass. Hands are clasped and ball is hit on the wrists. This pass is used when a player cannot get into position for a chest pass. It insures greater floor coverage and cleaner ball handling.

211

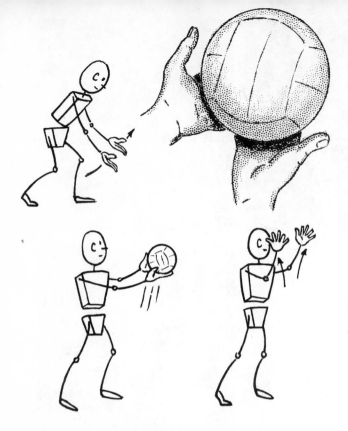

Underhand Pass. — The underhand pass is a last-resort pass, and is not allowed in tournament play. Many times the user of this pass is accused of holding the ball, which is a foul. The essential motion of the underhand pass is a batting one, not a lifting or throwing motion. Your fingers contact the ball only long enough to bat it in the opposite direction.

To start this pass spread your feet and lean forward with knees bent, both hands low, apart, and out in front of your body, palms up and fingers almost flat. As your fingers meet the ball, keep your arms and wrists rigid, and bat the ball. It must leave your hands instantly. Follow through by stepping in the direction of the pass and swinging your arms upward and slightly outward to the sides.

Net Recovery and Pass. — For playing balls from the net, use movements similar to those for the underhand pass. Anticipate the play by watching where the ball strikes the net. Get under it quickly, knees well bent and your side to the net. As the ball drops off the net, rise to meet it, straightening your legs, and batting your hands upward. Bat the ball high enough so that a teammate can come under and drive it over the net. Use the dig pass if you cannot get two hands on the ball.

If the ball strikes the top tape or below the center area of the net, it usually rebounds back into court; this recovery is easier to set for the spiker. If the ball strikes below the top tape but above the center of the net, it generally rolls down the net; crouch to get it before it hits the court. In this case, and if you are Number 2 in the playing series, attempt to project the ball back to a back player.

Serving Techniques

The serve puts the ball into play. Since in volleyball the teams rotate the service, every player must learn to serve well. The server may deliver the serve from anywhere within the serving area behind the end line. The underhand or straight serve is the easier to control and the most accurate; the overhand or power serve requires more skill and practice. You should not attempt the latter until you can consistently and accurately put the ball in play with the underhand serve.

Overhand Serve. — For the overhand serve your left foot is about a foot behind the end line, right foot a comfortable distance behind it. You face the net with knees flexed. Rotate your trunk a bit to the right, and put your weight on the rear foot. Draw your right arm behind your ear. Hold the ball in well-spread fingers of your cupped hand. Now, toss it about 6 inches in front of your face and about 3 feet above your full reach. Use an overarm swing, like the service in tennis, to bring your right arm forward, elbow leading. Whip forward to hit the ball with your palm and fingers at dead center as it descends on a level with your forehead. As you strike the ball your body pivots around to the left with the force of your swing, and your weight comes directly over your left foot. Keep your eyes on the ball on its way up and down, as timing of the hit is the essence of this serve. After contact, step forward with your right foot and follow through bringing your arm straight downward. Finish with your right arm in full extension in the direction of the flight of the ball.

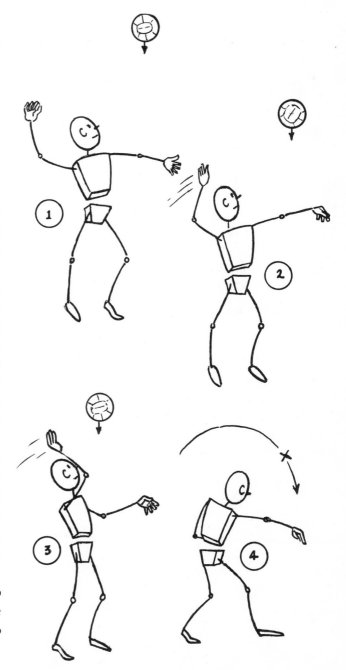

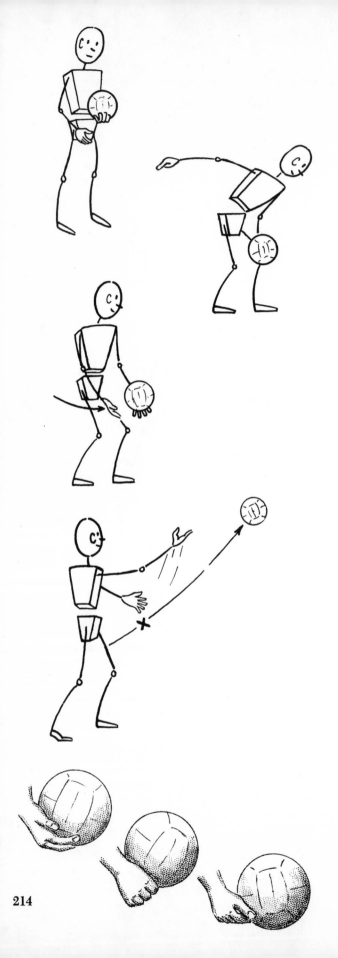

Underhand Serve. — For the straight open-hand underhand serve (right-handed player), first face the net with the left foot forward, knee slightly flexed, and body tilted forward. Hold the ball in your left hand, fingers well spread and pointed toward the right, thumb toward the net. Keep the ball close to and slightly to the right of your body. Now, rotate your trunk to the right as you swing your right arm backward and upward, your weight coming back on your rear foot. Swing your arm downward and forward, weight starting forward. Keep your eyes on the ball. Hit the ball from your left hand just below the center near the underside. Make the contact with the inside heel and palm of your right hand, merely knocking the ball off your left hand. As you strike the ball, stiffen your hand; shift your weight to your forward foot, and extend your ankle and knee. After striking, continue the forward and upward swing of your right arm to give the ball enough height to go over the net; your left arm swings off to the side for balance. Follow through in the intended direction of the flight of the ball.

Hand Position. — As soon as you have achieved a reasonable degree of skill with the straight underhand serve, the position of the hand can be varied from the open palm to improve your serving skill.

The position of the hand is changed by clenching the fist. There are two ways to hit the ball with the clenched fist; knuckles and heel of the hand and thumb side of fist. The more natural way is with the knuckles and heel of the hand, but some volleyball players prefer to hit the ball with the thumb side of the fist. Clenching the fist will enable the server to hit the ball harder but it will probably decrease his accuracy. The changes in hand position can be used in the overhand serve as well as the underhand. These underhand serve variations are frequently used by intermediate and advanced volleyball players; both boys and girls.

When you can control the ball accurately with the underhand deliveries, try to impart spin to the ball so that your opponents have more difficulty handling it. To give it spin, instead of hitting the ball slightly below the center and a little underneath, hit it a little on the right side with the fingers and palm rather than the heel and palm. As you hit, let your hand roll up the ball, thumb leading the way, and rotate your arm and hand inward, over the top of the ball. With enough force, the ball spins from right to left and curves toward the left boundary of your opponents' court. This left spin is called an outcurve.

To give the ball an incurve, strike it on the left side with the palm and fingers, little finger ahead. The spin imparted causes the ball to curve from left to right.

Another difficult ball to return is a floater. This is a serve with little or no spin which weaves through the air. To deliver a floater, flex the first and second joints of your fingers, thumb parallel to your index finger. Contact the ball with

the knuckles, fingernails, and the heel of your hand. A receiver finds this deceptive, but you should not attempt to serve a floater until you have mastered the underhand services.

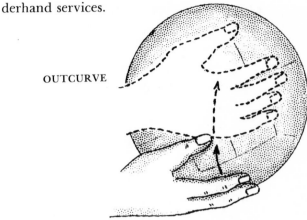

OUTCURVE

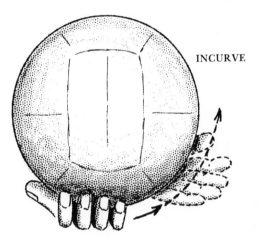

INCURVE

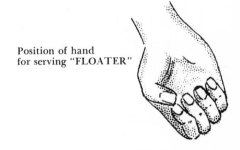

Position of hand
for serving "FLOATER"

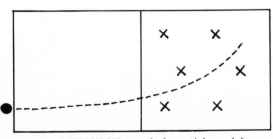

The OUTCURVE travels from right to left

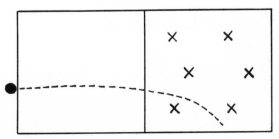

The INCURVE travels from left to right

Placement of Serves. — In serving you try to serve to your opponents' right or left back court, rather than to the center area. If your opponents in their rotation have the set-up in the center-forward area, direct the serve to the right-back area, left-back a second choice. This is because the receiver, in the right-back position in standard play, will pass to his set-up, in center-forward position, who has to turn away from his partner in left-forward position to get the pass; thus he is at a disadvantage. This would not be the situation if you direct your serve to the left-back position, the second choice.

If the opponents' spiker is in the center-forward area, with set-up players on either side, direct your serve to the left-back area, right-back area a second choice. The left-back receiver has to make a long pass to his set-up in the right-forward area; right-back receiver has an easier pass to execute.

Try to place your serve between two players rather than directly at one. The best position for the server is about one-third in toward the center of the serving area from the side line.

Advanced Techniques. — As a team game, volleyball has advanced to the point where team strategy has become highly developed. It includes signals given for team plays and skillful performance of all basic volleyball skills. A brief discussion of some of these techniques will be undertaken.

Screening. — In an endeavor to obstruct the view of the opponents as the server delivers the ball, the server's teammates sometimes set a screen for him. In a three-player screen the right forward,

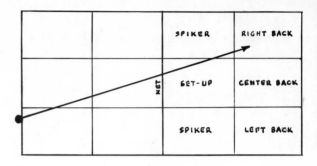

center forward, and center back, still in their respective areas of the court, group themselves together, the center back responsible for the placement. The forwards lean in toward each other, placing their hands behind their heads; the center back places his hands on his hips. All face the net; none can be in motion during the serve. The server stands behind the end line at the right third of the court to take advantage of the screen.

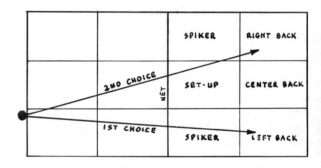

A more effective screen involves four players: left forward, center forward, left back, and center back. These players align similarly to the three-player screen, assuming positions in the corners of their respective areas. The server stands behind the end line at the left third of the court to take advantage of this arrangement. Screening is particularly effective when the server intends to deliver a low service.

Spiking Techniques. — The spike is the most colorful and spectacular play in volleyball, as well as the best point maker. The spiker strikes a rapidly descending ball, passed to him from the set-up, into the opponents' court. On a three-man offense where there are at least three spikers on a team, it is the third play. With the spiker and ball in motion at the same time, split-second timing is required to kill the ball at the proper height above the net. The sustained jumping and strain of the drive requires stamina, a good eye, and a sturdy pair of legs.

A spiker knows how to control the direction of the spike so that he either angles the ball or makes a long hit, how to hit the ball softly after feinting a hard kill, and how to hit between the opponents. He knows what kind of ball to tip instead of kill. He knows how rapidly and where a set pass will descend and how to time his run or jump to take it. He can control his weight so that when he jumps vertically he does not fall or step forward. In other words, a spiker possesses good judgment and skills, both of which he gains from practice and experience in the game.

The series of pictures on this page show Howie Gould putting beautiful wrist action into a Spike shot.

Jo Rae Turner, Los Angeles Genies, angles spike away from block in 1960 Nationals.

The Kill. — Three techniques are important in the kill: the run to align in position with the ball, the bent-arm action in the preparatory drive, and the impetus downward on top of the ball. You must time all movements of arms and legs in relation to the height of the descending ball. To get set for the spike, move toward it with the number of short steps necessary to bring you sideways to the net in line with the direction of the ball. Bring your feet together as you crouch for the jump; then leap from the balls of your feet and swing both arms upward, adding the force of your swing-

ing arms to the push from your legs. At the height of your jump your hitting arm is extended upward, ready to start down. As the ball descends into position for striking, bring the palm of your hand down on top of it. Your spiking movement carries your body around so that you land on the court facing the net, feet apart.

Throughout most of the spiking movement your elbow leads. On the upswing of your hitting arm, bring your arm back behind your head and shoulders, elbow raised in a bent position above your head. Your elbow leads the movement as you whip forearm and hand forward and downward on the ball. The elbow position permits the hand to trail first, like the end of a whip, and gives force to the slapping motion, like the cracking of the whip. A quick flexing of your wrist on the spike not only directs the ball downward but also adds force to the kill. Keep your other arm bent at the elbow in front of your body, chest high. Land on the balls of your feet, and flex your knees to absorb the impact and minimize the jar.

Though the bent-arm position is the more accurate for the spike, a straight-arm kill or a windmill spike are both effective techniques. In the straight-arm movement, extend your arm overhead and drive from the shoulder, contacting the ball with a straight arm. For the windmill arm movement, your extended arm starts in front of your body and continues backward in a circular motion. You complete the action when your arm comes in front of your face; then you snap your arm down on the ball.

Because a spiker and set-up function as a pair, both should practice the kill together until the placement of the pass and the timing of the spike become automatic. The spiker must keep the opposition guessing, varying close placements with long lobs and hard, straight drives; and he cannot do this unless he can read his teammate's mind almost instantly as to what kind of set-up play he will receive.

The Tip. — Instead of hitting the ball with all your power, as in making a kill, merely tip the ball on your spiking motion at the height of your jump. Try the tip as a change of pace when your set-up puts the ball close to the net. A tip shot has little or no arc and drops to the court rapidly. Inserting a tip play among kills may catch your opponents off their guard.

Three defensive players try to block a spike shot by John Brame, Hollywood Y.M.C.A. Star, during 1957 National Championships.

Blocking and Fielding Spikes. — To block a spike, two or more defenders raise their hands and arms to a position in the path of the spiked ball. They cut off the ball by jumping almost at the same instant the spiker jumps to meet the approaching ball well above the net. Blockers play close together and close to the net, directly in front of the opposing spiker. Predicting the exact instant the spiker intends to hit the ball, they jump in unison, arms thrust upward and forward, fingers spread, and hands tilted slightly backward. The blocker who plays the spike has two alternatives: he can tense his hands at contact and return the ball immediately to his opponents' court, keeping his team on the defensive; or he can give with the impact of the ball, tilting his hands and fingers farther backward so that the ball travels upward and backward into his own court, putting his team on the offensive.

Although all three forward players may block, it is better to have just two attempt to cut off the spike, with the third playing for a tip or lob. Success in blocking depends upon correct timing of the jump and getting the hands in line with the ball.

If the blockers fail to stop the spike, or if a blocker deflects the ball to his teammate in the back position, the back court players must field the ball. In fielding, players watch each movement of the spiker and keep in line with the direction they expect from the oncoming ball. In an alert position they keep the weight on the balls of their feet, semicrouch with hands chest high, fingers spread. Since there are three back players they cover the area on each side of the blockers, with the center-back defending against deep spikes or deflections going near the end line.

As the backs field the ball, the center and left forwards face the ball with left shoulders to the net when the fielder is in the left or center-back position, while the right-forward keeps the right side of his body to the net. If a fielder recovers the ball directly back of the forward, the latter must turn his back to the net.

If the spike has not been deflected, the fielder who plays the ball (Number 1) sends the ball to his set-up (Number 2). If a blocker has touched the ball, the retriever passes directly to his team's spiker (Number 3). Whenever possible the fielder uses a high chest pass to get the ball to the set-up. But if a ball is out of reach for a two-handed play, the one-handed dig pass may save a point.

Offensive Formations

The basic formations for offense play are the three spiker-three set passer plan, the standard; the six spiker offensive; and the four spiker-two set passer plan. Regardless of the offensive formation, teams follow the 1-2-3 system of play: the pass, set up, and spike combination. And though players move about the court as the fielding of the ball requires, they keep the same relationship to one another constantly. Therefore, each teammate knows where the others are without having to look for them.

Three Spiker-Three Set Passer Plan. — In the standard plan the players work in pairs, with the set-up preceding the spiker in rotation (except when the spiker is left-handed); therefore, only three players on the team need to be good spikers. This formation must be based on power spiking, because the defensive team is alerted in advance to the point of attack. Since the spiker and set-up work in pairs on practically every play, good teamwork can be developed. The disadvantages, however, of the standard formation are these: (1) there may be difficulty in working up a strong attack against good blockers and in passing the ball to the front line, especially when the set-up is in the right-forward area and the serve comes to the left-back; and (2) there are few opportunities for offensive plays and maneuvers.

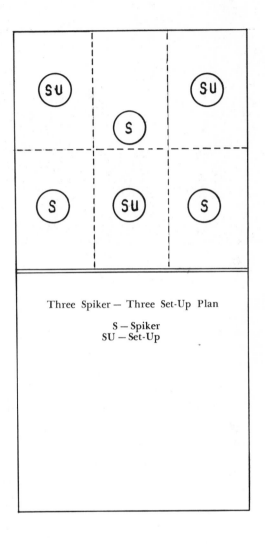

Three Spiker — Three Set-Up Plan

S — Spiker
SU — Set-Up

Below are two common plays made off the offensive plan above.

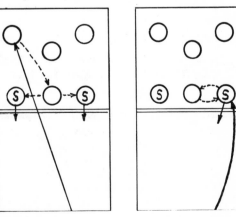

Play A   Play B

Play A (right) — Ball is served to right-back who passes to center-forward (set-up) who sets up ball for either forward spiker.

Play B (right) — Ball is served to left-spiker who passes to center-forward (set-up) who sets up ball for the left-spiker.

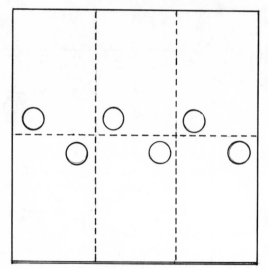

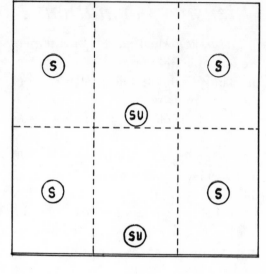

Using this formation, all six players must be good spikers.

Six Spiker Formation. — The six spiker formation concentrates spikers on the front line; therefore to use this offensive every player on the team has to be a good spiker. The alignment on receiving the service has six players staggered along an imaginary line between the front and back court, thus providing an effective means of handling the ball and of going into the attack. The formation is based on accurate and reliable passes; hence all players must be experienced in all phases of the game.

In executing this offensive, the first pass goes to any player on the front line; this player sets the ball to either of two spikers at a designated point at the net. The six spiker plan, based on power and deception offensively, sacrifices defensive strength. This may result in ineffective techniques in ball handling, fielding, and blocking.

Four Spiker-Two Set Passer Plan. — In the four spiker-two set passer formation the set-up is in the center-forward area near the net. When the set-up is in one of the other forward positions, the set-up and spiker switch immediately after the serve; therefore, the pass up is directed to the set-up advancing into the center position. This formation depends upon speed, power, deception, and good ball handling. It utilizes the abilities of highly specialized set-up players, and it is particularly effective against the three- or four-player block. With this formation the defense cannot anticipate the point of the spike, since both spikers usually occupy positions at the ends of the net. However, with one set-up stationed at the net, the formation is weak at the service. Five players have to cover six areas when receiving the serve, and difficulties arise in executing the switch when the ball is directed to players in the process of interchanging positions.

Defensive Formations

On defense, each player protects approximately one-sixth of the court. In general, the center-back, though officially a back line player, plays almost in the center of the court. Other backs vary their distances from the end line according to ability and height. Taller players stand farther forward in the court than shorter players who cannot reach so high. Forwards drop back a step or so from the net to be in a better position to receive the ball. While the opponents have the ball, all players face the net in a position of readiness and, as the ball comes over the net, all use a series of short steps or slides to shift into position to play it. Back line players seldom return the ball across the net after fielding it, because all offensive opportunities then are sacrificed. Back court players must not be concerned with plays at the net until they have adequately defended their own area in the back court.

Depending upon the type of defense, each defensive player has a more or less specific assignment on every play. If one leaves his position before his team's attack has developed, he will find the opponents taking advantage of his entire team.

Three-Player Block. — The standard defense formation is the three-player block. Three forwards in a line put up a solid block at the center of the net. The left- and right-backs cover the area behind the blockers and along the sides of the

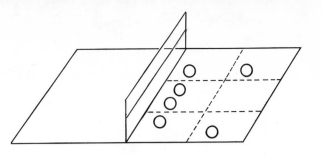

net, and the center-back covers the back court. A variation of this plan has the center-back roaming around the three-player block, and puts the responsibility on the left- and right-backs for covering the back court. With this variation, though, the roaming back often cannot see the opposing spiker approach the net; and consequently he is unable to determine whether the spiker will kill the ball or tip it over or around his three blockers.

Four-Player Block. — Another type of defense formation is the four-player block. Four players line up in a solid formation close to the center of the net. Three of these players are forwards; the fourth is the center-back who moves forward into the line when the opponents gain possession of the ball. He assumes inside responsibility and attempts to block the spiked ball. With four players blocking, the remaining backs cover the back area and shift with the offensive play. This formation is strong against the power spike but weak against offensive tips and volleys. To counteract these plays, the player in the four-player block farthest from the point of attack can slide away from the net leaving the three teammates to do the actual blocking. Thus the slide blocker can defend against tips and partially blocked angle spikes directed along the net. With this variation of the four-player block formation, the backs are relieved of covering the territory close to the net.

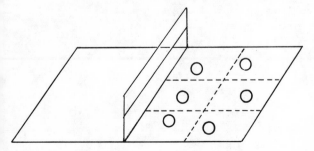

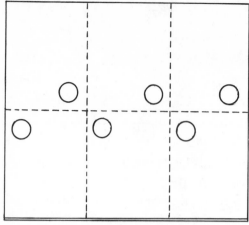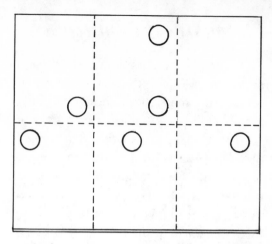

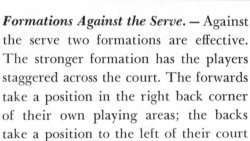

Formations Against the Serve. — Against the serve two formations are effective. The stronger formation has the players staggered across the court. The forwards take a position in the right back corner of their own playing areas; the backs take a position to the left of their court areas and near the dividing line. The second formation has five players along the dividing line, one player taking a position near the net. With this pattern the defense readily can switch to offense and into the attack.

Girls' and Women's Volleyball

The volleyball skills which have been described are as applicable to girls' and women's volleyball as boys' and men's. For girls and women, volleyball is becoming a very popular sport. Girls with a low level of skill in the sport enjoy it as do the most skillful. As a recreational game for young girls and older women it is unsurpassed.

The Division for Girls' and Women's Sports of the American Association for Health, Physical Education, and Recreation has done much to promote volleyball for girls and women. It publishes a bi-annual volleyball guide, rates game officials and provides leadership for local schools and clubs.

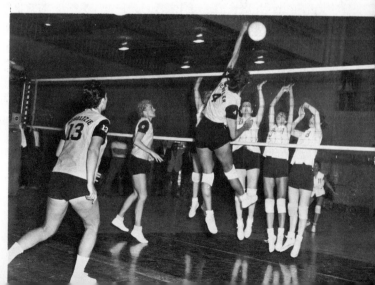

Co-Recreational Volleyball

Boys and girls, men and women, all enjoy playing volleyball together. A few slight modifications of volleyball rules are needed to adapt the game for age levels of both sexes. Three boys and 3 girls placed alternately on the court make up the team. But it is not uncommon to see teams of 5 boys and 5 girls. Boy and girl alternately hit the ball and the net is lowered to 7 feet for junior high school; 7 feet 6 inches for high school, college, and adults.

Modified Volleyball Games

Volleyball easily lends itself to modifications in the number of players, rule changes, and size of court. It can be played with as few as four players and as many as fifty or more. Only a few of the many modified volleyball games will be briefly described.

Volleyball Doubles. — In this modification the court is reduced to 20 feet by 40 feet with two players on each team. One player plays near the net and the other player in back court. Volleyball rules are followed with the exception that allows each player to hit the ball twice in succession but no more than three hits on a side. The serving team only can score points and 11 points is a game. It is a fast and exciting game when played by skilled players.

Twenty-Player Game. — Another volleyball modification allows for the number of players on each team to be increased to 10-20 players. No rule modifications are necessary except a limit on the number of hits on each side. A time limit can be placed for a game.

Keep-Away Volleyball. — Large numbers of players (20-40 per team) can play in this modified game. The ball is put in play by any player beginning the volley by hitting the ball with his hand. Any number of players can touch or relay the ball from either side. Points are scored when the opponents allow the ball to touch the floor or when it is volleyed into the net or out of bounds. The game is ended after a certain time limit or a point total (21).

Bibliography

Emery, Curtis R. *Modern Volleyball.* New York: The Macmillan Company, 1953.

Laveaga, Robert E. *Volleyball,* 2d edition. New York: The Ronald Press Company, 1960.

Welch, J. Edmund (ed.). *How to Play and Teach Volleyball.* New York: Association Press, 1960.

Division for Girls' and Women's Sports, *Volleyball Guide.* Washington, D.C.: American Association for Health, Physical Education, and Recreation, published biannually.

United States Volleyball Association. *Official Volleyball Rules.* Berne, Indiana: USVBA Printer, published annually.

WATER
SKIING

Herbert L. Loken

Origin and History

ON EVERY LAKE, pond, river, or ocean, wherever there are motorboats, water skiers of all ages are gaily riding and stunting behind them. In the past 30 years the sport has spread like wildfire; it now ranks as one of the top outdoor sports in the United States. The amazing spurt in interest and participation, implemented by the activities of the American Water Ski Association, paralleled the spectacular increase in family motorboating following World War II.

Early in the 1930s water skiers were in evidence around the Riviera resorts in southern France. Frequented by well-to-do people, and blessed with calm waters and warm climate, these resorts were ideal spots for the development of this outdoor activity. Not long after, water skiers were experimenting with skills on the coastal and lake resorts of the United States. Skiing forward only, they practiced takeoffs, landings, and wake jumping on one and two skis.

At a meeting of aquaplanists at Massapequa, New York, in 1936, time was set aside on the program for exhibitions of water skiing. For the first time, single and double ski techniques and ramp jumping were demonstrated. Dan B. Hains, who was in attendance, recognized the possibilities of this activity and within no time began to manufacture special equipment to use on the water. In 1939 he was instrumental in forming the American Water Ski Association which sanctioned the first national Water Ski Tournament at Jones Beach, New York, the same year. It has held annual tournaments ever since, with the exception of the war years of 1942-1945. Hains and Eugene Garvin, in an effort to encourage competition between nations, organized the World Water Ski Union. This group held its first worldwide competition at Juan-les-Pins on the French Riviera in 1949.

The American Water Ski Association formulates rules for competition and sanctions tournaments at local, regional, as well as national levels. It maintains qualifying judges and officials to administer rating tests devised for skiers to measure their skill on an absolute stand-ard. In addition, the AWSA conducts a program for summer camps, assists local clubs, sponsors a United States team to world tournaments, and publishes the rulesbook, tournament kits with scoring forms, and a magazine, *The Water Skier*.

Since the time of the first AWSA National Tournament competitive water skiing has been divided into three categories: trick riding, slalom, and jumping. Individual champions are named in each of these events. An overall winner is determined on point values based on placements in the three events which are weighted equally. Skiers compete in the following divisions:

Junior — to 13 years of age
Boys and Girls — 13 through 16
Men and Women — 17 through 34
Senior Men — 35 and over
Senior Women — 30 and over
Mixed Doubles (male and female), riding together.

Qualifications for major tournaments are required, based on previous competitive ratings or AWSA rating tests. In competition, skis must conform to given limitations; they must be at least 4 feet long, with a width of between 4 and 8 inches at the widest point.

Geoffrey Wolfe, World's Trick Champion, 1960-61.

Equipment

Essential equipment for water skiing consists of skis and bindings, towline and towbar, and towboat. In addition, the skier should have a well-fitting swim suit, a life belt with air chambers or a floatable vest for safety, and a windproof jacket to put on between rides.

Skis. — Conventional water skis are from 60 to 69 inches long (shorter for children), about 6¼ inches wide, and 9/16 of an inch thick. Some skis have parallel sides and a straight heel; others are tapered at both ends. All have semicircular or elliptical toes, with a front section curving gradually to a turnup of about 5 inches. Screwed on the underside of each ski near the heel are one or two wooden keels or fins. These runners guide the ski straight in the water and prevent skidding on turns.

Tough, resilient woods, such as white ash or hickory, make the best skis, although skis of fiberglass and aluminum are popular. In fact, skis of these materials may be better for learners. Since they are not as buoyant as wooden skis, the beginner may not have as much difficulty handling them in preparation for the takeoff. All kinds are equally easy to ride and handle if the binders are properly located on the ski.

Bindings. — Since a comfortable foot binding helps performance, a skier should secure an adjustable one and have it mounted properly on the ski. Heel and toe binders come in soft rubber or vinyl with aluminum fittings, and fasten to the ski on a plate, with the opening in the binding aft of center. Because the exact location for the binding varies with the shape and stiffness of the ski, the skier should experiment a little to determine the proper placement of the binding for the best ride. With a plate-type binding, the heel or toe or both can be moved a bit fore or aft — or reversed for backward skiing.

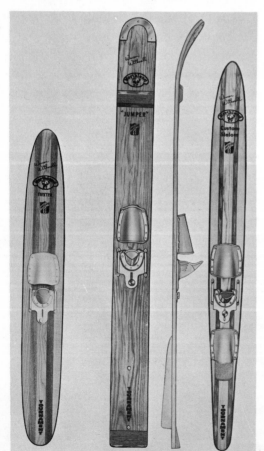

Standard binding

Slalom binding

Towline and Towbar. — The towline should be of first-grade manila or of braided polyethylene (plastic) ¼ of an inch in diameter. The conventional length is 75 feet from boat to towbar. The towline may be in two sections, a main section 70 feet long with a snap hook to clip to a 5-foot section which includes the bar. Since a new line always stretches, after a few rides it should be remeasured and shortened as required.

A new manila towline should be soaked and then dragged in the water awhile before being used; then it will untwist and not tangle when it is coiled.

With a manila towrope, a plastic float is advisable. This float, attached near the snap hook, keeps the rope from sinking and the towbar in clear view. A plastic line is much lighter and floats, therefore a float-attachment is not essential.

A hardwood bar about 14 inches long makes the most practical handle. The towline is passed through holes at each end of the bar and half-hitched around the bar. Then the towline is knotted about 15 inches from the bar. With this triangular arrangement good balance is assured. Double handles are also available and used by many skiers.

The popular single-handle towbar, which is best for beginners and for trick riding.

The double-handled towbar gives greater control in slalom skiing, as slack can be taken up with one hand.

231

Towboat. — Both outboard and inboard motorboats make good towers. The outboard leaves a flatter and smaller wake and the skier has an easier time riding behind. The inboard, a heavier boat, has a larger wake and offers the skier more obstacles because it roughs up the water. At least a 20 hp motor for an outboard and a 60 hp for an inboard is necessary for one driver and one skier.

The towboat should have a towing bar or pylon to keep the line high so that it will not touch the wake or catch on the ramp or a buoy. On the outboard, the pylon or bar can be installed above the motor, as shown in the photo below.

With a towing bar, a driver need not constantly steer to correct for a skier's pulling to one side, and he can turn or back up the boat without fouling the towline in the propeller. However, a rear-view mirror, mounted on the instrument panel, will allow the driver to keep his eyes straight ahead and also check on the skier, too. A second person in the boat, to keep an eye on the skier is a requirement in many states.

A skier, who is a poor or not a very strong swimmer should wear a life jacket or belt.

Fundamentals

Strangely enough, the most difficult skill in water skiing is the one you should master first — that of getting up on your skis for a takeoff in deep water. Once you have learned to do this, the remaining basic fundamentals are comparatively easy. These basics include taking off from shallow water or a float, maintaining good riding form, steering and balancing, and gliding to a landing. Then you will be ready for crossing the wake, riding a single ski, and trying simple tricks.

Since water skiing requires the skills of two persons — a driver and a skier — both must know how to communicate to facilitate learning the techniques.

Signals. — Both you and the driver must be familiar with the meanings of the following calls or signs.

A shout "In gear!" tells the driver to get ready — to put the motor in gear.

A shout "Hit it!" means that he immediately should start accelerating to planing speed.

Once you are up on skis and being towed, you communicate with these hand signals:

The latest method of communication, between skier and boat, is shown below. This is a two-way system and the other instrument is attached to the tow bar, which is shown in the pictures on page 235.

Slower Speed
Palm down, motion downward. Or shake your head "No."

Faster
Palm up, motion upwards. Or nod your head "Yes."

Speed Okay
Make the "okay" signal with thumb and forefinger.

Stop
Arm high in the air, fingers extended, hold it.

A Whip-off
Point out the direction, then make quick circular motion with hand.

A Turn
Palm vertical, motion in direction you want to go.

A Jump
Palm down, raise hand sharply.

Cut Motor
Make like you're cutting your throat.

233

Skier OK
Hands clasped over head.

Return to Dock
Bend your arm, then drop it, finger pointing down.

Proper fit, of the bindings, is important so Mike adjusts them to fit snugly on Nancy's feet.

Land Practice

Now that you are familiar with the equipment, you are ready for dry-land instruction, which is necessary before going out on the water.

In the sequence shown here, Mike Osborn and Nancy Legant, of Cypress Gardens, Florida, demonstrate the beginners technique of learning by practicing on the beach.

The first thing to do is fit your skis. The bindings are adjustable and should be set to fit snugly around the foot. Wet your feet first to prevent chafing.

The purpose of this instruction is to get accustomed to the feel of being pulled upright by the boat and learn proper form.

Hold the tow bar with both hands, then sit on the skis with the thighs pushed tight against the calves so that you are as far forward as possible. As a friend pulls you to a standing position do not try to help by pulling yourself up. Let the tow do the work.

Your form is important so remember to keep your arms straight and, as you rise, keep your knees slightly flexed and lean back against the tow.

Here Nancy starts out, in a seated position, with her knees tucked together and drawn up as high as possible, her elbows outside the knees. Her arms are extended but not tense.

Mike shows Nancy how the towboat will pull her erect but warns that she must not try to stand up too soon. Easy does it, AND KEEP THOSE ARMS EXTENDED.

Nancy is now up. Her arms are extended, but relaxed, her body erect with knees bent slightly to absorb the action of the waves.

Takeoffs

Learning to get on skis for a takeoff is easier if you wear a life belt or floatable vest to help keep you up in the water. Otherwise you have to add considerable treading and sculling to the job of getting and keeping in position. ***Shallow Water Takeoff.*** — Before attempting a shallow water takeoff, make certain that the water ahead is more than five feet deep. A fall in water less than this depth may result in an injury. You can take off from a beach safely as long as the water increases in depth. On a takeoff, always be sure the boat is pointing toward deeper water.

In a shallow water takeoff, put your skis on in water about waist deep. Follow the same procedure as you practiced in the dry-land instruction. With your feet in the bindings, sit in the water and rest the heels of your skis on the bottom. Get your balance, towbar between your skis, tips of the skis pointing up. As you shout "Hit it!" and feel the pull on the towline, let it pull you up just as you did on the beach. Remember — let the boat do the pulling.

In the sequence, starting at the top right, Nancy Legant and Mike Osborn take to the water to try out the takeoff technique that they practiced on the beach.

Nancy is now up — she is leaning back slightly with her arms extended. Her skis have leveled off, so that there is very little drag, and she is skimming over the water on her way to becoming an ardent water skier.

Here Nancy is just coming up out of the water and is concentrating on correct form — skis pointed toward the boat, still in a sitting position, arms extended and letting the boat do the work.

Nancy is now about halfway up and the boat is picking up speed. This is the point where many fall because they try to stand up too soon. Notice that Nancy still has her knees bent and is still not hurrying.

On your first takeoff you probably will think that you will never be able to manage your skis. They will seem unmanageable because your toe-up angle is high, because with little or no forward speed your skis are likely to be tilting inward or outward, and because you are uncertain and wobbly on your skis. With the initial pull of the towline, concentrate on keeping your skis level; this will keep them from crossing or spreading apart. If you feel you are going to fall backward, jerk on the towbar to regain your balance; then slacken your pull immediately. You must slacken quickly because you may need to jerk on the line another time to correct your balance. If you think you are going to fall forward, bend your knees quickly. This action should correct your balance and keep you on the water.

Once you are riding on the skis, lean back slightly. Hold your head in normal position, eyes focused on the center of the wake. Hold your back straight, knees relaxed, and arms out in front. With both hands, hold the towbar just above the waist. Later on, try holding on with one hand. With a straight arm your fingers can readily maintain a good grasp.

This picture shows proper skiing form. Check all the points, listed above, and see how well this girl is doing.

Deep Water Takeoff. — For a deep water takeoff, keep your body floating upright, a ski under each armpit and the towbar around your neck. Now:

1. With both hands push one ski down toward your foot. Simultaneously bend your knee so that you can reach the foot, and duck your head in the water. Get your foot in the front binder and then in the heel binder.

2. Raise your head out of the water and scull until you are in balance. Be sure the towbar is still around your neck.

3. Reach for the other ski and, with both hands, repeat procedure 1.

4. When you raise your head this time, right yourself in the water in a sitting position, sculling for balance. To keep your skis from floating up in front and pushing you backward, bend your knees against your chest and thrust your head forward.

5. Reach for the towbar. Keep your skis parallel, tips out of the water and up, and arrange the towline between your skis.

6. Turn in the water to face the back of the towboat. Scull with one hand for balance, hold the towbar with the other hand, and shout to the driver "In gear!"

7. As the boat moves and the towline tightens, grasp the bar with both hands and let yourself be dragged slowly for a second or two until your skis are aligned, tips up. Your driver will be watching you.

8. Shout "Hit it!" As the driver accelerates smoothly to about 20 mph, stay in a deep crouch until you are in balance. Keep your arms straight, and let the towline pull you to a standing position. Keep your skis parallel, level, and about a foot apart.

9. As you ride along, stay in the center of the boat's wake. Then you will not have to contend with the rough waves on either side. If your driver sees you are going too far to one side, he will steer the boat gradually to the other side as his speed picks up.

A young enthusiast gets a lot of help from his water skiing family.

Takeoff from a Float. — Take off from a float or dock from is a sitting position on the edge of the structure. Once your feet are in the binders, put the heels of your skis in the water under the float. The tips of the skis should be out of the water. Have the towline as it comes from the boat go between your skis. Have at least 3 yards of slack line coiled neatly beside you. With the towbar in both hands, face the stern of the boat and give the driver the "In gear!" signal. As the boat picks up the slack in the towline, shift your seat to the extreme edge of the structure. As the line tightens, put your weight on the skis, knees bent, hold the towbar low, arms straight out in front, shout "Hit it!" and lean back, bracing yourself for the jerk.

If you are bending forward rather than leaning backward, the jerk on the line may pull you out of your binders and cause you to fall headfirst into the water.

If you start to fall backward, pull on the towbar and release it quickly. If you start to fall forward, bend your knees deeply — squat. Either of these corrections may save a spill.

Driver's Part in Takeoffs. — For a takeoff in deep water the driver should maneuver the boat so that it will be crosswind or downwind of the skier in the water, towline loosely stretched out in the water. If he is upwind of the skier the boat will drift toward the skier and the slack in the line will cause trouble. The stern of the boat must face the skier, motor either off or in neutral gear.

When the skier calls "In gear!" the driver should shift to forward gear and let the engine idle. As the line tightens, the boat pulls the skier slowly a second or two. This gives him time to get the tips out of the water and his skis under control. When the skier signals "Hit it!" the driver accelerates steadily until the skier is planing. It should take about four seconds from idle to full throttle. The throttle should never be advanced quickly or the engine will buck or stall. The engine should respond smoothly to a continuously opening throttle.

To start a skier from a float or dock, the boat must have its stern toward the skier. If possible, the boat should be perpendicular to the side of the dock from which the skier is taking off. Since the skier has a lot of the line coiled beside him, the driver must watch the line after the "In gear!" signal, so that he can accelerate once the slack is taken up. Pickup speed must be faster for this start than for the deep-water takeoff, in order to keep the skier from sinking in the water.

238

If the takeoff is on one ski, pickup speed must be even faster, and the start of the pickup should occur before the slack of the towline has been entirely taken up. When a driver accelerates too soon he may jerk the skier forward. He may strain the skier's arms or pull him head over heels into the water if he picks up abruptly. With practice, driver and skier will soon synchronize to a perfect start.

Riding, Balancing, and Steering. — As you ride, the skis keep on the surface of the water by a process called "planing." Your weight on the skis pushes the water down as you are being pulled along by the boat. How much of the area of your skis you have on the water, how much weight you have on each ski, how fast the boat drags you along — these facts all affect your ride. With more weight and less speed, the tips of the skis will aim upward. On a takeoff you have to angle your skis about 45 degrees in order to compensate for the weight on the rear of the skis and the slow speed. With increasing speed the angle of your skis decreases. When your skis are riding practically flat you are planing. When you shift your weight from two skis to one, the supporting ski toes up more because of the additional weight. If the boat increases its speed, the ski flattens in spite of the additional weight it has to carry.

Riding directly behind the boat in the center of the wake is easy. You do not have to be concerned with steering since you have little toe-angle and your skis are straight and steady. Notice the form and position of the girl in the photo. If you want to make a turn you have to steer. In steering you must compensate for the centrifugal force of the turn and the pull on the towline by leaning to the side toward which you want to go, as demonstrated by the woman in the photo. This lean tilts or banks your skis toward that side. The sharper the turn the steeper you must lean your body and the more you must tilt the ski.

The angle of the toes of your skis, the tilt to the side, and the speed of the boat affect the radius of your turn. For examples, to make a sharp turn you must have both a greater toe-angle and tilt; for a wide turn at high speed you must ride your skis flatter. If you bank them correctly the runners on the bottoms of your skis will prevent the heels of the skis from slipping outward.

To turn abruptly requires a steep lean and a sharp tilting of the skis. At high speed it is possible to "jump" in the turn. To jump you take the weight off your skis for a mere second. You unweight the skis through a motion of rising up — a straightening of the knees immediately followed by a bending of the knees as your weight returns to the skis. In a jump you must keep your skis close together and parallel.

Crossing the Wake. — When you are in good riding form and familiar with the basic principles of steering, you are ready to learn how to cross a wake. Since you have to cross practically at a right angle, you must steer away from the wake in order to approach it at a perpendicular. To cross the edge of the wake to the right, for example, you first steer left, then turn sharply toward the right. As you go over the wave, bend your knees deeply to absorb the bump. You may want to jump slightly to unweight your skis as they take the bump. At any rate, be sure to hold up the toes of the skis as they leave the water.

To come back across the wave you must hit the edge at a wider angle because the wave is steeper. Therefore steer and pull to the side as far as you can; then make an abrupt turn toward the wake. If you approach the wake too timidly the wave may push your skis back toward the outside. When this happens, you will merely hang on to the side of the wave. You will have to steer out and away again, and come back to hit the wake at more of a right angle. As you go over, tips high, "give" with the bump. In other words, take the bump with your knees.

Riding on One Ski. — Once you can handle a two-ski takeoff, maneuver a wake, ride easily with one hand, you are ready to learn to ski on one ski. This is not too difficult. The main problem is one of balance because of a shift of weight.

If the driver is turning the boat one way or the other, you will have difficulty riding off the wake and even more difficulty getting back over the wake. This is because, on the inside of the turn, you lose speed and your skis are harder to control. You cannot hit the edge of the wave at a right angle. So, until the driver straightens the boat following a turn, you had better remain in the center of the wake behind the boat.

Controlling the Supporting Ski. — To begin, ride in the center of the wake on two skis holding the towbar with both hands. Lift one ski (this is now the free ski) slightly, but let it ride lightly and flat on the water. As you lift the free ski your weight will shift to the support ski. Because of the added weight, the toe of this ski rises and the ski starts to wobble or "fish." You must practice not to over-control when this occurs. Just try to keep the ski level and it will stop "fishing."

At first to help with balance, keep the free ski skimming the surface of the water until you get the supporting ski under control. Then lift the free ski completely out of the water, keeping the toe higher than the heel so that it cannot drop down and dig in. If you can control your balance on the supporting ski now, you can kick off the free ski and ride along on one.

Balancing on One Ski. — To cast off the free ski, first lift your heel out of the binder by pushing down on your toes, keeping your weight balanced on both skis. Now simultaneously shift your weight to the supporting ski and pull your toes out of the binder of the free ski. If you are successful the ski will drop away. As you ride on one ski, hold your free leg behind and to the side — you may need it to "step" onto the water for a second for balance. Once you are confident that you have the supporting ski under control, place your free foot behind the foot on the ski, transferring a little weight to this back foot. The "new" weight on the heel of the ski will cause the ski to toe up, and it may begin to "fish." Balance on the one ski is a bit troublesome at this point. Don't add too much weight to your back foot until you have controlled the wobbling. At that time you can divide your weight evenly

between your two feet and ride along with ease.

The next step is to ride on one ski holding the towbar with one hand. As you move from two skis to one ski, hold the bar with the same hand as the supporting leg. Your free arm can help with balance as you make the shift of weight. Later, switch the towbar from one hand to the other, with your free foot either off or on the ski. If you are under control with these exercises you are ready to tackle the wake.

Crossing the wake on one ski is much simpler than crossing on two skis. Since the toe of the ski rides higher you are not likely to dig it into the water as you come off the edge of the wake. Instead of bouncing over the edge as you did on two skis, you dig through the wave. Thus you have a smoother and easier ride.

Takeoffs on One Ski. — From deep water or from a float the techniques for a takeoff from one ski in many ways resemble those for the two-ski start. In deep water, with the rope of your towbar on the side of your free foot, bend the knee of your skiing leg deeply. As the pull on the towline begins, extend your free leg back and to the side. Rising out of the water, use the shin of your free leg for lift and balance — push down on the water. The pull on the line is harder than the pull on the two-ski takeoff, so straighten your body as soon as you can to get it out of the water and ease the pull.

In the initial learning of this deep water takeoff, let the toe of your ski rest against the towline during the pullup to help you control the wobbling of the ski. Later on, try the pullup with your free foot on the back of the ski.

In a takeoff from a float or dock you have to sit on the heel of your free foot, toes gripping the edge of the structure. Have your ski in the water, toe up. Your driver knows that the boat must take up the slack of the towline at a faster clip than was necessary for the two-ski takeoff. So prepare for a jerk on the towline. Time the snap of the line with a strong pushoff from the structure with your free foot. If your timing is right you will start out planing immediately.

Landings. — Once you let go of the towbar to land, the resistance of the water cuts down the forward momentum of your skis. If your driver has been towing you at a boat speed of 25 mph you will be able to glide about 75 feet. If you have been riding at 28 mph your glide will be about 100 feet; at 35 mph, about 150 feet. As you glide, the heels of your skis will begin to sink and the toes rise, causing an ever increasing drag. Finally your skis will stop gliding abruptly and sink. To make a good landing you have to know how quickly you will lose planing speed. You want your skis to sink at your landing spot.

On a Float. — With a speed of 25 mph the boat should be opposite the landing spot, about 40 feet from it and parallel to it, as you let go the towbar. As the boat nears the exact spot, you cut over the wake toward it. Then, pull hard on the towbar to give impetus to the glide, and let go the line. Glide in parallel to the side of the float so you will have some leeway as to the place on the float where you will end up. Since you know about how far you can glide at a given speed, your glide should bring you in near the landing spot.

On two skis, if you come in too fast, make an S-turn or weave to slow you down. On one ski, brake by shifting your weight to the heel of the ski to make it plough more deeply. If your glide is timed correctly, your skis or ski will sink as you reach your objective. Place your hands on the float or dock, lift your heels out of the binders, and twist your body to a sitting position. Your skis should be afloat somewhere near your feet, and you can retrieve them.

On a Beach. — For a beach landing your boat may have to be 100 or 150 feet out from your landing spot. Hence the boat speed must be greater — about 28 mph if you are 100 or more feet away — to give you sufficient speed to land near your objective. As the boat parallels the landing spot, cut over the wake and glide toward the place, angling at about 45 degrees. Your skis will sink fast at the landing. Since you can stand in the water, wade ashore with your skis on. Do not try to ski onto the beach. The skis will stick to the sand, and if you have any remaining momentum, you will pitch forward on your head.

Falls. — To protect yourself, you should learn to fall correctly. If you feel yourself going, throw the towbar aside, lower your head, and fling your hands overhead. You should get rid of the bar so that there is no possibility of catching an arm or leg on the handle or of tangling with the line. Try to fall to the side rather than forward in order to avoid hitting the toes of your skis. You will come out of your skis, but because the bindings are elastic there is little chance of hurting your ankles.

Sometimes a fall will knock your breath away. If this happens, don't panic. You will regain your breath in a very short time. Merely float quietly. If you can, grab a ski and hold on to it while you float. The boat will turn around and come back for you.

In his about-face, the driver should approach the skier to the side in order to return the towline to him. Just as the bow of the boat passes the skier, the

Good form in a beach landing.

driver should turn the boat sharply toward the skier to swing the stern away from the skier. He should then continue straight ahead until the line is within reach of the skier. As the skier reaches for the towbar, the driver should shift into reverse to stop the boat. He should stay in reverse momentarily only, or the towline will be sucked into the propeller. The driver should idle in forward gear as the skier prepares for the takeoff, awaiting the "Hit it!" signal.

Taking a header, once in a while, is all in the game.

Advanced and Competitive Skiing

This beautiful skier gives the skier's salute.

After you have learned the fundamental skills of water skiing, you will wish to start concentrating on the advanced types of skiing, namely: slalom, jumping, pair and group skiing and trick riding. Many of these will be pictured, in the following pages, without attempting any lengthy explanation of the maneuvers.

The slalom course consists of a series of buoys, on the water, around which the skier steers a zigzag course. The number of buoys, successfully made at pre-planned, progressively higher speeds, determines the score of the skier. Slalom competitions are exciting challenges to the skiing athlete.

Rounding a buoy, in a slalom course. The wake shows how the skier swung wide. then cut in close as he completed the turn.

This skier is not putting as much lean into his turn and not cutting as close, as the other skier.

Leaning way over, his arms pulled in close to take up the slack, this skier cuts close to the buoy.

247

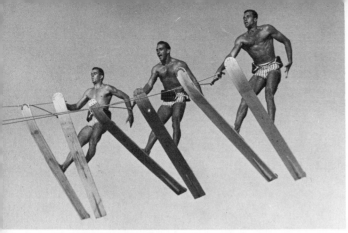

George Hughes, Jerry Imber and Simone Khoury, all champions, come flying off the ramp together.

Barbara Cooper, National Girl's Jumping Champion, demonstrates perfect jumping form.

These clowns, who perform at Cypress Gardens, make tricks, like this, look easy but don't try it.

Buster and Betty MacCalla execute a graceful Forward Swan.

The Twin Helicopter Turn requires perfect timing and expert skill.

This beautiful performer executes a graceful Backward Swan. Note the special harness for her foot.

A bird's-eye-view of a pretty miss skimming by on shoe skis.

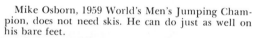

Here is a difficult one to perform, skiing backward on a short slalom ski.

Mike Osborn, 1959 World's Men's Jumping Champion, does not need skis. He can do just as well on his bare feet.

The difficult Toe-Hold Turnabout.

249

In this sequence, pretty Dolly Barrineau demonstrates the proper way to get the tow handle into position for this trick in which the skier is pulled with the tow handle behind the thighs.

On the opposite page, Dolly shows the various steps in performing the Heel-Tow trick. Notice that, while doing both of these tricks, Dolly is very graceful and has perfect balance.

Index